016.33
H62

Volume 24

History of Economic Thought

Economics Reading Lists,
Course Outlines, Exams,
Puzzles & Problems

Compiled by Edward Tower, *Duke University*, August 1990

NOTES TO USERS AND POTENTIAL CONTRIBUTORS

These teaching materials are drawn from both undergraduate and graduate programs at 93 major colleges and universities. They are designed to widen the horizons of individual professors and curriculum committees. Some include suggestions for term-paper topics, and many of the lists are useful guides for students seeking both topics and references for term papers and theses. Thus, they should enable faculty members to advise students more effectively and efficiently. They will also be useful to prospective graduate students seeking more detailed information about various graduate programs; to those currently enrolled in programs who are preparing for field examinations; and to librarians responsible for acquisitions in economics. Finally, they may interest researchers and administrators who wish to know more about how their own work and the work of their department is being received by the profession.

The exams, puzzles and problems include both undergraduate and graduate exams contributed by economics departments and individual professors. They should be especially useful to professors making up exams and problem sets and to students studying for comprehensive exams. They may also serve as the focus for study groups.

From time to time we will reprint updated and expanded versions. Therefore, we would welcome new or updated teaching materials, especially those which compliment material in this collection or cover areas we missed. Potential contributors should contact Ed Tower, Economics Department, Duke University, Durham, North Carolina 27706, U.S.A.

While Eno River Press has copyrighted the entire collection, authors of the various parts retain the right to reproduce and assign the reproduction of their own materials as they choose. Thus, anyone wishing to reproduce particular materials should contact the author of them. Similarly, those wishing to make verbatim use of department-wide examinations, except as teaching materials for one's own class, should contact the department chairperson concerned.

Acknowledgement

The associate compilers for this series are Cliff Carrubba, Maia Sisk, and Ron Temple. Cliff is a senior at Duke, majoring in Economics and Political Science. Maia is a senior at Duke, majoring in Economics and Computer Science. Ron is a graduate student at Harvard's John F. Kennedy School of Government. Andy Seamons, Kathy Shelley, and Geoff Somes also provided important help with production of the volumes. The cover was designed by the Division of Audiovisual Education, Duke University, and the volumes were printed by Multiprint, Inc., New York.

Eno River Press, Inc.$^{©}$1990. All rights reserved. No part of this publication may be reproduced, stored in a retrieval system, or transmitted, in any form or by any means, electronic, mechanical, photocopying, recording or otherwise, without the prior permission of Eno River Press.

Eno River Press
Box 4900, Duke Station
Durham, North Carolina 27706 U.S.A.

ISBN for this volume: 0-88024-152-7
ISBN Eno River Press for this series: 0-88024-128-4
Library of Congress Catalog Number: 90-082701

HISTORY OF ECONOMIC THOUGHT

Contents

TONY ASPROMOURGOS, *University of Sydney* Post Keynesian Economics, U	5
TONY ASPROMOURGOS AND PETER D. GROENEWEGEN, *University of Sydney* Economic Classics, R&E, G	12
WILLIAM J. BARBER, *Wesleyan University* History of Economic Thought, R&E, U	28
WILLIAM J. BAUMOL, *Princeton University* History of Economic Thought, G	38
RONALD G. BODKIN, *University of Ottawa* Histoire De La Pensée Économique, G	39
THOMAS BORCHERDING AND THOMAS ROCHON, *The Claremont Graduate School Center for Politics and Policy* The Nature of Social Science Inquiry, G	44
BRUCE J. CALDWELL, *University of North Carolina at Greensboro* History of Economic Thought, R&E, U	55
ROBERT B. EKELUND, JR., *Auburn University* History of Economic Thought: The Neoclassical Period Through Marshall and Veblen, G	68
RICHARD E. GIFT, *University of Kentucky* History of Economic Thought I & II, G	82
FRED R. GLAHE AND TRACY MOTT, *University of Colorado* Alternative Economic Paradigms, G	85
CRAUFORD D. GOODWIN, *Duke University* The History of Economic Thought: From Aristotle to the Present, U	97
PETER D. GROENEWEGEN, *University of Sydney* History of Economic Thought, R&E, U	104
D. WADE HANDS, *University of Puget Sound* History of Economic Thought, R&E, U	124

GEOFFREY C. HARCOURT, *University of Cambridge*
    History of Economic Thought 'Circus', U
    Lectures on Post-Keynesian and Growth Theory, U
    Capital and Growth in the Cambridge Tradition, U&G
    Keynes: from the <u>Treatise</u> to the <u>General Theory</u>, G
	133
	136
	142
	144

THOMAS J. KNIESNER, *Indiana University* **Kniesner's Guide to Doctoral Dissertations, G**	145
JOHN LODEWIJKS, *University of New South Wales* **Economic Methodology, R&E, U&G**	154
TOM MAYER, *University of California, Davis* **Orientation to Economic Research, G**	172
TRACY MOTT, *University of Colorado* **History of Economic Thought, R&E, G**	174
MARK PERLMAN, *University of Pittsburgh* **History of Economic Thought I: The History of Economic Thought and Society Until 1870, R&E, U&G**	177
History of Economic Thought II: The Evolution of Professional Specialization, 1870-1955, R&E U&G	197
LOUIS PUTTERMAN, *Brown University* **The History & Philosophical Context of Economic Thought, U**	225
JANE ROSSETTI, *Williams College* **Economics as Literature, U**	231
WARREN J. SAMUELS, *Michigan State University* **History of Economic Thought, U**	235
History of Economic Thought: A, G	237
History of Economic Thought: C, G	239
MARTIN C. SPECHLER, *Indiana University* **History of Economic Thought, U**	241
GEORGE J. STIGLER, *University of Chicago* **History of Economic Thought Before 1870, U&G**	244
History of Economic Thought After 1870, U&G	249
UNIVERSITY OF CHICAGO **History of Economic Thought Preliminary Exams, G**	253
UNIVERSITY OF MICHIGAN **History of Economic Thought Preliminary Exams, G**	260
PRINCETON UNIVERSITY **History of Economic Thought General Exams, G**	266

* * *

U = Undergraduate **G** = Graduate
R&E = Reading Lists & Exams and/or Problems

U
PKEGEN/EA

University of Sydney
DEPARTMENT OF ECONOMICS
ECONOMICS III - 1990

TONY ASPROMOURGOS   POST KEYNESIAN ECONOMICS
GENERAL INFORMATION

2 Lect.; year; Prereq. - Ec.II or Ec.II(P); T,W. 9.00am; MLR6

---

1. Course Content

The purpose of this course is to trace the main lines of development of a school of thought which has its origins in John Maynard Keynes's General Theory of Employment, Interest and Money (1936) and draws also upon the work of the classical economists, Marx and Michal Kalecki. The aim of the school has been to develop coherent alternative approaches to the theory of the capitalist economy, in contradistinction to the currently prevailing marginalist or "neo-classical" approach. This naturally involves alternative approaches to the study of all the constituent elements of a theory of the capitalist economy: income distribution and relative prices; money and interest; output and employment; growth and cyclical fluctuations; technological change. it also naturally leads to different policy implications.

The course is divided into three parts:

FIRST SEMESTER

Part I (10 weeks) -   I.   EFFECTIVE DEMAND AND THE THEORY OF PRICES

This topic is devoted to a reconstruction of the Keynesian theory of effective demand and its integration with a theory of prices and distribution not based upon supply and demand principles. The approach to prices and distribution is along the lines developed by Ricardo, Marx and Sraffa. Policy implications are drawn out - especially with regard to macroeconomic policy and welfare economics.

Part II (4 weeks) -   II.   GROWTH, FLUCTUATIONS AND DISTRIBUTION

This part of the course offers an exposition and a critique of Post-Keynesian macrodynamics. The aim of the lectures is to analyse the movement of the economy through 'historical time'. The underlying theme of the lectures is the need to construct a coherent long-run theory of economic growth that would be consistent with both History and Equilibrium, a theory that would be a guide to intelligent planning and policy.

SECOND SEMESTER
Part II(5 weeks, cont.)

Part III (8 weeks) —   III. CAPITAL, UTILIZATION AND UNEMPLOYMENT

This part of the course will look at the issue of capacity utilization in relation to: the structural composition of the capital stock; the formation of long run adjusted positions. In this context the connection between Malinvaud's *Profitability and Unemployment* and the above issues will be explored.

2. Assessment

The assessment for the course consists of

(1) two essays of a *maximum* 2,000 words each — 25% of total assessment *each*

(b) final exam, 3 hours, 4 essays (November) — 50% of total assessment.

A list of essay topics will be distributed early in first semester. The first essay will be due on or before Friday 6 July. The second essay will be due on or before Friday, 5 October.

3. Lecturers

The lecturers in the course are Tony Aspromourgos (Part I, 10 weeks), Louis Haddad (Parts II – III, 9 weeks) and Joseph Halevi (Part IV, 8 weeks). All enquiries concerning essays, exam and the course as a whole should be directed to Tony Aspromourgos.

Tony Aspromourgos
Lecturer-in-charge
Room 330, Phone: 692-3065

IIIPOSTK.js

Department of Economics

ECONOMICS III 1990

POST-KEYNESIAN ECONOMICS

18 Lectures   Tuesday and Wednesday at 9.00 a.m.

Tony Aspromourgos   Merewether Lecture Room 6

FIRST SEMESTER, PART I (10 WEEKS)

EFFECTIVE DEMAND AND THE THEORY OF PRICES

These lectures begin with an introductory overview of post-Keynesian economics — its sources, scope and content (Part A). Following this, an alternative account is provided of the determination of income distribution and prices in a competitive capitalist economy, an account contradistinct to that provided by marginalist or "neo-classical" theory (part B). The marginalist theory of prices and distribution entails a particular approach to the theory of output and aggregate employment — with a natural tendency towards full employment via the price mechanism. An alternative theory of value and distribution implies a rejection of the marginalist theory of output and aggregate employment, along with a rejection of marginalist distribution and price theory. Given the logical relation between the marginalist theory of distribution and the marginalist theory of employment, a critique of the former along "surplus" lines entails a critique of the latter (part C). This critique clears the way for a more important, positive task: a reconstruction of Keynes's "economics of effective demand", which reveals his distinctive results with respect to the theory of output and aggregate employment in a clearer light, unencumbered by marginalist predilections and opens the way for a clarification of the long-period implications of Keynes's economics. Policy implications will also be examined (part D).

Starred references below should be regarded as essential reading for the course. All references have been placed on closed reserve in Fisher Library and a number of core references are on closed reserve in Wolstenholme Library.

A.   INTRODUCTION (2 Lectures)

1.   What is Post-Keynesian economics?

2.   Sources of Post-Keynesian theory: Keynes, Kalecki, the Classical Economists and Marx.

3.   Scope and content of Post-Keynesian theories: consensus and disagreements.

Reading

Eichner, A.S. and J.A. Kregel (1975), "An Essay on Post-Keynesian Theory: a new paradigm in economics", Journal of Economic Literature 13, pp. 1293-1314.

The Editors (1978), "Statement of Purposes", Journal of Post-Keynesian Economics 1, pp. 3-7.

Dobb, Maurice (1973), Theories of Value and Distribution since Adam Smith, Cambridge U.P., Chs. 8 (pp. 211-40 only) and 9.

* Eatwell, John (1974), "Controversies in the Theory of Surplus Value: old and new", Science and Society, 38, pp. 281-303.

B.   THE SURPLUS APPROACH TO THE THEORY OF PRICES AND DISTRIBUTION
     (6 Lectures)

1. Production as a process of circulation.

2. "Normal" prices and the uniform rate of profit.

3. Real wage, rate of profit and relative prices - with a degree of freedom.

4. Price theory without demand theory.

5. Search for a relation to close the price system.

6. Economic Policy: distribution and employment.

Reading

* Sraffa, Piero (1960), Production of Commodities by means of Commodities, Cambridge U.P., Preface and Part I, pp. 3-40, a difficult work, but fundamental to the modern reconstruction of classical-Marxian theory.

Pasinetti, L.L. (1977), Lectures on the Theory of Production, Columbia U.P., esp. Chs. v, vi, pp. 71-179.

Walsh, Vivian and Harvey Gram (1980), Classical and Neoclassical Theories of General Equilibrium, New York: Oxford U.P., Chs. 11-13, 15, pp. 269-343, 371-96.

Roncaglia, A. (1978), Sraffa and the Theory of Prices, New York, Wiley.

* Bharadwaj, Krishna (1963), "Value through Exogenous Distribution", reprinted in G.C. Harcourt and N.F. Laing (Eds) (1971), Capital and Growth: selected readings, Penguin, pp. 183-195 - a valuable interpretation of the Sraffa system.

* Garegnani, P. (1983), "The Classical Theory of Wages and the Role of Demand Schedules in the Determination of Relative Prices", American Economic Review (Papers and Proceedings) 73, pp. 309-13 - isolates the fundamental difference between the classical and marginalist approaches to price theory.

* Garegnani, P. (1984), "Value and Distribution in the Classical Economists and Marx", Oxford Economic Papers 36, pp. 291-325 - essential reading on the method and content of the Surplus Approach; or "Surplus approach to value and distribution", in The New Palgrave: a dictionary of economics vol.4.

Sraffa Memorial Edition (1988), Cambridge Journal of Economics, Vol. 12, No. 1.

*Clifton, James A. (1977), "Competition and the Evolution of the Capitalist Mode of Production", Cambridge Journal of Economics 1, pp. 137-51.

Clifton, James A. (1983), "Administered Prices in the Context of Capitalist Development", Contributions to Political Economy 2, pp.23-38.

Harcourt, G.C. (1982), "The Sraffian Contribution: an evaluation", in I. Bradley and M. Howard (Eds.), Classical and Marxian Political Economy, London: Macmillan, Ch. 3.

Bharadwaj, K. (1978), Classical Political Economy and Rise to Dominance of Supply and Demand Theories (Orient Longman) - surplus and marginalist approaches in historical perspective.

C.   THE CRITIQUE OF MARGINALIST ECONOMIC THEORY (4 Lectures)

1.   Choice of technique

2.   The Marginalist notion of capital, substitution and the rate of profit.

3.   Reswitching of techniques and capital reversing.

4.   Reswitching, reversing and the theory of employment.

5.   Alternative theories of distribution and alternative theories of (un)employment.

Reading

*Dobb, Maurice (1970), "The Sraffa System and Critique of the Neo-classical Theory of Distribution", De Economist 118, pp.347-62, reprinted in E.K. Hunt and Jesse G. Schwartz (eds), A Critique of Economic Theory: selected readings, Penguin, 1972, pp.205-21 - an important interpretation of the critical implications of the Sraffa system.

Robinson, Joan (1961), "Prelude to a Critique of Economic Theory", Oxford Economic Papers 13, pp.7-14, reprinted in her Collected Economic Papers, Blackwell, 1965, vol. 3, pp.7-14, reprinted in Hunt and Schwartz (eds), op.cit., pp.197-204 - review of and commentary on Sraffa (1960).

*Harcourt, G.C. (1972), Some Cambridge Controversies in the Theory of Capital, Cambridge U.P., esp. ch.4 and Appendix, pp.118-204; or Harcourt, G.C. (1969), "Some Cambridge Controversies in the Theory of Capital", Journal of Economic Literature 7, pp.369-405 - the definitive references on the history of the Capital Debates.

*Kregel, J.A. (1976), Theory of Capital, London: Macmillan, esp. ch.3, pp.53-84 - a simple account of the issues covered in Harcourt (1969; 1972).

Garegnani, P. (1970), "Heterogeneous Capital, the Production Function and the Theory of Distribution", Review of Economic Studies 37, pp.407-38, reprinted in Hunt and Schwartz (eds), op.cit., pp.245-.

Garegnani, P. (1976), "On a Change in the Notion of Equilibrium in Recent Work on Value" in M. Brown et.al. (eds), Modern Capital Theory, Amsterdam: North-Holland, reprinted in Eatwell and Milgate (eds) (1983), Keynes's Economics and the Theory of Value and Distribution, London: Duckworth.

*Dobb, Maurice (1973), op.cit. ch.9, pp.247-72 - a useful interpretation of the Capital Debates.

Sraffa, Piero, op.cit., Part III, pp.81-87.

Pasinetti, L.L., et.al. (1966), "Paradoxes in Capital Theory: A Symposium", Quarterly Journal of Economics, 80, pp.503-83, esp. P.A. Samuelson, "A Summing Up", pp.568-83, reprinted in Harcourt and Laing (eds), op.cit., pp.233-50.

D.   VALUE AND DISTRIBUTION AND THE THEORY OF EMPLOYMENT (6 Lectures)

1.   Keynes and the Principle of Effective Demand.

2.   Marginalist interpretations of Keynes.

3.   A reconstruction of Keynes's theory.

4.   Short-period and long-period theories of employment.

5.   Elements for a long-period theory of employment: accumulation, growth and cycles.

6.   Applications to Economic Policy.

Reading

Keynes, John Maynard (1936), The General Theory of Employment, Interest and Money, Macmillan, esp. chs. 3, 10-13, 18-21.

*Garegnani, P (1978, 1979), "Notes on Consumption, Investment and Effective Demand", Cambridge Journal of Economics 2, pp.335-53; 3, pp.63-82, reprinted in Eatwell and Milgate (eds), op.cit.- essential reading on the reconstruction of Keynes's economics.

Milgate, Murray (1982), Capital and Employment, London: Academic Press, esp. ch.vi-viii, pp.77-142 - a useful account of Keynes.

Bharadwaj, Krishna (1983), "On Effective Demand: certain recent critiques", in J.A. Kregel (ed.), Distribution, Effective Demand and International Economic Relations, London: Macmillan, ch.1, pp.3-27.

*Garegnani, P. (1983), "Two Routes to Effective Demand", in Kregel (ed.) op.cit., pp.69-80 - summary statement on the "long-period" theory of employment.

Eatwell, J. and M. Milgate (1983), "Unemployment and the Market Mechanism", in Eatwell and Milgate (eds.), op.cit.

Magnani, M. (1983), "Keynesian Fundamentalism: a critique", in Eatwell and Milgate (eds), op.cit.

Eatwell, John (1983), "Theories of Value, Output and Employment", in Eatwell and Milgate (eds), op.cit.

Eatwell, John (1983), "The Long-period Theory of Employment", Cambridge Journal of Economics 7.

*Aspromourgos, T. (1987), "Unemployment, Economic Theory and Labour-Market Deregulation", Australian Economic Papers June, pp.130-144.

*Roncaglia, A. (1988), "Wage Costs and Employment: the Sraffian View", in J.A. Kregel, E. Matzner & A. Roncaglia (eds), Barriers to Full Employment (Macmillan).

*Aspromourgos, T. and G. White (1989), "The EPAC 'Growth Papers': An Assessment", Economic Record vol.65 (December).

Roncaglia, A. (1985), "Some Remarks on the Relevance of Sraffa's Analysis for Economic Policy", paper presented at the Sraffa Conference, Florence, Italy, 24-27 August [not to be quoted].

Tony Aspromourgos
February 1990

University of Sydney

Tony Aspromourgos and Peter Groenewegen

ECONOMIC CLASSICS
ECONOMICS IV - HONOURS 1990

This course is constructed to give an in-depth study of two of the great economic classics of the first half of the twentieth century, both of which still exercise a substantial influence upon economic theory and policy:

> Alfred Marshall, Principles of Economics
> (First edition, 1890; eighth and definitive edition, 1920, ninth variorum edition, 1961)
>
> John Maynard Keynes, The General Theory of Employment, Interest and Money, (first edition, 1936; new and augmented edition with prefaces to translations and associated material, 1973 as volume 7 of the Collected Writings of John Maynard Keynes).

The first semester is devoted to study of the Principles of Alfred Marshall; the second to Keynes's General Theory, in both cases prefaced with preliminary lectures on relevant background to the classics in question. The objective of the course is to acquaint students at first hand with the work of two economists who profoundly influenced the development of the discipline as it is taught and applied today.

Each semester of the course is divided into lectures and seminars commencing with the already mentioned introductory lectures. Seminars scheduled for each semester deal with topics in the two classics to be studied, and students are strongly advised to obtain their own personal working copy of each. Both are available in paper-covered editions, details of which are subsequently provided. The course is essentially a reading course, with private study the major course work apart from two seminar papers. The amount of reading to be done is extensive. Seminar performance counts for 50% of the final result, which includes participation by discussion during those seminars at which a student is not giving a paper.

Seminar papers are therefore an important part of course work assessment and students should consider the following in their preparation. Each paper should briefly discuss the major points raised by the topic set down for the seminar, drawing mainly on the reading from the classic itself. The secondary literature suggested is intended for supplementary guidance only and suggested readings of greater importance are marked with an *. Papers, which must be no longer than 2,000 words should be designed as vehicles for discussion at the seminar. Hence a listing of issues or questions considered particularly important for later discussion should be provided at the end of the paper. References should be provided as follows: Keynes (1973, p. 324), Marshall (1961 I 464n) and a bibliography in alphabetical order by author of the works consulted should be provided at the end of the paper.

The November examination paper is in two sections containing six questions each. Each section is devoted to the work of one semester respectively. Students have to attempt four questions in all, two from each section.

Paperback editions of the classics to be studied

Alfred Marshall, Principles of Economics, Papermac edition, Macmillan. [NB. This edition uses different pagination from the 8th edition because it was reset - a concordance of pagination is included as an appendix to allow easy transformation of page references from this version of the 8th edition to the earlier version.]

J.M. Keynes, General Theory of Employment, Interest and Money, in Collected Writings of John Maynard Keynes, Vol. 7, London, Macmillan: paperback edition available.

SEMESTER 1:

Marshall's Principles of Economics
(Lecturer: Peter Groenewegen)

This semester discusses Marshall's Principles of Economics from the perspective of the development of economics in the nineteenth century and towards the end, looking at some specific relationships between Marshall's economics and that of Keynes. The preliminary lectures provide the historical and theoretical settings for the 7 seminars on the Principles of Economics. 1990 marks the centenary of publication of the first edition of the Principles which took place in July 1890. A number of journals are devoting special issues to this event, including the Scottish Journal of Political Economy 37(1), February, and Economic Appliquee 43(1).

Introductory Reading

There is a wealth of introductory material on Marshall's economics and the following are listed as being of particular interest.

J.M. Keynes, 'Alfred Marshall', in Essays in Biography, Collected Works of John Maynard Keynes, Volume 10.

J.A. Schumpeter, 'Alfred Marshall', in Ten Great Economists.

Jacob Viner, 'Marshall's Economics in Relation to the man and to the his times', American Economic Review, 1941, reprinted in Viner, The Long View and the Short.

Alfred Marshall, 'On himself', in History of Economic Thought Newsletter, No. 8, Spring 1972, pp. 14-17. (This is circulated at the start of the course.)

J.K. Whitaker, 'Alfred Marshall 1842-1924' in The New Palgrave A Dictionary of Economics, Vol. 3, pp. 350-63.

N.B. Two of the above are reprinted in J.C. Wood (ed.), Alfred Marshall, Critical Assessments, London, Croom Helm, 1982, Vol. 1, section 1, while in subsequent volumes and sections much other relevant material can be found which those interested are invited to use.

A useful recent study of Marshall's economics is David Reissman, The Economics of Alfred Marshall, Macmillan, 1985 and his Alfred Marshall, Progress and Politics, Macmillan, 1987.

LECTURES 1 AND 2 (first two weeks):
The Growth of Economic Science

After an introduction to the course, these lectures examine the development of economics as seen by Marshall (Principles, Appendix B) with special reference to aspects of the work of Adam Smith, David Ricardo and John Stuart Mill.

Reading :

A. Marshall, Principles of Economics , **Appendix B, I.**

P. Groenewegen, 'Marshall on Ricado' (copies to be circulated).

D. O'Brien, 'Marshall's Work in Relation to Classical Economics' University of Durham, Department of Economics Working Paper 91, April 1988.

K. Bharadwaj, Classical Political Economy and Rise to Dominance of Supply and Demand Theories, R.C. Dutt Lectures on Political Economy, 1976, Centre for Studies in Social Sciences, Calcutta, 1978.

A. Campus, "Notes on Cost and Price: Malthus and the Marginal Theory", Political Economy: Studies in the Surplus Approach, 1987, Vol. 3, No. 1.

K. Bharadwaj, 'The Subversion of Classical Analysis: Alfred Marshall's early writing on Value', Cambridge Journal of Economics, 2(3), September, pp. 253-71.

LECTURES 3 and 4 (weeks 3 and 4):
Alfred Marshall (1842-1924) and Contemporaneous Developments in Economics

A biographical sketch of Alfred Marshall which places him in the context of the developments in economics during the second half of the nineteenth century and the early decades of the twentieth.

Reading:

Guillebaud, Introduction to variorum edition, Vol. II.

J.K. Whitaker, 'Alfred Marshall: The Years 1877-1885', History of Political Economy, Spring, 1972.

* Alfred Marshall, 'Mr. Jevons' Theory of Political Economy', (1872), and 'Mr. Mill's Theory of Value' (1876), both reprinted in A.C. Pigou (ed.), Memorials of Alfred Marshall, Part II, essays 1 and 3.

* J. Whitaker, introduction to The Early Economic Writings of Alfred Marshall 1867-1890, Macmillan 1975, Vol. I, pp. 3-113.

Ronald H. Coase, 'Alfred Marshall's Mother and Father', History of Political Economy, Vol. 16, no. 4, Winter 1984.

Peter Groenewegen, 'Alfred Marshall and the Establishment of the Cambridge Economics Tripos', History of Political Economy, 20(4), Winter 1988.

SEMINAR 1 (Week 5):
Preliminary Survey and Fundamental Notions

Designed to come to grips with aspects of Marshall's view of the subject in general, and methodology in particular.

Reading:

* Marshall, Principles, prefaces, Books I, II, Appendices A,C,D.

* Marshall, 'The Old Generation of Economists and the New' in Memorials of Alfred Marshall, ed. Pigou, ch. 13.

J.C. Wood, ed. Vol. I, essay 16, 21, 22.

David Reisman, Alfred Marshall, Progress and Politics, Ch.7.

Peter C. Dooley,'Alfred Marshall: Fitting the Theory to the Facts', Cambridge Journal of Economics, 9(3), September 1985, pp. 245-55.

SEMINAR 2: (Week 6)
Analysis of Consumer Behaviour: Theory of Demand and Consumption

Reading:

Marshall, Principles, Book III.

David Reisman, The Economics of Alfred Marshall, Chapter 3.

Peter C. Dooley, 'Giffen's Hint?' Australian Economic Papers, 24,(44), June 1985, pp. 201-5.

Michael White, 'Porter's Hint? A Note', Australian Economic Papers, 16(49), December 1987, 328-31.

SEMINAR 3: (Week 7)
The Theory of Production and the Theory of Supply

This seminar is designed to cover not only a discussion of issues arising from the theory of production - factors of production and their definition, laws of returns - but also the connection with the theory of supply in preparation for the subsequent seminar on the theory of value (supply and demand). The link between the theory of production and supply is not explicitly made till Book V chapter 3, though the underlying theory of costs is virtually fully presented in the main book set down for study for this seminar.

Reading:

* Marshall, Principles, Book IV, Book V, chapters 3, 4, 7, Appendices E and H.

Stigler, Production and Distribution Theories, chapter 4, pp. 61-83.

David Reisman, The Economics of Alfred Marshall, chapters 3-5.

Lionel Robbins, 'Certain Aspects of the Theory of Costs', Economic Journal, 1934.

SEMINAR 4: (Week 8)
The Theory of Value as a Theory of Supply and Demand

This seminar is designed to examine time periods in relation to the theory of value in particular, and hence needs to deal with market price determination, and the theory of short, long period value, secular price movements and the stationary state.

Reading:

Marshall, Principles, Book V, chapters 1-3, 5, 12-15, Bk. VI, ch. 12.

R. Opie, 'Marshall's time analysis', Economic Journal, 1931.

R. Frisch, 'Alfred Marshall's Theory of Value', Quarterly Journal of Economics, 1950, reprinted in H. Townsend (ed.),Readings in Price Theory, Penguin Modern Economics Readings

B.J. Loasby, 'Whatever happened to Marshall's Theory of Value', Scottish Journal of Political Economy, Vol. 25, no. 1, Feb., 1978, pp. 1-12, reprinted in revised form in Brian Loasby, The Mind and Method of the Economist, Brookfeld Gower, 1989, ch. 4.

Peter Newman, 'The Erosion of Marshall's Theory of Value',Quarterly Journal of Economics, Vol. 74, November 1960, pp. 587-601.

All articles above are included in J.C. Wood (ed.), Alfred Marshall, Critical Assessments, the last three in Vol. 3.

SEMINAR 5: (Week 9)
Theory of Distribution as an Application of the Theory of Value

This seminar is designed to present a general overview of Marshall's theory of distribution in the Principles, and is followed by two further seminars (6 and 7) on labour, wages and employment; capital, interest, quasi-rent and rent. The various forms of Marshall's distribution theory as identified by Stigler should be particularly examined for this seminar.

Reading:

Marshall, Principles, Book V, ch. 6, pp. 381-7; Book VI,chs, 1-2, 11, 13.

Stigler, <u>Production and Distribution Theories</u>, chapter 4, pp. 83-87, chapter 12, pp. 344-356.

D. H. Robertson, <u>Lectures on Economic Principles</u>, Volume II, ch. 2 (or Part II, ch. 2 in one volume edition).

J. Whitaker, 'The Distribution Theory of Marshall's Principles' in <u>Theories of Income Distribution</u>, ed. A. Asimakopulos, Kluwer Academic Publishers, Boston, 1987, chapter 5.

SEMINAR 6: (Week 10)
Labour, Wages and Employment

The Marshallian supply and demand approach to labour economics is the focus of this seminar, with an eye to second semester discussion of Keynes' analysis of the classical theory of employment.

Reading:

Marshall, <u>Principles</u>, Book IV, chapters 4-6 (aspects relevant to labour supply); Book VI chapters 3-5, Appendix J.

David Reisman, <u>The Economics of Alfred Marshall</u>, chapter 9.

George Stigler, <u>Production and Distribution Theory</u>, chapter 4, pp. 97-101.
[reference can also be fruitfully made to Whitaker's article listed for seminar 5, esp. pp. 112-7.]

SEMINAR 7: (Week 11)
Capital, Interest, Profits, Rent and Quasi-Rent

The focus on Marshall's treatment of other factor price (returns) determination in this seminar is also designed with an eye on the discussion which Keynes gave it in the <u>General Theory</u>.

Reading:

Marshall, <u>Principles</u>, Book IV, chapter 7, Book V, chapters 4, 8-11; Book VI chapters 6-10, Appendix E.

David Reisman, <u>The Economics of Alfred Marshall</u>, chapters 8, 10, Pascal Bridel, <u>Cambridge Monetary Thought</u> (London: Macmillan, 1987), ch. 2.

Pascal Bridel, Cambridge Monetary Thought (London: Macmillan, 1987), ch. 2.

George Stigler, Production and Distribution Theory, chapter 4, pp. 87-97, pp. 101-07.

F.W. Ogilvy, 'Marshall on Rent', Economic Journal, March 1930; M.T. Hollond, 'Marshallian Rent: a Reply to Professor Ogilvy', Economic Journal, 1930; both in Wood, Alfred Marshall, Critical Assessments, Vol. 3, Readings 49,52.

LECTURE 5: (Week 12)
From Marshall to Keynes: A Preliminary View

This lecture examines aspects of Marshall's work outside the Principles concerned with money and business fluctuations on which he wrote and lectured before (and after) completion of the Principles. Reading for this final section of the course for Semester 1 is largely drawn from secondary sources, but some references to Marshall's more accessible writings on these topics are provided.

Reading:

A. Marshall and M.P. Marshall, The Economics of Industry, London, Macmillan, second edition, 1881, Book III, chapter 1, reprinted in A.H. Hansen and R.V. Clemence (eds.), Readings in Business Cycles and National Income, London, George Allen and Unwin, 1953, Reading 7.

A. Marshall, 'Remedies for Fluctuations of General Prices', Contemporary Review 1887, reprinted in A.C. Pigou (ed.), Memorials of Alfred Marshall, London, Macmillan, 1925, pp. 188-211.

J.M. Keynes, 'Alfred Marshall 1842-1924', in Essays in Biography (Vol. X of the Collected Works, 1973, pp. 189-95)

David Reisman, Alfred Marshall: Progress and Politics, ch. 6.

A. Krishnaswamy, 'Marshall's Theory of Money and Interest', Indian Economic Journal, 1941, in Wood, Alfred Marshall: Critical Assessments, Vol. 3, Reading 55.

Eprime Eshag, From Marshall to Keynes, Oxford, Basil Blackwell, 1963.

* Pascal Bridel, Cambridge Monetary Thought (London: Macmillan, 1987), ch. 3.

SEMESTER 2

KEYNES'S GENERAL THEORY OF EMPLOYMENT, INTEREST AND MONEY (Lecturer: Tony Aspromourgos)

This semester consists of an intensive study of John Maynard Keynes's major work on economic theory, published in 1936. The preliminary lectures provide the historical and theoretical setting for the 7 seminars on The General Theory by examining the main currents in the development of economic theory from the 1870s to the 1930s and Keynes's life and intellectual work. They also outline in a preliminary way the main currents in interpretation of the GT, a theme returned to in the final double lecture.

LECTURES 6 and 7 (first two weeks)
The Development of Economic Theory 1871-1936

These 4 lectures examine the main currents in economic theory from the "first generation" of marginalist theorists to the 1930s, thereby providing the intellectual background, in particular from Marshall to Keynes:

1. From the first to the second generation of marginalist theorists.
2. Developments in the Marshallian/Cambridge School.
3. Aspects of heterodox economics 1883-1936.
4. Michal Kalecki.
5. The state of economics in February 1936.

Reading:

* M. Dobb (1973), Theories of Value and Distribution since Adam Smith (Cambridge: CUP), ch. 7, pp. 166-210 ("The 'Jevonian Revolution' ").

* P.D. Groenewegen (1988), "Neo-Classical Value and Distribution Theory: The English Speaking Pioneers", Department of Economics, Working Papers, No. 112, September.

* M. Kalecki (1933), 'Outline of a Theory of the Business Cycle", in Kalecki (1971), Selected Essays on the Dynamics of the Capitalist Economy 1933-1970 (Cambridge: CUP), ch. 1; pp. 1-14.

A.C. Pigou (1933). The Theory of Unemployment (reprint London: Frank Cass, 1968), passim.

G.L.S. Shackle (1967). The Years of High Theory: Invention and Tradition in Economic Thought 1926-1939 (Cambridge: CUP), ch. 10, pp. 94-128 ("Myrdal's Analysis").

P.Bridel (1987), Cambridge Monetary Theory: The Development of Saving-Investment Analysis from Marshall to Keynes (London: Macmillan).

LECTURES 8 and 9 (third and fourth weeks)
John Maynard Keynes and His Economics

These 4 lectures examine the life of Keynes with particular reference to his intellectual development and activities; and provide an account of the main currents in interpretation of the GT in the approximately 50 years subsequent to its publication:

1. Life and activities
2. Keynes's intellectual development with particular reference to the making of the GT (1930-36)
3. Reception of the GT; rise and fall of "Keynesian" economics.
4. Main currents in the interpretation of Keynes.

Reading

* R.F. Harrod (1951). The Life of John Maynard Keynes (Pelican, 1972), ch. 11, pp. 509-72 (" 'The General Theory of Employment, Interest and Money' ") and passim.

* J.R. Hicks (1937). "Mr. Keynes and the 'Classics': A Suggested Interpretation", Econometrica (reprinted in many places).

  A.C. Pigou (1936). "Mr. J.M. Keynes' General Theory of Employment, Interest and Money", Economica.

* A. Robinson (1947), "John Maynard Keynes, 1883-1946", Economic Journal, Vol. 57, 1-68.

  R. Skidelsky (1983). John Maynard Keynes: Hopes Betrayed 1883-1920 (London: Macmillan).

  C.H. Hession (1984), John Maynard Keynes (New York: Macmillan).

SEMINAR 8 (week 5)
"Classical" Economics and the Principle of Effective Demand

Reading

J.M. Keynes, GT, Preface (v-viii); chs. 1-3 (3-34),
5 (46-51), 6, sec II (61-65), 7, sec. V (81-85), 18 (245-54).

* M. Milgate (1982). Capital and Employment: A Study of Keynes's Economics (London: Academic Press), ch. 6, pp. 77-101 ("The Principle of Effective Demand: The Positive Part of the General Theory").

L.L. Pasinetti (1974). "The Economics of Effective Demand", in, Pasinetti, Growth and Income Distributon (Cambridge: Cambridge U.P.).

* J.T. Dunlop (1938), "The Movement of Real and Money Wage Rates", Economic Journal, Vol. 48, 413-34.

* J.M. Keynes (1939), "Relative Movements of Real Wages and Output", Economic Journal, Vol. 49, 34-51 (March) [reply to Dunlop].

C. Casarosa (1981), "The Microfoundations of Keynes's Aggregate Supply and Expected Demand Analysis", Economic Journal, Vol. 91, 188-94 (March).

SEMINAR 9 (week 6):
The Theory of Consumption and the Multiplier

Reading

J.M. Keynes, GT, chs. 8-10 (89-131).

* R.F. Kahn (1931), "The Relation of Home Investment to Unemployment", Economic Journal, reprinted in Kahn (1972), Selected Essays on Employment and Growth (Cambridge:Cambridge UP).

N. Cain (1979), 'Cambridge and its Revolution: A Perspective on the Multiplier and Effective Demand', Economic Record.

* G.L.S. Shackle (1967), The Years of High Theory (Cambridge UP), Ch. 14 ("The Multiplier").

* F. Targetti and B. Kinda-Hass (1982), "Kalecki's Review of Keynes' General Theory", Australian Economic Papers, Vol. 21, 244-60.

SEMINAR 10 (week 7):
Investment Demand and the Trade Cycle

Reading

J.M. Keynes, GT, chs. 11-12 (135-64), 22 (313-32).

* P. Garegnani (1983). "Notes on Consumption, Investment and Effective Demand" (Part I, Appendix and Addendum), in J. Eatwell and M. Milgate (eds.), Keynes's Economics and the Theory of Value and Distribution (London: Duckworth), pp. 21-41, 64-69.

* N. Kaldor (1938). "Economic Stability and Full Employment", Economic Journal,

H.P. Minsky (1975), John Maynard Keynes (New York: Columbia UP), Ch. 4 ("The Theory of Investment").

V. Chick (1983), Macroeconomics After Keynes (Oxford: Philip Allen), ch. 16, "Cyclical Fluctuations".

SEMINAR 11 (week 8):
Monetary Theory and the Rate of Interest

Reading

J.M. Keynes, GT, chs. 13-17 (165-244).

* R.F. Kahn (1954). "Some Notes on Liquidity Preference", The Manchester School, reprinted in Kahn (1972), op.cit.

J. Tobin (1958), "Liquidity Preference as Behaviour Towards Risk", Review of Economic Studies, Vol. 25, 65-86 (February).

* C. Panico (1988). Interest and Profit in the Theories of Value and Distribution (London: Macmillan), ch. 4, pp. 102-56 ("Keynes on the Interest Rate").

A.H. Meltzer (1989), Keynes's Monetary Theory (Cambridge CUP).

* G. Mongiovi (1989), "Keynes, Sraffa and Hayek: On the Origins of Chapter 17 of The General Theory", mimeo.

E.J. Nell (1983), "Keynes After Sraffa: The essential properties of Keynes's Theory of Interest and Money", in J. Kregel (ed.), Distribution, Effective Demand and International Economic Relations (London: Macmillan).

D. Patinkin (1976), Keynes' Mopnetary Thought (Durham: Duke UP).

SEMINAR 12 (week 9):
Money Wages, Price and Employment

Reading

J.M. Keynes, GT, chs. 19-21 (257-309)

* P. Garegnani, op.cit. (Part II and Conclusions), pp. 41-63.

* D. Patinkin (1948). "Price Flexibility and Full Employment", American Economic Review, corrected version in F.A. Lutz and L.W. Mints (eds.), Readings in Monetary Theory (Philadelphia,1951), pp. 252-83.

  E. Roy Weintraub (1979). Microfoundations (Cambridge UP), ch. 3, pp. 38-54 ("The 4,287th re-examination of Keynes's System").

* A. Leijonhufvud (1974), "Keynes' Employment Function", History of Political Economy, Vol. 6.

SEMINAR 13 (week 10):
Economic Policy

Reading

J.M. Keynes, GT, ch. 24 (372-84) with pp. 94-95, 119-20,128-31, 163-64, 196-99, 202-08, 217-21, 266-71, 315-20. (These pages bring together the more significant discussions of policy prior to ch. 24. Most come up in earlier seminars. They deal with monetary policy, fiscal policy, public works and public investment, and wages policy.)

* D. E. Moggridge and S. Howson (1974). "Keynes and Monetary Policy, 1910-1946", Oxford Economic Papers.

  A. Leijonhufvud (1968), On Keynesian Economics and the Economics of Keynes (New York: OUP), Ch. VI:2, pp. 401-16.

  D. Winch, op.cit., ch. 8 and Appendix, pp. 145-66, 339-50. ("Keynes and the Academic Community, 1919-1936", "Keynes and the British left in the inter-war period").

  S. Howson (1973), "A Dear Money Man'?: Keynes on Monetary Policy", Economic Journal (June).

* A.P. Thirlwall (ed.) (1982), Keynes as a Policy Advisor (London: Macmillan), passim.

SEE ALSO REFERENCES FOR SEMINAR 14.

SEMINAR 14: (week 11):
Social Philosophy and Politics

   Reading

   J.M. Keynes, GT, ch. 24 (372-84).

   J.M. Keynes (1972), Essays in Persuasion (London: Macmillan),
   Part IV, passim.

   J.M. Keynes (1932), "The Dilemma of Modern Socialism",
   Political Quarterly, Vol. 3, No. 2 (April-June).

* R. O'Donnell (1989).

* J. Steindl (1985), "J.M. Keynes: Society and the Economist",
   in F. Vicarelli (ed.), Keynes' Relevance Today, (London:
   Macmillan).

   P. Lambert (1963), "The Social Philosophy of John Maynard
   Keynes", reprinted in J.G. Wood, Critical Assessments, Vol. I.

* B. Schefold (1980), "The General Theory for a Totalitarian
   State? A Note on Keynes' Preface to the German Edition of
   1936", Cambridge Journal of Economics, Vol. 4.

   A. Fitzgibbons (1988), Keynes's Vision (Oxford: Oxford UP).

LECTURE 10 (week 12):
Keynesian Economics After Keynes

This lecture draws together the earlier lectures and seminars in
order to consider concluding Keynes's influence on theory and policy
on half a century after after the GT.

   Reading

* R.W. Clower (1969). "The Keynesian Counter-revolution: A
   Theoretical Appraisal", in Clower (ed.), Monetary Theory
   (Harmondsworth: Penguin).

* J. Eatwell (1983). "The Long-Period Theory of Employment",
   Cambridge Journal of Economics.

* A.C. Pigou (1950). Keynes's General Theory,
   (London:Macmillan).

                                        Peter Groenewegen
                                        Tony Aspromourgos

                                        February, 1990.

THE UNIVERSITY OF SYDNEY

FACULTIES OF ECONOMICS, ARTS, ETC.

ECONOMICS IV - Final Honours and
M.A. and M.Ec. (1st Year)

PAPER - ECONOMIC CLASSICS

November, 1989.   Time Allowed: Three Hours.

Answer FOUR questions, TWO from EACH section.
Answer each question in a separate book.

SECTION A

1. Critically examine the usefulness of the various time periods Marshall distinguished. To what extent do they explain his conception of quasi-rent?

2. "Two Marshalls - one the abstract theorist, the other the practical observer of everyday economic life - were blended in all of his writings." (William Barber). Discuss, illustrating your answer with examples of his treatment EITHER from the laws of returns OR from his discussion of market structure.

3. "For Marshall, not only was constant purchasing power of money a device for separating the theory of relative prices from monetary theory; it was also a bridge between the two." (Milton Friedman). Discuss, confining your illustrations to Marshall's work in the Principles.

4. "The framework for a mathematically determined market price by the intersection of the schedules of supply and demand was set out in Book V of Marshall's Principles, the section which he regarded with reason as containing the real nub of his own special contribution to economic theory." (Phyllis Deane). Discuss, including in your answer at least some reference to the implications of this statement for Marshall's own perception of his work as a continuous development from the British classical tradition in economics.

5. Critically examine the proposition that Marshall's theory of distribution is essentially a marginal productivity theory.

6. "If we shut our eyes to realities we may construct an edifice of pure crystal imaginations, that will throw side lights on real problems; and might conceivably be of interest to beings who had no economic problems at all like our own. Such playful excursions are often suggestive in unexpected ways: they afford good training to the mind: and seem to be productive only of good, so long as their purpose is clearly understood." (Alfred Marshall). Discuss, with reference to the extent this judgment may be argued to apply to Marshall's own work in the Principles.

../2

SECTION B

7. "... it is an outstanding characteristic of the economic system in which we live that, whilst it is subject to severe fluctuations in respect of output and employment, it is not violently unstable. Indeed it seems capable of remaining in a chronic condition of sub-normal activity for a considerable period without any marked tendency either towards recovery or towards complete collapse. Moreover, the evidence indicates that full, or even approximately full, employment is of rare and short-lived occurrence" (GT, 249-50). In the light of this conclusion, outline and appraise Keynes's formulation of the Principle of Effective Demand (in terms of Aggregate Demand and Aggregate Supply) in Book I of the GT, and the associated critique of "classical" economics.

8. "An increment of investment in terms of wage-units cannot occur unless the public are prepared to increase their savings in terms of wage-units. Ordinarily speaking, the public will not do this unless their aggregate income in terms of wage-units is increasing. Thus their effort to consume a part of their increased incomes will stimulate output until the new level (and distribution) of incomes provides a margin of saving sufficient to correspond to the increased investment. The multiplier tells us by how much their employment has to be increased to yield an increase in real income sufficient to induce them to do the necessary extra saving ..." (GT, p. 117). In light of this statement, outline and appraise the theory of consumption in Book III of the GT.

9. Outline and appraise Keynes's theory of investment in Book IV of the GT, and its relation to his Principle of Effective Demand and theory of the trade cycle.

10. "... the rate of interest is a highly psychological phenomenon ... It might be more accurate ... to say that the rate of interest is a highly conventional ... phenomenon. For its actual value is largely governed by the prevailing view as to what its value is expected to be ... Such comfort as we can fairly take from more encouraging reflections must be drawn from the hope that, precisely because the convention is not rooted in secure knowledge, it will not be always unduly resistent to a modest measure of persistence and consistency of purpose by the monetary authority" (GT, 202-04). Outline and appraise Keynes's monetary theory of interest, and his views on monetary policy, in the light of these comments.

11. Outline and appraise Keynes's theory of the relations between money wages, employment, prices and the quantity of money, especially in Book V of the GT.

12. EITHER

    (a) Outline and appraise Keynes's views on the relation between his own theory in the GT and that of his predecessors, orthodox and heterodox.

    OR

    (b) Outline and appraise how Keynes's theory of the capitalist economy, together with his political values, shape his views on economic policy and social reconstruction.

Economics 258　　　　　　**Wesleyan University**　　　　W. Barber
History of Economic Thought　　　　　　　　　　　　　　Fall 1989

Syllabus

Key:　x　- designates required reading
　　　(x) - indicates that one selection from a group of readings is required.
　　　　　Other readings on the list are recommended.

I. The Mercantilist Background

　　Texts: x　Mun, England's Treasure by Forraign Trade.
　　　　　　　Considerations Upon the East India Trade, 1701 in Early
　　　　　　　English Tracts on Commerce, McCulloch, ed.
　　　　　　　King, "Of the Naval Trade of England Anos. 1688 and the
　　　　　　　National Profit then Arising Thereby," in Two Tracts.

　　Commentaries:

　　Heckscher, "On Mercantilism" (in Spiegel, The Development of
　　　Economic Thought).
　　Heckscher, Mercantilism, Vol. I, Chapter VII.
　　Viner, Studies in the Theory of International Trade, Chapters I-II.
　　Senior, Three Lectures on the Transmission of Precious Metals.
　　Schumpeter, History of Economic Analysis, pp. 335-376.
　　Hinton, "The Mercantile System in the Time of Thomas Mun," Economic
　　　History Review, 1955.
　　Muchmore, "Gerald de Malynes and Mercantile Economics," History of
　　　Political Economy, 1969.
　　Barber, British Economic Thought and India, Part I.

　　For Comparison:

　　x　Keynes, "Notes on Mercantilism," The General Theory, Chapter 23.
　　　Viner, "Power versus Plenty as an Objective of Policy in the 17th
　　　　and 18th Centuries," World Politics, 1948 (Reprinted in The Long
　　　　View and the Short).
　　　Momtchiloff, "Schachtian Mercantilism," Journal of Industrial
　　　　Economics, 1954.

　　Historical Background:

　　Davis, English Overseas Trade, 1500-1700.

II. Transitions to Explicit Theorizing

　　Texts:　　Quesnay, "Tableau Economique," (Reprinted in Monroe, Early
　　　　　　　　Economic Thought).
　　　　　　　Turgot, Reflections on the Origins and Distribution of
　　　　　　　　Riches.
　　　　　x　Hume, "On Money," and "On the Balance of Trade," (Kapp,
　　　　　　　　Readings; also in Hume, Writings on Economics, Rotwein,
　　　　　　　　ed.).
　　　　　　　Steuart, Principles of Political Economy.

Economics 258   -2-   W. Barber
History of Economic Thought   Fall 1989
Syllabus (Continued)

Commentaries:

Meek, The Economics of Physiocracy.
Hutchison, Before Adam Smith.
Vaggi, The Economics of Francois Quernay.

For Comparison:

Phillips, "The Tableau Economique as a Simple Leontief Model," Quarterly Journal of Economics, 1955.
Tsuru, "On Reproduction Schemes, " Appendix A in Sweezy, The Theory of Capitalist Development.
Barber, "British Economic Thought and the Indian Monetary System During the Period of East India Company Rule," Journal of Oriental Studies, January 1970.

III. The Classical Model

　　A. Smith's Statement of the Classical Problem

　　　　Text:　x　Smith, The Wealth of Nations, Books I and II.

　　　　Commentaries:

　　　　Hollander, The Economics of Adam Smith.
　　　　Cole, "Puzzles in the 'Wealth of Nations'," Canadian Journal of Economics and Political Science, 1958.
　　　　Robertson and Taylor, "Adam Smith's Approach to the Theory of Value," Economic Journal, 1957.
　　　　Thweatt, "A Diagrammatic Presentation of Adam Smith's Growth Model," Social Research, 1957.
　　　　Adam Smith Bicentennial Issue: History of Political Economy, Winter 1976.

　　B. Elaborations of the Classical System

　　　　Texts: x　Malthus, Essay on the Principle of Population.
　　　　　　　 x　_____, Principles of Political Economy (Selections in Kapp, Readings).
　　　　　　　 x　Say, A Treatise on Political Economy, (Kapp, Readings).
　　　　　　　 x　Ricardo, Principles of Political Economy and Taxation.

　　　　Commentaries:

　　　　Sowell, Say's Law.
　　　　Meek, Studies in Labour Theory of Value.
　　　　Myint, Theories of Welfare Economics.
　　　　Blaug, Ricardian Economics.
　　　　Corry, Money, Savings and Investment in English Classical Economics.
　　　　Fetter, The Development of British Monetary Orthodoxy.
　　　　　　　Winch, Malthus.
　　　　　　　Fetter, "The Rise and Decline of Ricardian Economics," History of Political Economy, 1969.

29

Economics 258 -3- W. Barber
History of Economic Thought Fall 1989
Syllabus (Continued)

(Commentaries, continued):

Stigler, "Ricardo and the 93% Labor Theory of Value," <u>American Economic Review</u>, 1958.
Spengler, "Malthus's Total Population Theory," (reprinted in Spengler and Allen, <u>Essays in Economic Thought</u>).
Keynes, "Robert Malthus" in <u>Essays in Biography</u>.
Hollander, <u>The Economics of David Ricardo</u>.

C. The Utilitarian Strand in the Classical System

Texts: x   J.S. Mill, Principles of Political Economy, Book IV.
    _____, "Utilitarianism" (Patterson, <u>Readings</u>).
    Stark, ed., <u>The Economic Writings of Jeremy Bentham</u>.

Commentaries:

Viner, "Bentham and J.S. Mill: The Utilitarian Background," (in Spiegel, <u>Development of Economic Thought</u>).
Hutchinson, "Bentham as an Economist," <u>Economic Journal</u>, 1956.
Balassa, "John Stuart Mill and the Law of Markets," <u>QuarterlyJournal of Economics</u>, 1959.
Little, <u>Critique of Welfare Economics</u>, Chapter 1.
Myrdal, <u>The Political Element in the Development of Economic Theory</u>.

D. Classical Perspectives on Policy Questions

x   Robbins, <u>The Theory of Economic Policy in the English Classical School</u>, Lectures I, III, VI.
x   James Mill, "Testimony Before the Select Committee on East India Affairs," 1831.
    Hollander, "Malthus and the Post-Napoleonic Depression," <u>History of Political Economy</u>, 1969.
    Black, <u>The Classical Economists and the Irish Question</u>.
    Barber, "James Mill and the Theory of Economic Policy in India," <u>History of Political Economy</u>, 1969.
    Coats, ed., <u>The Classical Economists and Economic Policy</u>.
    Fetter, "Economic Controversy in the British Reviews, 1802-1850," <u>Economica</u>, 1965.

For Comparison:

x   Lewis, "Economic Development with Unlimited Supplies of Labour," <u>Manchester School</u>, 1954.
    Adelman, <u>Theories of Economic Growth</u>.
    Sraffa, <u>The Production of Commodities by Means of Commodities</u>.

Economics 258
History of Economic Thought
Syllabus (Continued)

W. Barber
Fall 1989

Historical Background:

Colquhoun, "An Attempt to Exhibit a General View of Society" (1821).
Jones, *The Development of English Agriculture, 1815-1870*.
Marshall, *The Old Poor Law, 1795-1834*.
Flinn, *British Population Growth, 1700-1850*.
Chapman, *The Cotton Industry in the Industrial Revolution*.

IV. Marxian Economics

Text: x   Marx, *Das Kapital*, Vol. 1.

Commentaries:

x Bronfenbrenner, "Das Kapital for the Modern Man," *Science and Society*, Fall 1965.
Robinson, *An Essay on Marxian Economics*.
Lange, "Marxian Economics and Modern Economic Theory," *Review of Economic Studies*, June 1935.
Schumpeter, "Marx the Economist," in *Capitalism, Socialism and Democracy*.
Bronfenbrenner, "The Vicissitudes of Marxian Economics," *History of Political Economy*, Fall 1970.
Samuelson, "Marxian Economic Models," *American Economic Review*, December 1957.
"Das Kapital: A Centenary Appreciation," *American Economic Review*, May 1967 (Papers by Samuelson, Erlich, and Bronfenbrenner).
Wolfson, *A Reappraisal of Marxian Economics*.
Elliott, "Marx and Contemporary Models of Socialist Economy," *History of Political Economy*, Summer 1976.
Sowell, *Marxism*.
Foley, *Understanding Capital*.
Roemer, *Analytical Marxism*.

For Comparison:

(x) Sweezy and Baran, *Monopoly Capital*, Chapter 3-4 (and Appendix).
-OR- (x) Baran, *The Political Economy of Growth*, Chapter 2.
-OR- (x) Baran and Sweezy, "The Tendency of Surplus to Rise," in *Economics: Mainstream Readings and Radical Critiques* (Mermelstein, ed.).
Sweezy, Essay in *Keynes' General Theory: Reports of Three Decades* (Lekachman, ed.).
Baran and Hobsbawm, "The Stages of Economic Growth," in *Economics: Mainstream Readings and Radical Critiques* (Mermelstein, ed.).
Sweezy, *The Theory of Capitalist Development*.
Dobb, *The Political Economy of Capitalism*.
Meek, *Studies in the Labor Theory of Value*.
Mandel, *Marxist Economic Theory*.
Kalecki, *Collected Economic Papers*.

Economics 258
History of Economic Thought
Syllabus (Continued)

W. Barber
Fall 1989

V. **Aspects of Neo-Classical Economics**

   Texts: x Marshall, <u>Principles of Economics</u>, Book I, Chapters 1-4; Book V, Chapters 1-5, 12; Book VI, Chapters 1-2, 11-13.
            x Schumpeter, "Bohm-Bawerk," in <u>Ten Great Economists</u>.
              Hutchinson, "L. Walras" in <u>Review of Economic Doctrines, 1870-1929</u>.
            x Pigou, <u>The Economics of Welfare</u>, Part I, Chapters 1, 3, 7-8; Part II, Chapter 2-11; Part IV, Chapters 1, 11-13.
              Clark, <u>The Ethics of Distribution</u>.
              Jevons, <u>The Theory of Political Economy</u>.

   Commentaries:

      x Friedman, "The Marshallian Demand Curve," <u>Journal of Political Economy</u>, 1949.
         "Papers on the Marginal Revolution in Economics," <u>History of Political Economy</u>, Fall 1972.

   Historical Background:

   Taylor, <u>Laissez-Faire and State Intervention in Nineteenth Century England</u>.
   Dorfman, <u>The Economic Mind in American Civilization</u>, Vol. 3, Part III, "The Heartbreaking Nineties."

VI. **Aspects of Institutionalism**

   Texts: x Veblen, "The Limitations of Marginal Utility," in Kapp, <u>Readings</u>.
            x Veblen, <u>The Theory of the Leisure Class</u>.
              Commons, <u>Institutional Economics</u>.
              Ely, <u>Problems of Today</u>.

   Commentaries:

   Dorfman, <u>Thorstein Veblen and His America</u>.
   Furner, <u>Advocacy and Objectivity</u>.

   Historical Background:

   Dorfman, <u>The Economic Mind In American Civilization</u>, Vol. 3, Part IV, "The Promise of the New Century."

   For Comparison:

   Galbraith, <u>The New Industrial State</u>.

Economics 258 -6- W. Barber
History of Economic Thought Fall 1989
Syllabus (Continued)

VII. **The Shifting Analytic Landscape in the 1920's and Early 1930's**

 A. Texts: x Sraffa, "The Laws of Returns Under Competitive Conditions," Economic Journal, 1926 (reprinted in AEA Readings in Price Theory).
 Viner, "Cost Curves and Supply Curves," Zeitschriftfur National Okonomie, 1931 (reprinted in AEA Readings in Price Theory).
 Berle and Means, "Corporations and the Public Investor," American Economic Review Supplement, 1930.
 Tugwell, "Planning and the Institution of Laissez-Faire," American Economic Review Supplement, March 1932.
 Robinson, The Theory of Imperfect Competition.
 Chamberlin, The Theory of Monopolistic Competition.

 B. Texts: Myrdal, Monetary Equilibrium, 1931, Chapter 3.
 Eshag, From Marshall to Keynes, Chapter 1.
 x Fisher, "Our Unstable Dollar and the So-Called Business Cycle," Journal of the American Statistical Association, 1925.
 Fisher, "The Stock Market Panic in 1929," Journal of the American Statistical Association, 1930.
 Keynes, A Treatise on Money, 1930.

 Commentary:

 Patinkin, "Keynes' Monetary Thought: A Study of Its Development," History of Political Economy, Spring 1976.

VIII. **The Keynesian Revolution and its Reception**

 Texts: x Keynes, "The End of Laissez-Faire," 1926 in Essays in Persuasion.
 x Kahn, "The Relation of Home Investment to Unemployment," Economic Journal, 1931.
 x Keynes, The General Theory, passim.
 x Hansen, "Mr. Keynes on Underemployment Equilibrium,". Journal of Political Economy, 1936.
 x Hansen, "Economic Progress and Declining Population Growth," American Economic Review, 1939 (Reprinted in AEA Readings in Business Cycle Theory).
 x Hicks, "Mr. Keynes and the Classics," Econometrica, 1937 (Reprinted in AEA Readings in the Theory of Income Distribution and in Mueller, Readings in Economics).
 Fisher, "The Debt-Deflation Theory of Great Depressions," Econometrica, 1933.
 Simons, "Rules versus Authorities in Monetary Policy," Journal of Political Economy, 1936.

Economics 258　　　　　　　　　　　-7-　　　　　　　　　　　W. Barber
History of Economic Thought　　　　　　　　　　　　　　　　　Fall 1989
Syllabus (Continued)

Commentaries:

x　Hicks, "Recollections and Documents," <u>Economica</u>, 1973.
x　Shackle, "Keynes and Today's Establishment in Economic Theory: A View," <u>Journal of Economic Literature</u>, 1973.
　　Shackle, <u>The Years of High Theory</u>.

For Comparison:

Heller, <u>New Dimensions of Political Economy</u>.
Winch, <u>Economics and Policy</u>.

IX.　**The Nature of Scientific Revolutions in Economics**

　　Texts:　x　Bronfenbrenner, "The 'Structure of Revolutions' in Economic Thought," <u>History of Political Economy</u>, 1971.
　　　　　　x　Coats, "Is There a Structure of Scientific Revolutions in Economics?" <u>Kyklos</u>, 1969.
　　　　　　x　Blaug, "Kahn versus Lakatos, or Paradigms versus Research Programmes in the History of Economics," <u>History of Political Economy</u>, Winter 1975.

<u>**General Reference Works**</u>:

Schumpeter, <u>History of Economic Analysis</u>.

Blaug, <u>Economic Theory in Retrospect</u>.

Seligman, <u>Main Currents in Economic Thought</u>.

Spiegel, <u>The Growth of Economic Thought</u>.

Barber, <u>A History of Economic Thought</u>.

Cochrane, <u>Macroeconomics Before Keynes</u>.

Breit and Ransom, <u>The Academic Scribblers</u>.

Stigler, <u>Essays in the History of Economics</u>.

Mitchell and Deane, <u>Abstract of British Historical Statistics</u>.

Bureau of the Census, <u>Historical Statistics of the United States</u>.

Economics 258
History of Economic Thought

W.J. Barber
Fall, 1989

MID-TERM EXAMINATION
October 19, 1989

PART I. Select one question (50 per cent)

1. Evaluate the argument that the focus of analysis in the classical tradition shifted from an interpretation of the causes of economic growth (in the late 18th century) to the consequences of economic growth (in the early to mid-19th century). What analytic developments might account for such a shift?

2. What theoretical rationale underlies the positions of classical economists from Smith through J.S. Mill on appropriate policies toward agricultural protection, relief of the poor, and taxation?

3. What, if anything, is "classical" in Arthur Lewis's model of the growth process in underdeveloped economies?

PART II. Select one question (25 per cent)

1. Assess the attempts of Smith and Ricardo to explain value in terms of labor content.

2. How did Hume arrive at the conclusion that the pursuit of mercantilist strategies was self-defeating? How might an orthodox mercantilist have responded to this indictment?

3. If the price of the products of land is determined on "zero-rent" land, how can the rent share of income be greater than zero?

PART III. Define and comment briefly on the significance of five of the following (25 per cent)

1. productive vs. unproductive labor

2. partial vs. general "glut"

3. the nature of "laws" in economics

4. positive vs. preventive checks

5. natural vs. market price

6. the stationary state

7. the "scientific" tax

Economics 258　　　　　　　　　　　　　　　　W.J. Barber
History of Economic Thought　　　　　　　　　Fall, 1989

FINAL EXAMINATIONS

INSTRUCTIONS: Follow the directions for each part. Each part will be weighted equally.

PART I. Select ONE question.

1. In the development of economic doctrines, some "master models" are primarily "supply-oriented"; others are primarily "demand-oriented." Discuss the properties of each with attention to their respective approaches to theories of value, distribution, and the behavior of aggregate income.

2. Trace the development of and the differing interpretations assigned to FOUR of the following within various traditions of economic analysis:

    a. the role of money in economic activity
    b. the behavior of the rate of profit
    c. the nature of "laws" in economics
    d. the definition of productive activity
    e. the concept of "surplus"
    f. the concept of "exploitation"

3. It has sometimes been argued that much is revealed about the intellectual style of the "big thinkers" in economics through an analysis of the portions of earlier traditions with which they choose to identify and the portions they choose to reject. How then might one interpret:

    a. the sympathetic reading Keynes gives to the mercantilist tradition in light of the treatment it received from most classical and neo-classical writers;

    b. the difference between Marx's views of the contributions of Ricardo and of Malthus;

    c. Veblen's attitude toward his neo-classical inheritance.

PART II. Select ONE question.

1. In what crucial respects is the neo-classical program fundamentally different from the Marxian one?

2. What differentiates the Veblenian conception of class from the Marxian one? How and why do their readings of the problems of capitalism diverge?

3. Why did the phenomenon of increasing returns to scale (long-run decreasing supply price) present a problem for Marshall? How did he attempt to solve it?

4. What claims did Marshall make for the novelty of his conception of the "scissors"? What presuppositions underlie his derivation of the demand "blade"?

Economics 258
History of Economic Thought
Final Examination (Continued)

-2- W.J. Barber
Fall, 1989

PART III. Select ONE question.

1. How might a "Say's lawyer" have explained the persistence of unemployment during the Great Depression? From Keynes's perspective, what was unsatisfactory about this explanation?

2. Set out the reasoning underlying the divergent views of neo-classical economists and Keynes on the effectiveness of wage-cutting as a remedy for unemployment.

3. What, if anything, is "revolutionary" about The General Theory?

PART IV. Identify and discuss briefly the significance of FIVE of the following statements.

1. "We regard the state as an educational and ethical agency whose positive aid is an indispensable condition of human progress....(W)e hold that the doctrine of laissez faire is unsafe in politics and unsound in morals....We hold that the conflict of capital and labor has brought to the front a vast number of social problems whose solution is impossible without the united efforts of church, state, and science."

2. "Interest today rewards no genuine sacrifice, any more than does the rent of land."

3. "An abstract law of population exists for plants and animals only and only in so far as man has not interfered with them."

4. "Abstract reasoning as to the effects of economies in production which an individual firm gets from an increase of its output are apt to be misleading, not only in detail, but in their general effect."

5. "...that which determines the magnitude of the value of any article is the amount of labor socially necessary, or the labor time socially necessary for its production."

6. "It is a Physiocratic illusion to hold that rents grow out of the soil and not out of society."

7. "Whatever form of expenditure the consumer chooses, or whatever end he seeks in making his choice, has utility to him by virtue of his preference. As seen from the point of view of the individual consumer, the question of wastefulness does not arise within the scope of economic theory proper....But it is, on other grounds, worth noting that the term 'waste' in the language of everyday life implies deprecation of what is characterized as wasteful."

8. "The influence of the rate of interest on the amount actually saved is of paramount importance, but is in the opposite direction to that usually supposed."

PRINCETON UNIVERSITY
Department of Economics

Economics 506   Professor William Baumol
History of Economic Thought   Fall 1988

Smith, Adam, **Wealth of Nations**, 1776, Book I, Chapters 1, 2, 3, 5, 6, 7, 8 (first 20 pages), 10 (first 17 pages); Book II, Chapter 3; Book IV, Chapters 1, 2, 8.

Malthus, T. R., **An Essay on the Principle of Population**, 1798, Pelican Edition, 1970, Introduction by Anthony Flew, Chapters 1-5, 18, 19.

Ricardo, David, **On the Principles of Political Economy and Taxation**, London, 1817, Chapters I-X, XIX-XXI, XXX-XXXI.

*Ricardo, David, **Notes on Malthus**, Piero Sraffa, Editor, Cambridge, Cambridge University Press, 1951, Editor's Introduction and pp. 300-382.

Marx, Karl and Friedrich Engels, **Manifesto of the Communist Party**.

Marx, Karl, **Capital** (three volumes), New York, International Publishing Company.

  Volume I: Author's Prefaces; Chapter 1; Chapter 3, Sections II
               a, b; Chapter 5; Chapter 6; Chapter 7, Section 2;
               Chapter 8; Chapter 9, Sections 1, 3, 4; skim Chapter 10;
               Chapter 15, Section 6; Chapter 16; Chapter 24; Sections 2,
               3, 5; Chapter 25.

  Volume II: Preface; Chapter 9; Chapter 16, Part 3; pp. 390-396
               (Chapter 17, last 6 pages on Simple Reproduction);
               Chapter 20; pp. 576-9 (Chapter 21, I, Accumulation in
               Department 1 (1) formation of a hoard).

  Volume III: Preface; Chapters 1, 2, 8, 9, 10, 13, 14, 15, 22, 27,
               37, 38, 48.

*Marx, Karl, **A Critique of the Gotha Program**, Moscow, Progress Publishers, 1937.

----

*On reserve at Firestone Library.

UNIVERSITÉ D'OTTAWA
UNIVERSITY OF OTTAWA

FACULTÉ DES SCIENCES SOCIALES
FACULTY OF SOCIAL SCIENCES

ECO 5532

HISTOIRE DE LA PENSÉE ÉCONOMIQUE

Prof.: Ronald G. Bodkin
Bureau: #293 pavillon Tabaret
Tél.: 564-4987

Janvier-avril 1990

Heures de
 bureau: Tous les matins, entre 10h et 11h.
en dehors de ces heures, par rendez-vous

Le manuel obligatoire sera Henri Denis, <u>Histoire de la Pensée économique</u>, 4ième édition (Paris: Presses universitaires de France, 1974), 36.00$ (à peu près).

Deux autres sources utilisées seront:

1. I.H. Rima, <u>Development of Economics Analysis</u>. troisième édition (Homewood, Illinois: Richard D. Irwin, Inc., 1978), et

2. H.W. Spiegel (rédacteur), <u>The Development of Economic Thought</u>, édition abrégée (New York, John Wiley & Sons, Inc., 1964).

Des commentaires à propos du cours:

Les sujets d'étude de ce cours seront les pensées, les théories, et les vies (en partie) des grands économistes du passée. On fera cela, et pour son propre intérêt et aussi comme aide à la compréhension de la théorie économique courante. Chaque ère réinterprète les grands penseurs du passé, et nos critères seront les théories et concepts actuels. Puisque l'interprétation peut varier, on incite l'etudiant(e) à lire autant des sources originales que possible, étant donné les contraintes du temps disponible (lesquelles sont très sévères dans un cours d'un seul trimestre). D'ailleurs, une introduction très limitée aux commentateurs actuels qui sont rénommés serait donnée.

SCIENCE ÉCONOMIQUE/ECONOMICS

Il y aura un examen de mi-trimestre et aussi un examen final. L'examen de mi-trimestre comptera entre 33 1/3 pour cent et 40 pour cent de la moyenne finale des examens, tandis que l'examen final comptera entre 66 2/3 pour cent et 60 pour cent de la moyenne finale des examens (selon l'avantage de l'étudiant). Si l'étudiant(e) n'écrit pas de travail majeur, la moyenne finale des examens deviendra la note finale pour le cours, sauf que le professeur se réserve le droit d'augmenter la note finale pour la participation exceptionnelle dans la discussion de la classe. Un travail majeur ou un essai ne sera pas requis, mais il est facultatif. J'incite l'étudiant(e) à faire un tel travail puisque celui-ci pourra élever (mais ne pas abaisser) la note finale. Spécifiquement, si la note pour le travail majeur est supérieure à la moyenne finale des examens (comme décrite en haut), alors la note pour le travail majeur comptera pour 25 pour cent de la note finale. (Encore, le professeur se réserve le droit d'augmenter la note finale pour la participation exceptionnelle dans la discussion de la classe.)

Le sujet du travail majeur peut être n'importe quel sujet dans l'histoire de la pensée économique, si discuté dans le cours ou non. Cependant, je préconise que l'étudiant(e) qui considère la possibilité d'écrire un tel travail majeur fasse une consultation avec le professeur tôt dans le trimestre, pour éviter le gaspillage de son temps (et celui du professeur).

Le plan de cours et les lectures recommandées

I. Introduction; pourquoi étudier l'histoire de la pensée économique? (1/2 semaine):

   1. Denis, pp. 1-6

   2. Rima, chapitre 1

   3. (facultatif) Ronald G. Bodkin and Edwin G. West, "Conjectural Nobel Prizes in Economics: 1770 to 1890", Eastern Economic Journal, July-September 1983, pp. 151-165.

II. La pensée économique de l'Antiquité et du Moyen-Age. (1/2 semaine):

   Denis, pp. 7-88.

- 3 -

III. Le Mercantilisme et ses critiques; Petty, Hume, et Galiani.
(1 semaine):

1. Denis, pp. 91-151

2. Spiegel (réd.), article par Hecksher sur le mercantilisme

3. Keynes, John Maynard, <u>La théorie générale de l'emploi, de l'intérêt et de la monnaie</u>, chapitre 23, les cinq premières sections (à peu près 20 pages).

IV. Richard Cantillon et les Physiocrates
(1 semaine):

1. Richard Cantillon, <u>Essai sur la nature du commerce en générale</u> (édition bilingue traduit par Henry Higgs), les parties 1 et 2,

ou

2. (alternativement) A.E. Monroe, <u>Early Economic Thought</u>, abrègement de l'<u>Essai de Cantillon</u>

3. Denis, pp. 161-186.

4. Norman S. Ware, "The Physiocrats: A Study in Economic Rationalization", <u>The American Economic Review</u>, Vol. XXI (1931), pp. 607-619.

V. Adam Smith
(1 semaine)

1. Denis, pp. 187-220

2. Smith, <u>La richesse des nations</u>
   a. Vol. I, chapitres 1-4
   b. Vol. I, chapitre 10, partie I
   c. (facultatif) Vol. IV, chapitre 1
   d. (facultatif) Vol. V, chapitres 1 et 2

3. (facultatif) Nathan Rosenberg, "Some Institutional Aspects of the Wealth of Nations", <u>Journal of Political Economy</u>, décembre 1960.

- 4 -

VI. T.R. Malthus et David Ricardo
(1 semaine):

1. Denis, pp. 293-308, 317-350

2. Spiegel (réd.), articles par Bonar, Fay, et Keynes sur Malthus et par Marshall sur Ricardo.

VII. EXAMEN DE MI-TRIMESTRE (12 février)

VIII. Jean Baptiste Say
(1/2 semaine):

Denis, pp. 309-316.

IX. Nassau Senior, John Stuart Mill, et le bilan de l'Ecole Classique
(1 semaine):

1. Denis, pp. 226-230, 467-481.

2. Emile James, <u>Histoire sommaire de la pensée économique</u>, 4ième édition, Deuxième partie, Chapitre V, "Bilan des écoles classiques"

3. John Stuart Mill, <u>Principes de l'économie politique</u>

    a. Vol. III, chapitres 1-3

    b. (facultatif) Vol. III, chapitres 4-6

    c. Vol. IV, chapitre 4

4. (facultatif) Spiegel (réd.), article par Viner sur Mill et sur Bentham.

X. Les romantiques, les nationalistes, l'école historique allemande, et les socialistes avant Marx
(1 semaine)

1. Denis, pp. 390-463

2. Marx, <u>Le Capital</u>, livre 1, chapitre 10

3. Joseph A. Schumpeter, <u>Capitalism, Socialism, and Democracy</u>, chapitre 3 de la partie I, "Marx the Economist".

XII. Les marginalistes (Cournot, Gossen, von Thünen, Jevons, et les autrichiens)
(1 semaine):

    1. Denis, pp. 481-500, 520-522, 524-526

    2. Spiegel (réd.), articles par keynes sur Jevons et par Hayek sur Menger

    3. Augustin A. Cournot, Principles mathématiques de la théorie des richesses, Introduction et premier chapitre.

XIII. L'Ecole de Lausanne et Pareto comme sociologue
(1 semaine):

    1. Denis, pp. 500-519, 526-531, et 615-619

    2. Léon Walras, Eléments d'économie politique pure, partie II

    3. (facultatif) Milton Friedman, "Leon Walras and His Economic System", American Economic Review, décembre 1955, pp. 900-909.

XIV. J.B. Clark et Alfred Marshall
(1 semaine)

    1. Denis, pp. 522-524 et 531-544

    2. Spiegel (réd.), article par J.M. Clark sur J.B. Clark

    3. Marshall, Principles d'économie politique, le livre 3 et les chapitres 1-3 du livre 5.

* * * * * * * * * *

The Claremont Graduate School
Center for Politics and Policy
and
Department of Economics

The Nature of Social Science Inquiry

Thomas Borcherding
201 Harper East
(x-3355)

Thomas Rochon
216 Harper East
(x-3366)

Structure of the Course

This seminar is designed to provide an introduction to the nature of empirical social science. The stress will be on philosophical assumptions underlying the empirical observation of political and economic phenomena, on the advantages and disadvantages of the approaches most commonly adopted by political scientists and economists, and on strategies for designing research that can provide empirical tests of social science theories. There will be a special focus on the problems associated with evaluating public policy and analyzing policy processes. This is not a course in statistics or on specific techniques for gathering and analyzing quantitative data, but those subjects will be touched on.

Requirements for the course include reading of the starred (*) material in the syllabus, all of which is available on reserve in Honnold. A packet of required articles may also be purchased from Kinko's, at 216 West Second St. The following books are recommended for purchase and are available at the Huntley Bookstore:

Donald Campbell and Julian Stanley <u>Experimental and Quasi-Experimental Designs for Research</u>

Donald Fiske and Richard Shweder <u>Metatheory in Social Science</u> (recommended)

Robert Frank <u>Passions Within Reasons</u>

Thomas Kuhn <u>The Structure of Scientific Revolutions</u>

Mancur Olson <u>The Logic of Collective Action</u>

For students with a particular interest in the public choice approach, we have also asked Huntley to stock a few copies of Dennis Mueller, <u>Public Choice</u>, second edition. This is a comprehensive survey of the field, at a moderately advanced level. Students in CPP may also benefit from a review of

Richard McKenzie and Gordon Tullock, <u>The Best of the New World of Economics</u>, which contains a wide range of short, clearly written examples of economic research. Professor Borcherding will hold a one-evening review session on economic theory near the beginning of the semester, designed to give CPP students a grounding in the basics.

All students are expected to be active participants in the weekly seminar meetings and to write three papers. The first paper is a short essay of about five pages on the possibilities and limitations of a social science. It must be written after the first segment of the course. The second paper is also an essay of about five pages contrasting the rational and cultural approaches to social science and making an argument for one of those approaches in a substantive field of interest to you. This second paper is an opportunity to summarize your views on social science and to apply them to a concrete problem area. The final paper will be a report of about ten pages, critiquing a specific piece of empirical research from the standpoint of research design. A sample research design critique is available on reserve.

PART I: THE PHILOSOPHY OF SOCIAL SCIENCE

WEEK 1.   Introduction: Methods of Social Science Inquiry

There is no assigned reading for the first session

WEEK 2.   What are we trying to do?

* Ralph Bunche, "Presidential Address," <u>American Political Science Review</u> 47 (December 1953), pages 961-974

* David Truman, "Disillusion and Regeneration: The Quest for a Discipline," <u>American Political Science Review</u> 59 (December 1965), pages 865-873

* Charles Lindblom, "Another State of Mind," <u>American Political Science Review</u> 76 (March 1982), pages 9-21

* George Stigler, "Economists and Public Policy," <u>Regulation</u> 6 (May/June 1982), pages 13-17

* Steven Kelman, "'Public Choice' and Public Spirit," <u>Public Interest</u> (Spring 1987), pages 80-94

* Ryan Amacher, Robert Tollison and Thomas Willett, "The Economic Approach to Social Policy Questions," pages 18-37 in Ryan Amacher, Robert Tollison and Thomas Willett (eds.), <u>The Economic Approach to Public Policy</u>

* Mancur Olson and Christopher Clague, " Dissent in Economics," pages 79-99 in Ryan Amacher, Robert Tollison and Thomas Willett (eds.), The Economic Approach to Public Policy

WEEK 3. The Natural Science Model of Social Science

* Karl Popper, "Unity of Method in the Natural and Social Sciences," in David Braybrooke, Philosophical Problems of the Social Sciences

* Milton Friedman, "The Methodology of Positive Economics," pages 3-43 in Essays in Positive Economics

* Gabriel Almond and Stephen Genco, "Clouds, Clocks and the Study of Politics," World Politics 29 (1977), pages 489-522

* Philip Converse, "Generalization and the Social Psychology of 'Other Worlds'," pages 42-60 in Donald Fiske and Richard Shweder (eds.), Metatheory in Social Science

* Vernon Smith, "Experimental Economics: Induced Value Theory," American Economic Review (May 1976), pages 274-279

* Samuel Eldersveld, "Experimental Propaganda Techniques and Voting Behavior," American Political Science Review 50 (1956), pages 154-165

* Murdock Pencil "Salt Passage," (unpublished manuscript)

Karl Popper, "Of Clouds and Clocks," pages 206-255 in Objective Knowledge

Max Weber, "Objectivity in Social Science and Social Policy," in Fred Dallmayr and Thomas McCarthy (eds.), Understanding and Social Inquiry

Paul Secord, "Explanation in the Social Sciences and in Life Situations," pages 197-221 in Donald Fiske and Richard Shweder (eds.), Metatheory in Social Science

Abraham Kaplan, The Conduct of Inquiry

Charles Plott, "The Applications of Laboratory Experimental Methods to Public Choice," in Clifford Russell (ed.), Collective Decision Making, pp 137-160 and 170-171

WEEK 4. Philosophical and Political Critiques of Social
        Science

* Charles Taylor, "Interpretation and the Sciences of Man,"
Review of Metaphysics 25 (September 1971), pages 3-51. Also
in Fred Dallmayr and Thomas McCarthy (eds.), Understanding
and Social Inquiry

* Sheldon Wolin, "Political Theory as a Vocation," American
Political Science Review 63 (December 1969), pages 1062-1082

* Peter Hall, "Conclusion: The Politics of Keynesian Ideas,"
pages 361-391 in Peter Hall (ed.), The Political Power of
Economic Ideas

* Kathy Ferguson, "Male-Ordered Politics: Feminism and
Political Science," chapter 9 in Terence Ball (ed.), Idioms
of Inquiry

* Dennis Quinn, "The End of the End of Ideology: The
Reemergence of Ideology in Economic Policy." Paper
presented at the American Political Science Association
meetings, September 1989.

* Donald McCloskey, "The Rhetoric of Economics," Journal of
Economic Literature (June 1983), pages 481-517

Arjo Klamer, Conversations with Economists

Roy D'Andrade, "Three Scientific World Views and the
Covering Laws Model," pages 19-41 in Donald Fiske and
Richard Shweder (eds.), Metatheory in Social Science

Roger Spegele, "Deconstructing Methodological
Falsificationism in International Relations" American
Political Science Review 74 (March 1980), pages 104-122

John Gunnell, "American Political Science, Liberalism, and
the Invention of Political Theory," American Political
Science Review 82 (March 1988), pages 71-87

Eugene Miller, "Positivism, Historicism and Political
Inquiry," American Political Science Review 66 (September
1972), pages 796-817. Read also the "Comments" by
Braybrooke and Rosenberg, Rudner, and Landau, and the
"Rejoinder" by Miller

Richard Rorty, Philosophy and the Mirror of Nature, chapters
7 and 8

John Gunnell, "Encounters of a Third Kind: The Alienation
of Theory in American Political Science," American Journal
of Political Science 25 (August 1981), pages 440-61

Charles Taylor, "Neutrality in Political Science," pages 139-170 in Alan Ryan (ed.), The Philosophy of Social Explanation

Peter Winch, The Idea of a Social Science, chapters 1 and 5

Martin Landau, Political Theory and Political Science

James Farr, "Historical Concepts in Political Science: The Case of 'Revolution'" American Journal of Political Science 26 (November 1982), pages 688-708

T.W. Hutchison, Knowledge and Ignorance in Economics

Stephen Salkever, "Cool Reflexion and the Criticism of Values," American Political Science Review 74 (March 1980), pages 70-77

John Nelson, "Accidents, Laws and Philosophic Flaws," Comparative Politics 7 (April 1975), pages 435-457

WEEK 5. The Evolution of Social Science

* Thomas Kuhn, The Structure of Scientific Revolutions

* William Riker, "The Two-Party System and Duverger's Law," American Political Science Review 76 (December 1982), pages 753-766

* Walter Salant, "The Spread of Keynesian Doctrines and Practices in the United States," pages 27-51 in Peter Hall (ed.), The Political Power of Economic Ideas

* Robert Clower, "The Ideas of Economists," in Arjo Klammer, Donald McCloskey and Robert Solow (eds.), The Consequences of Economic Rhetoric

Arend Lijphart, "The Structure of the Theoretical Revolution in International Relations," International Studies Quarterly 18 (March 1974), pages 41-74

J.D. Moon, "The Logic of Political Inquiry," in Fred Greenstein and Nelson Polsby (eds.), Handbook of Political Science, volume 1.

Martin Landau Political Theory and Political Science, chapter 2

John Rodman, "Paradigm Change in Political Science," American Behavioral Scientist 24 (September-October 1980), pages 49-78.

THE FIRST PAPER SHOULD BE WRITTEN AFTER THIS SESSION.
IT IS DUE IN CLASS NEXT WEEK.

WEEK 6. The Basic Model of Rationality

* James DeNardo, "Introduction"

* Donald McCloskey, "The Limits of Expertise: If You're So Smart, Why Ain't You Rich?" American Scholar 57 (Summer 1988), pages 393-406

* Gordon Tullock The Vote Motive, pages xiv-xv and 1-58

* Terence Ball, "Is There Progress in Political Science?", chapter 1 in Terence Ball (ed.), Idioms of Inquiry

* Fred Glahe and Dwight Lee, "The Economic Analysis of Political Decision Making," pages 517-544 in Glahe and Lee (eds.), Microeconomics: Theory and Applications

* Garrit Hardin, "The Tragedy of the Commons," Science 162 (December 1968), pages 1243-1248

* Gordon Tullock, "The Welfare Costs of Tarrifs, Monopolies, and Theft," Western Economic Journal (June 1967), pages 224-232

George Tsebelis Nested Games: Rational Choice in Comparative Politics, chapters 1-2

Richard McKenzie and Gordon Tullock, The Best of the New World of Economics

Morris Fiorina, "Formal Models in Political Science," American Journal of Political Science 19 (February 1975), pages 133-159

WEEK 7. Advanced Models and Some Applications

* Thomas Schelling, "Micromotives and Macrobehavior," pages 9-43 in Schelling (ed.), Micromotives and Macrobehavior

* Robert Axelrod, The Evolution of Cooperation, pages 3-26

* George Tsebelis, "Nested Games: The Cohesion of French Electoral Coalitions," British Journal of Political Science 18 (April 1988), pages 145-170

Gary Becker, "A Theory of Competition Among Pressure Groups for Political Influence," Quarterly Journal of Economics (August 1983), pages 371-400

Colin Camer, "Gifts as Economic Signals and Social Symbols," <u>American Journal of Sociology</u> (Supp. 1988), pages S180-S214

Peter Ordeshook, <u>Game Theory and Political Theory: An Introduction</u>

Dennis Mueller, <u>Public Choice</u> (second edition)

Eric Rasmussen, <u>Games and Information: An Introduction to Game Theory</u>

WEEK 8. Anomalies and Critiques of Rationality

* Kenneth Arrow, "Risk Perception in Psychology and Economics," <u>Economic Inquiry</u> 20 (January 1982), pages 1-9

* Albert Hirschman, "Morality and the Social Sciences," chapter 14 in Hirschman, <u>Essays in Trespassing</u>

* Michael McPherson, "Limits on Self-Seeking: The Role of Morality in Economic Life," pages 71-85 in David Colander (ed.), <u>Neoclassical Political Economy</u>

* Clifford Geertz, "Blurred Genres," in Geertz, <u>Local Knowledge</u>

* Amos Tversky and Daniel Kahnemann, "Judgement Under Uncertainty: Heuristics and Biases," in Kahnemann and Tversky, <u>Judgement Under Uncertainty</u>

* Robert Lane, "Political Observers and Market Participants: The Effects on Cognition," <u>Political Psychology</u> 4 (1983), pages 455-473

WEEK 9. The Cultural Alternative

* David Elkins and Richard Simeon, "A Cause in Search of its Effect, or What Does Political Culture Explain?" <u>Comparative Politics</u> 11 (January 1979), pages 127-146

* Clifford Geertz, "Thick Description: Toward an Interpretive Theory of Culture," chapter 1 in Geertz, <u>The Interpretation of Cultures</u>

* James S. Coleman, "Norms as Social Capital," in Gerard Radnitzky and Peter Bernholz (eds.), <u>Economic Imperialism</u>

* Gerald Scully, "The Institutional Framework and Economic Development," <u>Journal of Political Economy</u> (June 1988), pages 652-662

* Douglass North, "Institutions, Transaction Costs and Economic Growth," Economic Inquiry 25 (April 1987), pages 419-428

* Martin Wiener English Culture and the Decline of the Industrial Spirit, 1850-1980, chapters 1-3

* David McClelland, "The Achievement Motive in Economic Growth," in William Lambert and Rita Weisbrod (eds.), Comparative Perspectives on Social Psychology

Stephen Chilton, "Defining Political Culture," Western Political Quarterly 41 (September 1988), pages 419-445

Michel Foucault, Madness and Civilization, chapters 1-4,9

Brian Barry, Sociologists, Economists and Democracy

Aaron Wildavsky, "Choosing Preferences by Constructing Institutions: A Cultural Theory of Preference Formation," American Political Science Review 81 (March 1987), pages 3-21

David Laitin/Aaron Wildavsky, "Political Culture and Political Preferences," American Political Science Review 82 (June 1988), pages 589-596

Harry Eckstein, "A Culturalist Theory of Political Change," American Political Science Review 82 (September 1988), pages 789-804

Robert Putnam, "Studying Elite Political Culture: The Case of Ideology," American Political Science Review 65 (September 1971), pages 651-681

Ronald Rogowski, Rational Legitimacy, introduction

Harry Eckstein, "A Theory of Stable Democracy," appendix B in Eckstein, Division and Cohesion in Democracy

PART II. THREE APPLICATIONS

WEEK 10. Who Represents Whom in Government?

* Edmund Burke, "Letters to the Sherrifs of Bristol."

* Warren Miller and Donald Stokes, "Constituency Influence in Congress," American Political Science Review 57 (March 1963), pages 45-56

* Richard Fenno, "Observation, Context and Sequence in the Study of Politics," <u>American Political Science Review</u> 80 (March 1986), pages 3-15

* Barry Weingast and Mark Moran, "Bureaucratic Discretion or Congressional Control," <u>Journal of Political Economy</u> 92 (October 1983), pages 765-800

* Joseph Kalt and Mark Zupan, "Capture and Ideology in the Economic Theory of Politics," <u>American Economic Review</u> (June 1984), pages 279-300

* Douglas Nelson and Eugene Silberberg, "Ideology and Legislator Shirking," <u>Economic Inquiry</u> (January 1987), pages 15-25

* John McArthur and Stephen Marks, "Constituent Interest vs. Legislator Ideology: The Role of Political Opportunity Cost," <u>Economic Inquiry</u> 26 (July 1988), pages 461-470

WEEK 11. When Does it Pay to Organize?

* Mancur Olson, <u>The Logic of Collective Action</u>, chapters 1-2, 6 and appendix

* Mancur Olson, "The Logic," pages 17-35 in Olson, <u>The Rise and Decline of Nations</u>

* Stanley Kaplowitz and Bradley Fisher, "Revealing the Logic of Free-Riding and Contributions to the Nuclear Freeze Movement," pages 47-64 in Louis Kriesberg (ed.), <u>Research in Social Movements, Conflicts and Change</u>, volume 8.

* Bruce Fireman and William Gamson, "Utilitarian Logic in the Resource Mobilization Perspective," pages 8-44 in Mayer Zald and John McCarthy (eds.), <u>The Dynamics of Social Movements</u>

WEEK 12. Why is there Altruism?

* Robert Frank, <u>Passions Within Reasons: The Strategic Role of the Emotions</u>

THE SECOND ESSAY SHOULD BE WRITTEN AFTER
THIS WEEK'S CLASS. IT IS DUE IN CLASS NEXT WEEK.

PART III. RESEARCH DESIGN

WEEK 13. Experimental and Quasi-Experimental Design

* Donald Campbell and Julian Stanley, _Experimental and Quasi-Experimental Designs for Research_

Roger W. Benjamin, "Strategy versus Methodology in Comparative Research," _Comparative Political Studies_ 9 (January 1977), pages 475-484

Arend Lijphart, "Comparative Politics and the Comparative Method," _American Political Science Review_ 65 (September 1971), pages 682-693

Arend Lijphart, "The Comparable-Cases Strategy in Comparative Research," _Comparative Political Studies_ 8 (July 1975), pages 158-177

Paul Spector, _Research Designs_

Adam Przeworski and Henry Teune, _The Logic of Comparative Social Inquiry_, pages 3-46

Theodore Meckstroth, "Most Different Systems and Most Similar Systems: A Study in the Logic of Comparative Inquiry," _Comparative Political Studies_ 8 (July 1975), pages 132-157

Donald Campbell, "Reforms as Experiments," _American Psychologist_ 24 (1969), pages 409-429

Herbert Blalock, _Causal Inferences in Non-Experimental Research_, chapter 1

Fred Kerlinger, _Foundations of Behavioral Research_, chapters 15-17

WEEKS 14 AND 15. Evaluating Research Designs

* Shanto Iyengar, "Television News and Citizens' Explanations of National Affairs," _American Political Science Review_ 81 (September 1987), pages 815-831

* Jarol Manheim and Robert Albritton, "Changing National Images: International Public Relations and Media Agenda Setting," _American Political Science Review_ 78 (September 1984), pages 641-657

* Thomas D. Willett et al., "Inflation Hypotheses and Monetary Accommodation: Postwar Evidence from the Industrial Countries," pages 200-236 in Thomas Willett (ed.), Political Business Cycles

* Robert Ayanian, "Political Risk, National Defense and the Dollar," Economic Inquiry 26 (April 1988), pages 345-352

* Maurice East, "Size and Foreign Policy Behavior," World Politics 25 (July 1973), pages 556-576

THE FINAL PAPER, A CRITIQUE OF THE RESEARCH DESIGN OF AN ARTICLE OF YOUR CHOICE, IS DUE ON THE LAST DAY OF CLASSES

University of North Carolina at Greensboro

SYLLABUS

Economics 555
History of Economic Thought
Fall 1990

Bruce J. Caldwell
Office: 444 B&E Bldg.
Phone: 334-5463

Required Texts:
H.W. Spiegel, *The Growth of Economic Thought*. Revised edition, 1983.
Adam Smith, *The Wealth of Nations*. Univ. of Chicago edition, 1976.
Robert Tucker, ed. *The Marx-Engels Reader*. 2nd. edition, 1978.
Bruce Caldwell, ed. *Carl Menger and his Legacy in Economics*. 1990.
(There are also two articles on reserve at the Library)

Course Requirements:
Term Paper: 50%
Final Exam: 50%

COURSE OUTLINE

I. Introduction - Goals, Purposes, Procedures

II. Pre-Classical Economics   Readings:

    A. Scholastics   Speigel: Chapter 3 (S-3)

    B. Transition to Mercantilism

    C. Mercantilism - French and English   S-5

    D. Transition to Liberalism   S-6 on Petty (pp. 122-35)
                                                     S-7
                                                     S-8 (pp. 171-183)

    E. Physiocrats   S-8 (pp. 183-200)

III. Classical Economics

    A. Smith   Book I (*except* pp. 163-269)
                                                       Book II (*except* pp. 314-50)
                                                     Book III - Chapter 1
                                                     Book IV - Chapters 1, 2, 3,
                                                     and 9 (*except* pp. 503-13)

    B. Malthus   S-12
                                                     S-13 (pp. 292-99)

    C. Ricardo   S-14

IV. The Marxian System

    A. Precursors and Origins

    B. Marx's System

    C. Evaluation

Readings:

Tucker: see list of readings on the Study Questions sheet handed out on the first day of class.

V. The Marginal Revolution

    A. Origins and Jevons   S-22

    B. The Austrians   S-23
                                  Caldwell: selected articles

    C. Walras and Pareto   S-24

    D. Marshall and the Cambridge School   S-25

    E. Assessment of the Marginal Revolution

Article on Reserve by Mirowski: "Physics and the Marginalist Revolution"

VI. The Twentieth Century - Selected Topics

    A. Overview   See list of famous works

    B. Institutionalism   S-27, pp. 628-43

    C. The Austrian Revival   Caldwell: selected articles
Article on Reserve by Caldwell: "Hayek's Transformation"

Economics 555
History of Economic Thought
Study Questions to Help
Your Reading

Questions to think about as you read various sections. You may wish to outline rough answers before class, and perhaps to add some questions of your own for discussion by the class.

I. Scholastics

   1. What is a "just price"? Do modern economists speak of just prices? Why or why not? Do others speak of justice in the marketplace? Do you? (e.g. Have you ever felt overcharged for a good? Do you think it is fair for new Ph.D.'s in accounting to be paid more than new Ph.D.'s in economics, who are paid more than new Ph.D.'s in English?)

   2. What is usury? Why was it perceived as bad by the Scholastics, and by many people since? What are some modern examples of anti-usury doctrines? Do _you_ think it is bad? Be prepared to defend your answer.

   3. Do the beliefs of Scholastics "make sense" to you? What do you like and dislike, and why?

II. Mercantilism

   1. The English mercantilists were primarily businessmen. Did they favor free trade? Why or why not? Do modern businessmen favor free trade? (Think of Lee Iococca, or the textile industry.)

   2. Some mercantilists believed that a net inflow of bullion (gold and silver) would make a country prosperous. Do you agree? Carefully figure out what would happen to such a country. If not gold and silver, what is the cause of the wealth of nations?

III. The Rise of Science (not in readings - just think about these)

   1. What is science? What is the scientific method? Have you ever used it? Where has _your_ knowledge come from? (Answer honestly.) What do you mean by "knowledge"?

   2. How do we evaluate scientific theories? (Think about how you answered some of the questions above about the Scholastics and Mercantilists.) Are there any theories that you believe to be true in economics? What kind of evidence would make you give up your belief?

IV. Physiocracy

   1. Mark Blaug states that physiocracy was "an effort to provide agrarian reform with a watertight theoretical argument." Explain.

   2. Contrast the Mercantilists and the Physiocrats on the source of value. Was Physiocracy a reaction against "Colbertism," or French mercantilism?

3. Some terms and concepts to remember - Quesnay's Tableau Economique, the produit net, the 3 classes, the circular flow.

V. Adam Smith - **Wealth of Nations** - Book I - Things to look for in reading.

Chapter 1	- Why is division of labor important? Pin factory; how division of labor improves productivity.
Chapter 2	- Did someone have to invent the division of labor?
Chapter 3	- What limits are there on the extent of the division of labor?
Chapter 4	- What are the functions of money; compare to modern approach.
Chapter 5	- Looking for a _measure_ of value.
Chapter 6	- Looking for determinants of value.
Chapter 7	- Same as 6, but more fully developed.

Chapters 5, 6, and 7 are tough. Read them, try to come to an interpretation. Marx said Smith had a labor theory of value, but botched the representation. Your thoughts?

Chapter 8-11	- Theory of Distribution, or Factor Markets.
Chapter 8	- A variety of theories of wage determination.
Chapter 9	- Theory of profits. Many have criticized Smith on this chapter. Do _you_ see any problems?
Chapter 10	- Causes of wage differentials.
Chapter 11	- A differential surplus theory of rent. (What does that mean?)

VI. Marxism Section - Instead of questions, I've summarized the readings below. The readings are drawn from Robert Tucker, ed. The Marx-Engels Reader (New York: Norton, second ed. 1978).

1. Preface - A useful overview of the organization of the volume, mostly for your information.
2. Introduction - I. The early Marx, the influences of Hegel and Feuerbach. II. Das Kapital III. Revolutionary theory and practice. IV. Marx & Engels.
3. Theses of Feuerbach (pp. 143-45) - materialism, religion, philosophy, vs. action.
4. Working Class Manchester (pp. 579-85) - a view of living conditions of workers.
5. Engels' Speech at the Graveside of Marx (pp. 679-81) - a summary and eulogy.
6. Socialism - Utopian and Scientific (pp. 681-717) - Engel's popularization of Marxism - the pamphlet which introduced Marxism to the West. This is easy and interesting reading - everything from intellectual history to emergence of capitalism, anarchy under capitalism, the business cycle, to the proletarian revolution.
7. The Communist Manifesto, Sections, I, II, and IV (omit III) - (pp. 473-491, 499-500). Enjoy the alternating short, staccato sentences and longer passages on the history of the class struggle. In their agenda, they even explain why middle class readers like you won't like what you're reading. The concluding sentences are ones you've heard before.
8. A taste of _Das Kapital_ (361-76).

Economics 555
Guidelines for a Perfect Term Paper

Your required term paper will count for 50% of your grade. My past experience indicates that some students have a hard time writing papers. The guidelines outlined below should be carefully followed by everyone. If you are unclear on anything, be sure to see me to get the problem straightened out.

I. Your paper will be evaluated according to three criteria: research, style, and presentation of theme.

A. Research - your research should be thorough. Your sources should include both primary and secondary sources. A primary source is a book written by the economist studied (e.g., Adam Smith's Wealth of Nations; Petty's Political Arithmetick); a secondary source is a scholarly book or article which examines some aspect of the chosen economist's work (e.g., Ronald Meek, Turgot on Progress, Sociology and Economics; Thomas Sowell, Say's Law; Joseph Spengler, "The Physiocrats and Say's Law of Markets," Journal of Political Economy). Do not make the common error of using history of economic thought textbooks as secondary sources. While these books can be used to suggest topics or to provide biographical background material on your subject (and this latter legitimate use should be footnoted), such texts should not be used as secondary sources. It is also best to avoid the common but sophomoric practice of padding you bibliography with citations of books you either have not read at all or have read only sparingly.

B. Style - In any written presentation, style is truly important. Poor sentence structure and incorrect grammar detract from the presentation and distract the reader. If you are not confident in this area, you should purchase Strunk & White's Elements of Style. It is an inexpensive, short paperback that is worth its weight in gold.

Style also includes the proper use of footnotes and bibliographical citations. Two standard guidebooks here are the MLA Handbook and the Chicago Manual of Style. Remember, both direct quotes and reworded ideas taken from other authors must be footnoted. Two common errors with regard to footnotes are:

1. Too many footnotes - in this case, the paper consists of line after line of quotations. It indicates that you have not synthesized the material yourself, but merely patched together a number of other people's ideas.

2. Too few footnotes - this is especially dangerous if you use language which is not your own and do not cite your source, for it constitutes plagiarism.

A word of warning - be extremely careful about plagiarism. By now, you should be well aware of what does and what does not constitute a violation; if not, check your student handbook. You should be forewarned - unintentional plagiarism will result in a poor grade or a demand that the paper be rewritten; intentional plagiarism will be prosecuted to the full extent of the law. And remarkably, I am not as dumb as I look.

C. Presentation of the theme - This category involves the substantive content of your paper. Did you accomplish the task as it is set out in your title and introduction? Did you include a conclusion? Is your conclusion based on the arguments made in the body of the paper? If you plan on studying the major economic contributions of some economist, did you do so, or did you spend two thirds of the paper telling me about his or her life and times? Does your conclusion indicate that you have fully synthesized the material you studied?

Finally, your paper should be <u>typed</u>, <u>doubled-spaced</u>, and <u>handed in on time</u> - the week before classes end. You should <u>proofread</u> it before handing it in. The average length of good papers in the past has been 15 pages.

II. Plausible Types of Topics

    A. An aspect of a major economist's work. Past A papers have included:

        Marshall's theory of demand   Ricardo's rent theory
                     Marx on surplus value

        Such a paper would also include comments from the secondary literature and your own conclusion.

    B. A survey of a minor economist's work. Past A papers have included:

        Petty's economic thought   Turgot's contributions
               Fisher's theory of interest

        Again, citations from secondary sources and a conclusion are essential.

    C. A study of the contributions of a major school in economic thought. Past A papers have included:

        Quesnay and the Physiocrats   The Institutionalists
              Precursors of the Marginalists

        You will probably use more secondary sources in a paper like this.

    D. A topic of your own choosing.

        About three weeks into the semester, I will ask you for a paper proposal, in which you will state your topic of study and which should include some bibliographical citations.

III. How to find a topic

    A. Read over the bibliographic citations at the end of Spiegel. One reason I chose this book as our text is because it has one of the best and most complete bibliographies available.

    B. Read the shelves in the library. The history of thought section is HB70-160. The major journal in the field is <u>History of Political Economy</u>.

    C. Desperate? See me.

History of Economic Thought

A List of Famous Works in the Twentieth Century

1899 - Thorstein Veblen - Theory of the Leisure Class

1906 - Knut Wicksell - Lectures on Political Economy, English translation in 1933/34

1910 - Philip Wicksteed - The Common Sense of Political Economy

1911 - Irving Fisher - The Purchasing Power of Money

1915 - E. Slutsky - "On the Theory of the Budget of the Consumer," Giorgnale degli Economisti

1917 - A.C. Pigou - "The Exchange Value of Legal Tender Money," QJE

1919 - E. Lindahl - "Just Taxation - A Positive Solution"

1920 - A.C. Pigou - The Economics of Welfare

1921 - Frank H. Knight - Risk, Uncertainty and Profit

1921 - T. Veblen - The Engineers and the Price System

1926 - Piero Sraffa - "The Laws of Returns under Competitive Coditions," Economic Journal

1927 - W.C. Mitchell - Business Cycles: The Problem and Its Setting

1928 - Lionel Robbins - "The Representative Firm," Economic Journal

1930 - J.M. Keynes - A Treatise on Money

1930 - I. Fisher - The Theory of Interest

1932 - L. Robbins - An Essay on the Nature and Significance of Economic Science

1932 - A.A. Berle and G. Means - The Modern Corporation and Private Property

1933 - E.H. Chamberlin - Theory of Monopolistic Competition

1933 - Joan Robinson - Economics of Imperfect Competition

1934 - John R. Hicks and R.G.D. Allen - "A Reconsideration of the Theory of Value," Economica

1936 - J.M. Keynes - The General Theory of Employment, Interest and Money

1937 - F. A. von Hayek - "Economics and Knowledge," Economica

1937 - J.R. Hicks - "Mr. Keynes and the Classics: A Suggested Interpretation," Econometrica

1938 - Abraham Bergson - "A Reformulation of Certain Aspects of Welfare Economics," QJE

1938 - Paul Samuelson - "A Note on the Pure Theory of Consumer's Behavior," Economica

1939 - P. Samuelson - "Interaction Between the Multiplier Analysis and the Principle of Acceleration," REStat

1939 - J.R. Hicks - Value and Capital

1939 - R.L. Hall and C.J. Hitch - "Price Theory and Business Behaviour," Oxford Economic Papers

1939 - Paul Sweezy - "Demand under Conditions of Oligopoly," JPE

1939 - Nicholas Kaldor - "Welfare Propositions of Economics and Interpersonal Comparisons of Utility," Economic Journal

1941 - Tibor Scitovsky - "A Note on Welfare Propositions in Economics," Review of Economic Studies

1942 - Joseph A. Schumpeter - Capitalism, Socialism and Democracy

1944 - F.A. von Hayek - The Road to Serfdom

1944 - John von Neumann and Oskar Morgenstern - The Theory of Games and Economic Behavior

1947 - P. Samuelson - Foundations of Economic Analysis [First published in 1941]

1948 - P. Samuelson - Economics

1948 - P. Samuelson - "International Trade and the Equalization of Factor Prices," Economic Journal

1949 - Ludwig von Mises - English translation of Human Action

1950 - I.M.D. Little - A Critique of Welfare Economics

1951 - Kenneth J. Arrow - Social Choice and Individual Values

1953 - Milton Friedman - "The Methodology of Positive Economics"

1954 - J.A. Schumpeter - History of Economic Analysis

1954 - K.J. Arrow and G. Debreu - "Existence of Equilibrium for a Competitive Economy," Econometrica

1955 - Lawrence Klein and Arthur Goldberger - An Econometric Model of the U.S., 1929-1952

1956 - Richard G. Lipsey and Kelvin Lancaster - "The General Theory of Second Best," Review of Economic Studies

1956 - Milton Friedman - "The Quantitiy Theory of Money: A Restatement"

1956 - Robert Solow - "A Contribution to the Theory of Economic Growth," QJE

1956 - T. Swan - "Economic Growth and Capital Accumulation," Economic Record

1957 - Herbert Simon - Models of Man

1958 - John Kenneth Galbraith - The Affluent Society

1958 - James Tobin - "Liquidity Preference as Behavior Towards Risk," Review of Economic Studies

1958 - A.W. Phillips - "The Relation Between Unemployment and Rate of Change of Money Wages in the United Kingdom, 1861-1957," Economica

1958 - F. Modigliani and M. Miller - "The Cost of Capital, Corporation Finance and the Theory of Investment," AER

1959 - R. Musgrave - The Theory of Public Finance

1960 - R.H. Coase - "The Problem of Social Cost," Journal of Law and Economics

1960 - W.W. Rostow - The Stages of Economic Growth

1960 - P. Sraffa - Production of Commodities by Means of Commodities

1961 - George Stigler - "The Economics of Information," JPE

1961 - J.F. Muth - "Rational Expectations and the Theory of Price Movements," Econometrica

1962 - James Buchanan and Gordon Tullock - The Calculus of Consent

1963 - M. Friedman and D. Meiselman - "The Relative Stability of Monetary Velocity and the Investment Multiplier in the U.S., 1897-1958," Stabilization Policies

1963 - M. Friedman and Anna J. Schwartz - A Monetary History of the U.S., 1861-1960

1963 - R.M. Cyert and J.G. March - A Behavioral Theory of the Firm

1964 - Gary Becker - Human Capital

1965 - Don Patinkin - Money, Interest, and Prices

1965 - Robert Clower - "The Keynesian Counter-Revolution: A Theoretical Appraisal," in Clower, The Theory of Interest Rates, 1969.

1966 - P. Baran and P. Sweezy - Monopoly Capital

1966 - K. Lancaster - "A New Approach to Consumer Theory," JPE

1966 - H. Leibenstein - "Allocative Efficiency vs. X-Efficiency," AER

1967 - Edmund Phelps - "Phillips Curves, Expectations of Inflation and Optimal Unemployment," Economica

1968 - M. Friedman - "The Role of Monetary Policy," AER

1968 - Axel Leijonhufvud - On Keynesian Economics and the Economics of Keynes

1969 - Luigi Pasinetti - "Swithes of Technique and the 'Rate of Return' in Capital Theory," Economic Journal

1970 - G. Akerlof - "The Market for 'Lemons': Quality Uncertainty and the Market Mechanism," QJE

1970 - E. Phelps, ed. - Microeconomic Foundations of Employment and Inflation Theory

1970 - Amartya K. Sen - Collective Choice and Social Welfare

1971 - John Rawls - A Theory of Justice

1971 - R. Barro and H. Grossman - "A General Disequilibrium Model of Income and Employment," AER

1974 - M. Spence - Market Signalling

1975 - Robert Lucas - "An Equilibrium Model of the Business Cycle," JPE

1982 - Richard Nelson and Sidney Winter - An Evolutionary Theory of Economic Change

Economics 555
Potential Exam Questions

* Evaluate the economic doctrines of the Scholastics. A favorable assessment might stress (e.g.,) how the ideas were those of a religious community, and how those ideas reflect a morality which is too often lacking in the modern world. A negative judgement might be based on (e.g.,) how those ideas might have caused economic growth to be retarded. I do not care which side you take, and you may wish to offer a more balanced judgement in which both pros and cons are discussed. But your answer should explicitly address the seven or eight points of Scholastic economic doctrine covered in class.

* Mercantilism took both an English and a French form. In which ways were the two forms similar? In which ways were they different?

* Intellectual history is often shaped by cultural, political, social, economic (etc.) contexts - that is to say, it often seems in retrospect that the ideas of great writers are shaped by the times in which they live, or those just preceding. Discuss, using examples from the Scholastic and mercantilist periods.

* It is the year 1758. You are Henri LeFou, chief assistant to Quesnay, and an intimate associate of the other Physiocrats. A group of English intellectuals is visiting Paris, and you have been asked by Quesnay to describe the Physiocratic system to them. A typical French person, you assume that your English audience is comprised of ignorant dolts who are nonetheless eager for Enlightenment. What would you tell them about Physiocratic thought? Do not neglect to include in your answer:
   a. The background assumptions of Physiocratic thought
   b. The three classes, and their interaction as revealed by the Tableau Economique
   c. The policy implications of your ideas. Are you a free trader?

* Outline and comment upon Smith's contributions in Book I of *The Wealth of Nations*. Be sure to discuss the following points.
   a. What does Smith have to say concerning the origin of, advantages conferred by, and limitations faced by the division of labor?
   b. Certain later commentators claimed that Smith confused the distinction between measures of value and determinants of value. Discuss Chapters 5 - 7, and in the process clear up this confusion.
   c. Describe his theory of distribution. Why have some commentators called this theory incomplete, and others called it inconsistent?
   d. It would seem that in a system of perfect liberty there should be no differences in the wages paid to different professions. If such a differential existed, freely mobile workers would leave the low-paying fields and enter the high-paying ones, and this movement would raise wages in the former and lower them in the latter until equality was reached. Smith points out that even in a system of perfect liberty, wage differentials would exist. Reproduce his argument.

* Implicit in the writings of the Classicals is a theory of economic growth, a theory which would hold if the system of natural liberty were left undisturbed.
    a. Outline the theory.
    b. Describe how it could lead to a happy progressive state (a la Smith). Are there any inconsistencies in Smith's model?
    c. How did Malthus' theories of population and commodity gluts challenge this happy vision? What policy conclusions does Malthus draw from this?
    d. Show how Ricardo reached his conclusion that the growth process would end up in a stationary state.

* Some economists claim that the Classicals (excluding Malthus) embraced a strict interpretation of Say's Law - supply creates its own demand, general overproduction is impossible, money has no effect on the real variables in the economy. Others deny this, claiming that the Classicals did understand that gluts were possible and that money had effects. Discuss the evidence offered by both sides in this debate within the history of thought.

* Detail Thomas Malthus' contribution to economics in the areas of population, diminishing returns, and the question of commodity gluts.

* Answer the following questions on classical theories of value.
    a. What is a theory of value?
    b. Some claim that Adam Smith held a labor theory of value. Did he? Explain.
    c. One economist has stated that Ricardo held a "93% labor theory of value." What does this mean?
    d. Ricardo outlines the assumptions necessary for a labor theory of value to work. Explain in detail what these assumptions are.

* In Marx's vision of the laws of motion of capitalism, capitalism is doomed to destruction due to certain contradictions inherent in its structure.
    a. Beginning with the capitalist's tendency to substitute capital for labor (i.e., omit Marx's derivation of the origins of surplus value, and simply accept it as a premise of his argument), describe the process leading to socialist revolution and the millennium as Marx envisioned it.
    b. Point out which of his predictions held true and which went wrong. Assess his argument and draw a conclusion.

* In five short sentences (no major compound sentences, please) summarize the most important points of the Communist Manifesto. Then write a short essay defending why you chose these five particular points as revealing the essence of the essay.

* Outline the major arguments contained in either "The Communist Manifesto" or "Socialism - Utopian and Scientific."

* "Competition ensures that social welfare is maximized." Discuss this idea, using your knowledge of the history of economic thought. Mention Smith, Marx, the relevant marginalists, and 20th century welfare economics in your answer.

* Jevons, Menger and Walras are known as the founders of the "Marginal Revolution."
  a. How are their analyses similar?
  b. How do they differ from one another?
  c. In what ways was the Marginal Revolution a true break with the past?
  d. In what ways was there a continuity with the past?

* Marshall's treatment of utility theory and his method of deriving a demand curve differs from the modern indifference curve approach. Compare the two approaches, espcially in terms of their assumptions. Is one approach "better" than the other? Defend your answer.

* "Economics hasn't changed much since Marshall's Principles; will that be your text?" quipped one historian of thought, interviewing me for a job (which I did not get offered). Do a better job than I did by:
  a. Discussing those areas in which Marshall made contributions which have lasted.
  b. Mentioning some of Marshall's suggestive hints that led followers to break new ground.
  c. Mentioning certain areas whose development Marshall neither originated nor anticipated.

* One of the many tasks that academics face is refereeing articles for professional journals. The editors of journals receive manuscripts from authors, then send them to other academics for an evaluation. The referee's report usually consists of a brief restatement of the major themes of the paper, an assessment of the plausibility of the arguments, and comments on such things as style, appropriateness for the specific journal in question, originality, and so on. In a sense, such a report is like a book review of a paper. The editors use these reports to decide whether or not to publish the papers submitted.
    Write such a report for either Mirowski's "Physics and the Marginalist Revolution" or Caldwell's "Hayek's Transformation."

G

ECONOMICS 657
AUBURN UNIVERSITY
ROBERT B. EKELUND, JR.

HISTORY OF ECONOMIC THOUGHT: THE NEOCLASSICAL PERIOD

THROUGH MARSHALL AND VEBLEN

TEXTS

> Schumpeter, Joseph A. History of Economic Analysis (1954). The work should form the core of every serious student's library on the history of economic analysis. (optional).
>
> Ekelund, R. B. Jr. and Hebert, R. F. A History of Economic Theory and Method (New York: McGraw-Hill Book Company, 3rd edition, 1990). Page references to the third edition. (optional)

SELECTED REFERENCES

The following books are suggested for further general reading and/or for graduate student research paper-secondary source materials. There is no substitute for reading in primary sources!!!

1. Mark Blaug. Economic Theory in Retrospect, Any edition Blaug's book contains excellent "readers guides" to the great books and the most meticulous treatment of Marshallian economic and its development in the literature.

2. H. J. Davenport. The Economics of Alfred Marshall.

3. T. W. Hutchison. A Review of Economic Doctrines 1870-1929.

4. Wesley Clair Mitchell. Notes on Types of Economic Theory. Vol. II.

5. Eric Roll. A History of Economic Thought (1956). A reasonable secondary source on Marx by a Marxist.

6. Joseph J. Spengler and William Allen. Essays in Economic Thought: Aristotle to Marshall.

7. George J. Stigler. Essays in the History of Economics (1965).

8. -------. Production and Distribution Theories: The Formative Period. Stigler's doctoral dissertation and a brilliant, if idiocyncratic, source on neoclassical theory in these areas.

READINGS

I. INTRODUCTION: HISTORY OF ECONOMIC THOUGHT AND ANALYSIS

1. Schumpeter, History of Economic Analysis, Part I.

2. Kuhn, Thomas S. The Structure of Scientific Revolutions. Revised edition (Chicago: University of Chicago Press).

3. Fetter, Frank. "The Relations of the History of Economic Thought to Economic History," American Economic Review (May 1965).

4. Hutchison, T. W. "Insularity and Cosmopolitanism in Economic Ideas, 1870-1914," American Economic Review (May 55).

5. Spengler, Joseph J. "Exogenous and Endogenous Influences in the Formation of Post-1870 Economic Thought: A Sociology of Knowledge Approach," in Robert Eagly (ed.), Events, Ideology and Economic Theory. (Detroit: Wayne State University Press, 1968).

6. Stigler, George J. "The Influence of Events and Policies on Economic Theory," (May 1960), repinted in Essays in the History of Economics (1965).

7. Stigler, George J. "The Nature and Role of Originality in Scientific progress," Economica (November 1955), reprinted in Essays in the History of Economics (1965).

8. Chalk, A. F. "Schumpter's Views on the Relationship of Philosophy and Economics," Southern Economic Journal (January 1958).

II. THE DECLINE OF CLASSICAL ECONOMICS (1848-1890)

A. The Wages Fund Doctrine: Original Sources

Early Attacks

1. Longe, Francis. A Refutation of the Wages Fund Theory of Modern Political Economy (1866).

2. Thornton, William T. On Labour: Its Wrongful Claims and Rightful Dues, Its Actual Present and Possible Future (London, 1869, second edition, 1870).

3. Mill, John Stuart. "Thornton on Labour and Its Claims," Fortnightly Review (May and June, 1869), pp. 505-518 and pp. 680-700.

4. Taussig, Frank W. Wages and Capital. Chapter 12, pp. 241-

2

256.

Cairnes' Restatement of the Wages Fund Doctrine

1. Cairnes, John E. Some Leading Principles of Political Economy, Newly Expounded, Pt. II, Chs. I, II, III, V (Sec. 6-9).

2. Taussig, F. W. Wages and Capital, Chapter 12, pp. 256-265.

Later Criticisms of the Wages Fund Doctrine

1. Walker, Francis Amasa. The Wages Question. Chapters 8 and 9. (Reader may also refer to his Principles of Political Economy, Part IV, Sections 4 and 5; Part IV, Section 5).

2. George, Henry. Progress and Poverty, Book I, Chapters 1-5.

3. Taussig, F. W. Wages and Capital, Chapter 14, pp. 280-300.

4. Hutchison, T. W. A Review of Economic Doctrines, 1870-1929, pp. 1-31.

B. The Wages Fund Doctrine: Secondary Sources

1. Breit, William L. "Some Neglected Early Critics of the Wages Fund Theory," Southwestern Social Science Quarterly, 48 (June, 1967), pp. 53-60.

2. Breit, William L. "The Wages Fund Controversy Revisited," The Canadian Journal of Economics and Political Science, 33 (November 1967), pp. 509-528.

3. Ekelund, Robert B. and Olsen, Emilie S. "Comte, Mill and Cairnes: The Positivist-Empiricist Interlude in Late Classical Economics," Journal of Economic Issues (September 1973), pp. 383-416.

4. Ekelund and Hebert, 2nd edition, Chapter 8.

5. Ekelund, Robert B. "A Short-Run Classical Model of Capital and Wages: Mill's Recantation of the Wages Fund," Oxford Economic Papers (March 1976), pp. 66-85.

6. West E. G. and Hafer, R. W. "J. S. Mill, Unions, and the Wages Fund Recantation: A Reinterpretation," The Quarterly Journal of Economics 92 (November 1978), pp. 603-19.

7. Ekelund, Robert B. and Kordsmeier, William. "J. S. Mill, Unions, and the Wages Fund Recentation: A Reinterpretation: Comment," The Quarterly Journal of Economics (1981).

8. Negishi, Takashi. "Comments on Ekelund: Mill's Recantation of the Wages Fund," Oxford Economic Papers 37 (1985), pp.

3

148-51.

9. Ekelund, Robert B. "Mill's Recantation Once Again: Reply to Professor Negishi," Oxford Economic Papers 37 (1985), pp. 152-53.

10. Negishi, Takashi. "Thornton's Criticism of Equilibrium Theory and Mill," History of Political Economy 18 (1986), pp. 567-77.

11. Ekelund, Robert B. and Thommesen, Sven. "Disequilibrium Theory and Thornton's Assault on the Laws of Supply and Demand," History of Political Economy 21 (1989), pp. 567-592 and Negishi's "Reply," same issue, pp. 593-600.

III. JOHN STUART MILL, EDWIN CHADWICK, AND NASSAU SENIOR: LAISSEZ FAIRE, SOCIAL JUSTICE AND CLASSICAL ECONOMIC POLICY

A. Original Source Materials

1. Mill, J. S. Essays on Economics and Society, Volumes 4 and 5 in J. S. Mill's Collected Works, edited by J. M. Robson, with an introduction by Lord L. Robbins (Toronto: University of Toronto Press, 1967). The entire canon of J. S. Mill's works has now been published by the University of Toronto Press. It includes virtually all of Mill's published works and is composed of 17+ volumes. This collection is definitive and gives all a good look into Mill's catholic interests and incredible mind).

2. [Mill, J. S.] "The Employment of Children in Manufactories," The Examiner (January 29, 1832), pp. 67-68.

3. [Mill, J. S.] "On Mr. Walter's Pamphlet Against the Poor Law Amendment Bill," Morning Chronicle (May 12, 1834), p. 2.

4. [Mill, J. S.] "The Claims of Labour," Edinburgh Review LXXXI (April 1845), reprinted in J. S. Mill, Essays on Economics and Society, edited by J. M. Robson (Toronto: University of Toronto Press, 1967), Volume V, pp. 363-89.

5. Mill, J. S. "Endowments," Fortnightly Review, N. S., Volume V (April 1869), pp. 337-90. Reprinted in J. S. Mill, Essays on Economics and Society, Volume V.

6. Mineka, F. E. The Earlier Letters of John Stuart Mill, 1812-1848; and Mineka, F. E. and Lindley, D. N. The Later Letters of John Stuary Mill, 1848-1873, Volumes 12-17 of the Collected Works (Toronto: University of Toronto Press, 1963- and 1972).

7. Chadwick, Edwin. "Results of Different Principles of

Legislation and Administration in Europe; of competition for the Field, as compared with Competition within the Field of Service," *Royal Statistical Society Journal* 22 (1959), pp. 381-420

8. Senior, Nassau W. *Selected Writings on Economics* (New York: Augustus M. Kelley, 1966).

9. Senior, Nassau W. *Industrial Efficiency and Social Economy* (New York: Henry Holt, 2 vols., 1928).

B. *Secondary Sources: Mill, Chadwick, Senior and Economic Policy*

1. Schwartz, Pedro. *The New Political Economy of J. S. Mill* (Durham, North Carolina: Duke University Press, 1972).

2. Hollander, Samuel. *The Economics of John Stuart Mill* (Toronto: University of Toronto Press, 1986), 2 Volumes.

3. Ekelund, Robert B. and Tollison, Robert D. "The New Political Economy of J. S. Mill: The Means to Social Justice," *Canadian Journal of Economics* (June 1976).

4. Ekelund, R. B. and Crain, Mark. "Chadwick and Demsetz on Competition and Regulation," *Journal of Law and Economics* (April 1976), pp. 149-162.

5. Ekelund, R. B. and Price, Edward O. III. "Sir Edwin Chadwick on Competition and the Social Control of Industry: Railraods," *History of Political Economy* (Summer 1979), pp. 213-239.

6. Hebert, Robert F. "Edwin Chadwick and the Economics of Crime," *Economic Inquiry* (October 1977), pp. 539-550.

7. Harris, Abram L. "J. S. Mill on Monopoly and Socialism: A Note," *Journal of Political Economy* (December 1959), pp. 604-11.

8. Schwartz, Pedro. "John Stuart Mill and Laissez Faire: London Water," *Economica* N.S. (February, 1966), pp. 71-83.

9. West, E. G. "Tom Paine's Voucher Scheme for Public Education," *Southern Economic Journal* 33 (1967), pp. 378-82.

10. West, E. G. "J. S. Mill's Redistribution Policy: New Political Economy or Old," *Economic Inquiry* (October 1978), pp. 570-586.

11. Ekelund, R. B. and Tollison, R. D. "J. S. Mill's New Political Economy: Another View," *Economic Inquiry* (October 1978), pp. 587-592.

12. Marvel, Howard P. "Factory Regulation: A Reinterpretation of Early English Experience," *Journal of Law and Economics* 20 (1977), pp. 379-402.

13. Anderson, Gary M., Ekelund, R. B., and Tollison, R. D., "Nassau Senior as Economic Consultant: The Factory Acts Reconsidered," *Economica* (February 1989), pp. 71-82.

14. O'Donnell, Margaret. "Pigou: An Extension of Sidgwickian Thought," *History of Political Economy* (Winter 1979), pp. 589-605.

15. Davis, Elynor. "Mill, Socialism, and the English Romantics: An Interpretation," *Economica* (August 1985), pp. 345-358.

IV. AUSTRIAN CONTRIBUTIONS

A. The Early Austrians: Primary Sources

1. Menger, Carl. *Principles of Economics* (Glencoe, Ill.: The Free Press, 1871). Chapters 1, 2, and 3.

2. Wieser, Friedrich von. *Natural Value* (1884). Books I, II, III and V. Translated by A. Malloch, with a preface by William Smart. (new York: Kelley and Millman, 1956).

3. Wieser, Friedrich von. *Social Economics*. Translated by A. Ford Hinrichs (New York: Augustus M. Kelley, 1967), originally published in 1914.

4. Wieser, Friedrich von. *The Law of Power* (Das Gesetz der Macht) (Vienna: Julius Springer, 1926). Translated by W. E. Kuhn, edited with an introduction by Warren J. Samuels. (Lincoln: Bureau of Business Research, University of Nebraska, 1983).

5. Bohm-Bawerk, Eugene von. *Positive Theory of Capital*. Book I, Chapters II, IV, V, and VI. Book II, Chapters I - V. Vook V. (Also see his *Capital and Interest* for a brilliant critique of early interest theories).

B. Second and Third Generation Austrians

1. F. A. Hayek. *Individualism and Economic Order* (Chicago: University of Chicago Press, 1948).

2. Mises, Ludwig von. *Human Action: A Treatise on Economics* (New Haven: Yale University Press, 1949).

3. Kirzner, Israel. *Competition and Entrepreneurship* (Chicago: University of Chicago Press, 1972).

C. The Austrians: Other Sources

1. Ekelund, Robert B. "Power and Utility: The Normative Economics of Friedrich von Wieser," Review of Social Economy (September 1970), pp. 179-196.

2. Ekelund and Hebert, 2nd ed., Chapters 13 and 21.

3. Hutchison, T. W. Review of Economic Doctrines, Chapters 2, 9, 10, and 11.

4. Roll, Erich. History of Economic Thought (3rd edition), pp. 374-394.

5. Stigler, George J. Production and Distribution Theories, Chapters 2, 6 and 7 (highly recommended).

6. Stigler, G. J. "The Development of Utility Theory," Journal of Political Economy 58 (August and October 1950), reprinted in Essays in the History of Economics, pp. 78-97.

7. Ekelund, R. B. "Wieser's Social Economics: A Link to Modern Austrian Theory?" Austrian Economics Newsletter (Fall 1986), pp. 1, 4, 9-11. Also see Ekelund, R. B., and Thornton, Mark. "Wieser and the Austrian Connection to Social Economics," Forum for Social Economics 16 (Spring 1987), pp. 1-12.

8. Smart, William. An Introduction to the Theory of Value. (New York: Augustus Kelley, 1966).

9. Veblen, Thorstein. "The Limitations of Marginal Utility," Journal of Political Economy (November 1909). Reprinted in W. C. Mitchell (editor), What Veblen Taught, pp. 151-175.

10. Jaffe, William. "Menger, Jevons, and Walras De-homogenized," Economic Inquiry 14 (December 1976), pp. 511-524.

11. Howey, R. S. The Rise of the Marginal Utility School, 1870-1889 (Lawrence, Kansas: The University Press of Kansas, 1960).

12. Kauder, Emil. A History of Marginal Utility Theory (Princeton, N. J.: Princeton University Press, 1965).

V. THE EMERGENCE OF SCIENTIFIC ECONOMICS (I): NINETEENTH CENTURY CONTINENTAL AND BRITISH CONTRIBUTIONS TO ECONOMIC ANALYSIS

A. Original Sources

1. Baumol, William J. and Goldfeld, Stemphen M. (eds).

7

Precursors in Mathematical Economics: An Anthology. (London: London School of Economics and Political Science, 1968).

2. Cournot, Augustin. Researches into the Mathematical principles of the Theory of Wealth. Translated by Nathaniel T. Bacon with an essay by Irving Fisher.

3. Dupuit, Jules. "On the Measurement of the Utility of Public Works," translated by R. H. Barback, Annales des Ponts et Chaussees, 2nd Series, VIII (1844). Translation in the International Economic Papers, No. 2 (London: Macmillan, 1952).

4. Dupuit, Jules. "On Tolls and Transport Charges," translated by Elizabeth Henderson, Annales des Ponts et Chaussees, 2nd Series, XVII (1849). Translation in the International Economic Papers, No. 11 (London: Macmillan, 1962).

5. Jenkin, Fleeming. The Graphic Representation of the Laws of Supply and Demand, and Other Essays, 1868-1884 (London School of Economics Reprint, 1931). Jenkin's major paper, published in 1871, is reprinted in Readings in the Economic of Taxation, edited by R. A. Musgrave and C. S. Shoup (1959).

6. Jevons, William Stanley. The Theory of Political Economy, 4th edition. (1st edition, 1871). (New York: Augustus Kelley), Chapters 1-5.

7. Jevons, William Stanley. Papers and Correspondence of William Stanley Jevons, edited by R. D. Collison Black and Rosamond Konekamp (New York: Augustus M. Kelly with the Royal Economic Society, 1972) 6 volumes.

8. Lardner, Lionysius. Railway Economy (New York: Harper and Brothers, 1850). Reprinted by Augustus M. Kelley, 1968.

9 Pantaleoni, Maffeo. Pure Economics, translated by T. Boston Bruce (New York: Augustus M. Kelley, 1965). Original Italian edition, 1889; English translation first published, 1898. Part II, "The Theory of Value," Chapters I, II, III.

B. Secondary Sources

1. Calsoyas, C. D. "The Mathematical Theory of Monopoly in 1839: Charles Ellet, Jr.," Journal of Political Economy (April 1950).

2. Ekelund, R. B., "Jules Dupuit and the Early Theory of Marginal Cost Pricing," Journal of Political Economy (May/June 1968).

3. Ekelund, R. B., "A Note on Jules Dupuit and Neo-Classical Monopoly Theory," Southern Economic Journal (January 1969), pp. 257-62.

4. Ekelund, R. B. and Gramm, W. P., "Early French Contributions to Marshallian Demand Theory," Southern Economic Journal (January 1970), pp. 277-286.

5. Ekelund, R. B., "Price Discrimination and Product Differentiation in Economic Theory: An Early Analysis," Quarterly Journal of Economics (May 1970), pp. 268-279.

6. Ekelund, R. B., "Professor Stigler on Dupuit and the Development of Utility theory: Comment," Journal of Political Economy (Sept/Oct. 1972), pp. 1056-1059.

7. Ekelund, R. B. and Hebert, R. F. "Jules Dupuit and Marginal Utility: Context of the Discovery," History of Political Economy (Summer 1976), pp. 266-73.

8. Fry, C. L. and Ekelund, R. B., "Cournot's Demand Theory: A Reassessment," History of Politcal Economy (Spring 1971), pp. 190-97.

9. Ekelund, R. B., Furubotn, E. and Gramm, W. P. (eds.) The Evolution of Modern Demand Theory (Lexington: D. C. Heath and Co., 1972), pp. 29-31 on Fleeming Jenkin.

10. Hooks, Donald L. "Monopoly Price Discrimination in 1850: Dionysius Lardner," History of Political Economy (Spring 1971).

11. Robertson, R. M., "Jevons and His Precursors," Econometrica (July 1951).

12. Theocharis, Reghinos D. Early Developments in Mathematical Economics, 2nd edition. (Philadelphia: Porcupine Press, 1983). Especially good source on Cournot.

13. Ekelund, R. B. and Shieh, Yeung-Nan. "Full Price Competition and Dupuit's Defense of the Long-Haul and Short-Haul 'Discrimination'," Journal of Regulatory Economics 1 (1989), pp. 359-371.

14. Ekelund, R. B. and Hebert, R. F., "Cournot and His Contemporaries: Is an Obituary the Only Bad Review?" Southern Economic Journal (forthcoming, 1990).

15. Ekelund, R. B., and Hebert, Robert F. "Dupuit's Characteristics-Based Theory of Consumer Behavior and Entrepreneurship," Kyklos (forthcoming 1990).

16. Ekelund and Hebert, Chapters 12 and 14.

VI. THE EMERGENCE OF SCIENTIFIC ECONOMICS (II): SOME NINETEENTH CENTURY MODELS IN LOCATION THEORY

A. Original Sources

1. Cheysson, Emile, "La Statistique geometrique: ses applications industrielles et commerciales," Le genie civil, x, Nos 13 and 14 (Jan 29 and Feb 5 1887), pp. 206-10, 224-28. Translation available.

2. Ellet, Charles. "The Laws of Trade applied to the determination of the most advantageous fare for passengers on railraods." Edited by Thomas P. Jones, Philadelphia, in Journal of the Franklin Institute of the State of Pennsylvania, Vol. 30 (1840).

3. Ellet, Charles. "A popular exposition of the incorrectness of the tariffs of tolls in use of the public improvements of the United States," Journal of the Franklin Institute of the State of Pennsylvania, Vol. 29 (1840).

4. Thunen, Johann H. von. von Thunen's Isolated State, an English edition of Der Isolierte Staat. Translated by Carla M. Wartenberg and edited by Peter Hall. (Oxford: Pergamon Press, 1966).

B. Secondary Sources

1. Ekelund, R. B. and Hooks, D. L., "Joint Demand, Discriminating Two-Part Tariffs and Location Theory: An Early American Contribution," Western Economic Journal 10 (March 1972). On Ellet.

2. Hebert, Robert F. "A Note on the Historical Develpment of the Economic Law of Market Areas," Quarterly Journal of Economics (November 1972).

3. Greenhut, M. L. Microeconomics and the Space Economy (Chicago: Scott Foresman, 1963), Chapter 7, especially pp. 160-163 on von Thunen. Also see references to Launhardt and others.

4. Ponsard, Claude. Histoire des theories economiques spatiales. (Paris: Armand Colin, 1958).

5. Shami, Charles H. Charles Ellet, Jr., Early American Economic Theorist and Econometrician. (Unpublished Ph.D. dissertation: Columbia University, 1968).

6. Blaug, Mark, "The German Hegemony of Location Theory: A Puzzle in the History of Economic Thought," History of Political Economy 11 (1979), pp. 21-29.

7. Ekelund, R. B. and Shieh, Yeung-Nan, "Dupuit, Spatial Economics, and Optimal Resource Allocation: A French Tradition," Economica 53 (November 1986), pp. 483-496.

VII. THE EMERGENCE OF SCIENTIFIC ECONOMICS (III): SOME NINETEENTH CENTURY ORIGINS OF ECONOMIC EMPIRICISM

A. Original Sources

1. Belpaire, Alphonse. Traite des depenses d'exploitation aux chemin de fer. (Bruxelles: Librairie Polytechnique, 1847).

2. Ellet, Charles, Jr., "Cost of Transportation on Railways," Journal of the Franklin Institute of the State of Pennsylvania, edited by Thomas P. Jones. (September, October, November, December, 1842; November, 1843; January, February, 1844).

3. Jevons, W. S. "A Serious Fall in the Value of Gold Ascertained and its Social Effects Set Forth," (April, 1863), reprinted in Jevons, Investigations in Currency and Fianance, edited by H. S. Foxwell (London: Macmillan, 1909), pp. 11-111.

4. Jevons, W. S. "The Variation of Prices and the Value of the Currency Since 1782," (Originally in the Journal of the Statistical Society of London, June, 1865), reprinted in Investigations, pp. 112-142.

5. Minard, Charles Joseph. "Notions elementaires d'economie politique appliquees aux travaux publics," Annales des Ponts et Chaussees 14, 2nd Series (1850), pp. 1-125.

B. Secondary Sources

1. Ekelund, R. B., "Economic Empiricism in the Writing of Early Railway Engineers," Explorations in Economic History (Winter 1971), pp. 180-196.

2. Ekelund, R. B., and Hebert, R. F., "Public Economics at the Ecole des ponts et Chaussees: 1830-1850," Journal of Public Economics (July 1973), pp. 241-256.

3. Spengler, J. J., "On the Progress of Quantification in Economics," in Hang Woolf, editor, Quantification (Indianapolis: Bobbs-Merrill, 1961).

4. Stigler, Stephen M. "Francis Ysidro Edgeworth, Statistician." Journal of the Royal Statistical Society, Series A 141 (1978), pp. 287-322.

5. Ekelund, R. B., and Thornton, Mark. "Geometric Analogies and Market Demand Estimation: Dupuit and the French Contribution," History of Political Economy (forthcoming, 1991).

VIII. LEON WALRAS: THE ORIGINS OF GENERAL EQUILIBRIUM

A. Original Sources

1. Walras, Leon. Correspondence of Leon Walras and Related Papers. Edited by William Jaffe. (Amsterdam: North Holland Publishing Co., 1965, 3 Volumes).

2. Walras, Leon. Elements of Pure Economics. Translated by W. Jaffe. (Homewood, Illinois: Richard D. Irwin, 1954). Lessons 5, 6, 7, 8, 9, 10, 11, 12, and 15 give the essense of general equilibrium theory.

B. Secondary Sources

1. Ekelund and Hebert, Chapter 16.

2. Jaffe, William, "A. N. Isnard, Progenitor of the Walrasian General Equilibrium Model," History of Political Economy (Spring 1969).

3. Kolm, Serge Christophe, "Leon Walras' Correspondence and Related Papers: The Birth of Mathematical Economics," American Economic Review (December 1968).

4. Walker, Donald A., "Leon Walras in the Light of his Correspondence and Related Papers," Journal of Political Economy (July/August 1970).

5. Friedman, Milton, "Leon Walras and His Economic System," American Economic Review 45 (December 1955), pp. 900-909.

IX. NEOCLASSICAL ECONOMIC THEORY: ALFRED MARSHALL AND OTHERS

A. Alfred Marshall

1. Value: Marshall, Principles of Economics 8th edition, Book III, Chapters I, II, III VI, Book V, Chapters 2-5, 8-9, and 12-15.

2. Wages: Marshall, Principles, Book VI, Chapters 1-5.

3. Interest: Marshall, Principles, Book VI, Chapter 6.

4. Profits: Marshall, Principles, Book VI, Chapters 7 and 8.

5. Rent: Marshall, Principles, Book VI, Chapter 9.

   6. Summary: Marshall, Principles, Book VI, Chapters 11 and 12.

B. General

   1. Ekelund and Hebert, Chapters 15, 22 and 23.

   2. Stigler, G. J., Production and Distribution Theories, Chapter 4.

   3. Roll, Erich. History of Economic Thought, pp. 394-402.

   4. Schumpeter, J. A., History, pp. 834-840; 990-998.

   5. Schumpeter, J. A., "Alfred Marshall's Principles: A Semi-Centennial Appraisal," American Economic Review (June 1941).

   6. Culbertson, W. P., and Ekelund, R. B., "John A. Hobson and the Theory of Discriminating Monopoly," History of Political Economy (1977), pp. 273-283.

   7. Uhr, Carl G. Economic Doctrines of Knut Wicksell (Berkeley: University of California Press, 1962).

   8. Cross, Melvin and Ekelund, R. B., "A. T. Hadley on Monopoly Theory and Regulation: An American Contribution to Economic Analysis and Policy," History of Political Economy (Summer 1980), pp. 214-233.

   9. Cross, Melvin and Ekelund, R. B., "A. T. Hadley: The American Invention of the Economics of Property Rights and Public Goods," Review of Social Economy (1981).

X. BRITISH HISTORICISTS AND AMERICAN INSTITUTIONALISTS: A HETERODOX REACTION

A. Original Sources

   1. Keynes, John Neville. The Scope and Method of Political Economy (New York: Augustus M. Kelley, 1963), First Edition, 1890.

   2. Ingram, John Kells. "The Present Position and Prospects of Political Economy," Address of the President of Section F (Economic Science and Statistics) of the British Association for the Advancement of Science (August 15, 1878), reprinted in R. L. Smyth (ed.), Essays in Economic Method, paperback (1963).

   3. Ingram, J. K. History of Political Economy (New York: Augustus M. Kelley, 1967), originally published 1888. Chapters V and VI.

4. Veblen, Thorstein, "The Preconceptions of Economic Science," in W. C. Mitchell (ed.) What Veblen Taught, pp. 39-150.

   5. Veblen, Thorstein, "Why is Economics not an Evolutionary Science?", Quarterly Journal of Economics (July 1898), pp. 373-97.

B. Secondary Sources

   1. Coats, A. W., "The Historicist Reaction in English Political Economy, 1870-1890," Economica N. S. (May 1954).

   2. Ekelund, R. B., "A British Rejection of Economic Orthodoxy," Social Science Quarterly (September 1966).

   3. Ekelund and Hebert, Chapter 17.

   4. Hofstadter, Richard. Social Darwinism in American Thought (Boston: Beacon Press, 1955).

   5. Ault, Richard W. and Ekelund, R. B. "Habits in Economic Analysis: Veblen and the Neoclassicals," History of Political Economy 20 (Fall 1988), pp. 431-446.

ECO 665, History of Economic Thought I, University of Kentucky
Professor R. E. Gift (BE 207H, 7-7640)

I. COURSE DESCRIPTION

The purpose of this course is to understand the <u>foundations of modern economics</u> as seen in the eighteenth century works of Smith, Cantillon, Turgot, Quesnay, Petty, Steuart, Malthus, and Hume and to appreciate the literary background of the analysis as seen in works by such writers as Mun, Serra, Bodin, Oresme and Aquinas. (This course sets the stage for Economics 666, which begins with Ricardo's <u>Principles</u> and outlines the <u>technical history of modern economics</u>.)

II. COURSE OUTLINE

The plan of work in the course is to proceed with a reading of <u>The Wealth of Nations</u> in its entirety. Other reading assignments will be made from the reference list.

There will be a mid-term examination and a final examination, both essay type. Grading is by subjective letter grades. There will be no term paper, but the student will do a literature search in order to submit a working bibliography on some special problem in <u>The Wealth of Nations</u> such as human capital, wilderness preservation, or public debt. Regular class attendance is required.

III. REFERENCES

Primary:
  Smith, <u>The Wealth of Nations</u>, Cannan edition (purchase)
  Heckscher, <u>Mercantilism</u>, 2 vols.
  Monroe, <u>Early Economic Thought</u>
  Viner, <u>Studies in the Theory of International Trade</u>

Secondary:
  Angell, <u>The Theory of International Prices</u>
  Bell, <u>History of Economic Thought</u>
  Blaug, <u>Economic Theory in Retrospect</u>
  Campbell and Skinner, <u>Adam Smith</u>
  Ginzberg, <u>House of Adam Smith</u>
  Glahe, <u>Adam Smith and The Wealth of Nations</u>
  Haney, <u>History of Economic Thought</u>
  Hirschman, <u>The Passions and the Interests</u>
  Malthus, <u>Essay on Population</u>
  Malthus, <u>Principles of Political Economy</u>
  Monroe, <u>Monetary Theory Before Adam Smith</u>
  Murrow and Stebbins, <u>Adam Smith and The Wealth of Nations</u>
  O'Driscoll, <u>Adam Smith and Modern Political Economy</u>
  Schumpeter, <u>History of Economic Analysis</u>
  Smith, <u>The Theory of Moral Sentiments</u>
  Smith, <u>Lectures on Jurisprudence</u>
  Spengler and Allen, <u>Essays in Economic Thought</u>
  Teichgraeber, <u>Free Trade and Moral Philosophy</u>
  Wood, <u>Adam Smith</u>, 4 vols.

ECO 666, History of Economic Thought II
University of Kentucky
Professor R. E. Gift (BE 207H, 7-7640)

I. COURSE DESCRIPTION

The purpose of this course is to understand the **technical history of modern economics** as seen in the literature from Ricardo to Sraffa and Georgescu-Roegen. Primary attention is devoted to topics having to do with **value and distribution**. The emphasis is on the **classical**, **neoclassical**, and **Marxian** doctrines, but other schools of thought are also kept in view. Much of the class discussion deals with the significance of the **neoclassical production function** and with problems in the theory of capital. Several philosophical systems will be used, and special importance is assigned to Whitehead, Sartre, and Jaspers.

This course is a sequel to ECO 665, which deals with the **foundations of modern economics** as found in The Wealth of Nations and other writings from Aquinas to Malthus.

II. COURSE OUTLINE

The plan of work is to move in an orderly manner through the evolution of value and distribution theory from Ricardo to the present, following Blaug. Frequent references are to be made to books in the library, and the student will make intensive use of this material. Use will also be made of two journals, **History of Political Economy** and **Journal of Economic Literature**, as well as Research in the History of Economic Thought and Methodology (annual).

There will be a mid-term and a final examination, both essay type. There is no term paper, but there will be homework. Regular class attendance is required.

III. REFERENCES

Primary:

Blaug, Economic Theory in Retrospect (purchase, 4th edition)
Hunt, History of Economic Thought (purchase)

Secondary:

AEA, Readings in Business Cycle Theory
AEA, Readings in Monetary Theory
AEA, Readings in Price Theory
AEA, Readings in the Theory of Income Distribution
Backhouse, A History of Modern Economic Analysis
Bell, History of Economic Thought
Bohm-Bawerk, Capital and Interest
Bohm-Bawerk, Positive Theory of Capital
Brems, Pioneering Economic Theory
Commons, Legal Foundations of Capitalism
Conard, Theory of Interest

Dow, *Macroeconomic Thought*
Georgescu-Roegen, *The Entrophy Law and the Economic Process* (recommended purchase)
Haney, *History of Economic Thought*
Hayek, *Pure Theory of Capital*
Hicks, *Capital and Growth*
Hicks, *Value and Capital*
Hoover, *The Economy, Liberty, and the State*
Klein, *The Keynesian Revolution*
Malthus, *Essay on Population*
Malthus, *Principles of Political Economy*
Marget, *Theory of Prices*
Marshall, *Principles of Economics*
Marx, *Capital*
Mill, *Principles of Political Economy*
Mitchell, *Lecture Notes on Economic Theory*
Musgrave, *Theory of Public Finance*
Negishi, *Economic Theories in a Non-Walrasian Tradition*
Pareto, *Manual of Political Economy*
Pasinetti, *Lectures on the Theory of Production*
Patinkin, *Money, Interest, and Prices*
Pribram, *History of Economic Reasoning*
Ricardo, *Principles of Political Economy and Taxation*
Robinson, *Economics of Imperfect Competition*
Samuelson, *Foundations of Economic Analysis*
Schumpeter, *History of Economic Analysis* (recommended purchase)
Spengler and Allen, *Essays in Economic Thought*
Sraffa, *Production of Commodities by Means of Commodities* (recommended purchase)
Stigler, *Production and Distribution Theories*
Veblen, *Theory of the Leisure Class*
Walras, *Elements of Pure Economics*
Wicksell, *Lectures*
Wicksell, *Value, Capital, and Rent*
Wicksteed, *Common Sense of Political Economy*

ECONOMICS 610
Alternative Economic Paradigms
Professors Glahe and Mott
Spring 1988
University of Colorado

Assigned Texts:

Alexander H. Shand, <u>The Capitalist Alternative: An Introduction to Neo-Austrian Economics</u> (New York: New York University Press, 1984). Hereafter, <u>Capitalist Alternative</u>.

Edwin G. Dolan, ed., <u>The Foundations of Modern Austrian Economics</u> (Kansas City: Sheed and Ward, 1976). Hereafter, <u>Foundations</u>. Out of print.

Donald Harris, <u>Capital Accumulation and Income Distribution</u> (Stanford: Stanford University Press, 1978). Hereafter, <u>Capital Accumulation</u>.

Michal Kalecki, <u>Selected Essays on the Capitalist Economy</u> (Cambridge: Cambridge University Press, 1971). Hereafter, <u>Capitalist Economy</u>.

Maurice Dobb, <u>Welfare Economics and the Economics of Socialism</u> (Cambridge: Cambridge University Press, 1969). Hereafter, <u>Welfare Economics</u>.

John Maynard Keynes, <u>The General Theory of Employment Interest and Money</u> (New York: Harcourt Brace Jovanovich, 1964). Hereafter, <u>General Theory</u>.

General Texts:

Mises, Ludwig von <u>Human Action</u>, 3rd. rev. ed. (Chicago: Henry Regnery Co., 1966).

Rothbard, Murray N. <u>Man, Economy, and State</u>, 2 vols. (Los Angeles: Nash Publishing, 1970).

Chiaki Nishiyama and Kurt R. Leube, eds., <u>The Essence of Hayek</u> (Stanford: Hoover Press, 1984). Hereafter, <u>Essence</u>.

Lachmann, Ludwig M., <u>Capital, Expectations, and the Market Process</u> (Kansas City: Sheed and Ward, 1977). Hereafter, <u>Market Process</u>.

Moss, Laurence S., ed., <u>The Economics of Ludwig von Mises</u> (Kansas City: Sheed and Ward, 1976). Hereafter, <u>von Mises</u>.

O'Driscoll, Gerald P. Jr., *Economics as a Coordination Problem* (Kansas City: Sheed Andrews and McMeel, 1977). Hereafter, *Coordination*.

Spadaro, Louis M., ed., *New Directions in Austrian Economics* (Kansas City: Sheed Andrews and McMeel, 1978). Hereafter, *New Directions*.

Joan Robinson, *The Accumulation of Capital* (3rd ed., 1969, reprinted 1986, Philadelphia: Porcupine Press).

_____, *Essays in the Theory of Economic Growth* (London: Macmillan, 1962), out of print. Hereafter *Essays*.

_____, *Economic Heresies* (New York: Basic Books, 1973).

Nicholas Kaldor, *Essays on Economic Stability and Growth* (Glencoe, Illinois: Free Press, 1960).

Topic I.
Historical and Methodological Background

Required reading:

Stanley L. Jaki, "Knowledge in an Age of Science," in *Chance or Reality and other Essays* by Stanley L. Jaki (Lanham, Maryland: University Press of America, 1986), pp. 119-43.

Bruce J. Caldwell, "Praxeology and Its Critics: An Appraisal," *History of Political Economy*, 16:3, 1984, pp. 363-79.

G. C. Harcourt, "Post-Keynesianism: Quite Wrong and/or Nothing New?", in Philip Arestos and Thanos Skouras, *Post Keynesian Economic Theory* (Sussex, England, Wheatsheaf Books, 1985).

Harris, *Capitalist Accumulation*, Chapters 1 and 2.

Alfred Eichner, "Introduction," in Eichner, ed., *A Guide to Post-Keynesian Economics* (White Plains, N.Y.: M. E. Sharpe, 1979).

Shand, *Capitalist Alternative*, pp. xi-xii, 1-42.

Supplemental:

Mises, *Human Action*, pp. 11-71.

Rothbard, *Man, Economy, and State*, pp. 1-28, 61-66.

Dolan, "Austrian Economics as Extraordinary Science," in *Foundations*, pp. 3-18.

Rothbard, "Praxeology, the Methodology of Austrian Economics," in *Foundations*, pp 19-39.

Dobb, *Theories of Value and Distribution since Adam Smith* (Cambridge: Cambridge University Press, 1973), Chaps. 8,9.

T. W. Hutchison, *The Politics and Philosophy of Economics: Marxians, Keynesians, and Austrians* (New York: New York University Press, 1984).

Eichner and Jan Kregel, "An Essay on Post-Keynesian Theory: A New Paradigm in Economics," *Journal of Economic Literature* (1975).

Robert Kuttner, "The Poverty of Economics," *The Atlantic Monthly*, February 1985, pp. 74-84.

Hayek, "Economic Thought: The Austrian School," *International Encyclopedia of the Social Sciences*, Vol. 4, pp. 458-62.

Mises, *The Historical Setting of the Austrian School of Economics* (New York: Arlington House, 1969).

Rothbard, "New Light on the Prehistory of the Austrian School," in *Foundations*, pp. 52-74.

Nina Shapiro, "The Revolutionary Character of Post-Keynesian Economics," *Journal of Economic Issues* (1977).

Menger, Carl, *Problems of Economics and Sociology* (Champaign: University of Illinois Press, 1963), pp. 33-94.

Mises, *Theory and History*, (New York: Arlington House, 1969), pp. 1-15.

Rothbard, "In Defense of Extreme a Priorism," *Southern Economic Journal* (January, 1957) pp. 314-20.

Rothbard, "The Mantle of Science," in H. Schoeck and J. W. Higgins (eds.), *Scientism and Values* (New York: Van Nostrand, 1960).

Hayek, *The Counter-Revolution in Science* (Glencoe, Illinois: The Free Press, 1955), pp. 13-43.

Kirzner, "On the Austrian Method in Economics," in *Foundations*, pp. 40-51.

Kirzner, *The Economic Point of View* (Kansas City: Sheed and Ward, 1976), pp. 146-85.

Lachmann, "The Significance of the Austrian School of Economics in the History of Ideas," in *Market Process*, pp. 45-64.

Rizzo, Mario J., "Praxeology and Econometrics: A Critique of Positivist Economics," in *New Directions*, pp. 40-56.

Stanley L. Jaki, "The Fate of Physics in Scientism," in *The Relevance of Physics* (Chicago: University of Chicago Press, 1966), pp. 461-500.

Yeager, Leland B., "Measurement as Scientific Method in Economics," *The American Journal of Economics and Sociology* (July, 1957), pp. 337-46.

White, Larry H., *Methodology of the Austrian School* (New York: Center for Libertarian Studies, 1977).

Thomas C. Taylor, *The Fundamentals of Austrian Economics* (San Francisco: Cato Institute, 1980).

Topic II.
The Theory of Value

Required reading:

Shand, *Capitalist Alternative*, pp. 43-62.

Harris, *Capital Accumulation and Income Distribution*, Chaps. 3-7.

Robinson, *Essays*, pp. 1-21.

Supplemental:

Mises, *Human Action*, pp. 92-98, 119-42.

Rothbard, *Man, Economy, and State*, pp. 67-108.

Sraffa, Piero, *The Production of Commodities by Means of Commodities* (Cambridge: Cambridge University Press, 1960), Chaps. 1-6.

Robinson, "The Theory of Value Reconsidered," *Collected Economic Papers* (Oxford: Blackwell, 1980).

Robinson, "The Philosophy of Prices," *Collected Economic Papers* (Oxford: Blackwell, 1980).

Levine, David, "Production Prices and the Theory of the Firm," *Journal of Post Keynesian Economics* (1980).

Levine, "Aspects of the Classical Theory of Markets," *Australian Economic Papers* (1980).

Menger, Carl, *Principles of Economics* (New York: New York University Press, 1981), pp. 257-85.

Mises, *Theory of Money and Credit* (Irvington-on-Hudson, New York: 1971), pp. 38-49.

Rothbard, *Toward a Reconstruction of Utility and Welfare Economics* (New York: Center for Libertarian Studies, 1977).

Buchanan, James M., *Cost and Choice* (Chicago: Markham, 1969), pp. 38-50.

Littlechild, S. C., "The Problem of Social Cost," in *New Directions*, pp. 77-93.

Jaffe, William, "Menger, Jevons, and Walras De-Homogenized," *Economic Inquiry* (December, 1976), pp. 511-24.

Topic III.
Theory of Capital and Interest

Required reading:

Kirzner, "The Theory of Capital", in *Foundations*, pp. 133-44.

Lachmann, "On the Austrian Theory of Capital," in *Foundations*, pp. 145-51.

Harris, *Capital Accumulation*, Chaps. 8 and 9.

Robinson, *Essays*, pp. 22-87.

Keynes, *General Theory*, Chaps. 13-16.

Supplemental:

Mises: *Human Action*, pp. 479-537.

Rothbard: *Man, Economy, and State*, pp. 273-90, 313-63.

Harcourt, G. C., "Some Cambridge Controversies in the Theory of Capital," *Journal of Economic Literature*, 7 (1969).

Harcourt, *Some Cambridge Controversies in the Theory of Capital* (Cambridge: Cambridge University Press, 1972).

Robinson, "Capital Theory Up to Date," *Collected Economic Papers* (Oxford: Blackwell, 1980).

Robinson, *et al*, "Symposium on Reswitching," *Quarterly Journal of Economics* (1975).

Robinson, "The Rate of Interest," in *The Rate of Interest and Other Essays* (London: Macmillan, 1952).

Hayek, *Prices and Production* (New York: Augustus Kelly, 1967), pp. 32-68.

Kirzner, *An Essay on Capital* (New York: Augustus Kelly, 1966).

Kirzner, "Ludwig von Mises and the Theory of Capital and Interest," in *von Mises*, pp. 51-65.

Lachmann, *Capital and Its Structure* (London: G. Bell and Sons, 1956), pp. 1-34.

Lachmann, "Complimentarity and Substitution in the Theory of Capital," in *Market Process*, pp. 197-213.

O'Driscoll, *Coordination*, pp. 66-91.

Kuenne, Robert E., *Eugen von Bohm-Bawerk* (New York: Columbia University Press, 1971), pp. 1-25.

Nicholas Kaldor, "Speculation and Economic Stability," *Review of Economic Studies* (1939).

Tracy Mott, "Towards a Post-Keynesian Formulation of Liquidity Preference," *Journal of Post-Keynesian Economics* (Winter, 1985-86).

Topic IV.
Competition and Monopoly

Required reading:

Shand, *Capitalist Alternative*, pp. 63-97, 125-35.

Hayek, "The Meaning of Competition," in *Individualism and Economic Order*, pp. 92-106.

Kalecki, *Capitalist Economy* (Cambridge: Cambridge University Press, 1971), Chaps. 5, 14.

Lachmann, "On the Central Concept of Austrian Economics: Market Process," in *Foundations*, pp. 126-32.

Kenyon, Peter, "Pricing," in Alfred Eichner ed., *A Guide to Post-Keynesian Economics*.

Mott, "Kalecki's Principle of Increasing Risk and the Relation between Markup Pricing, Investment Fluctuations, and, Liquidity-Preference," *Economic Forum* (Winter 1985-86).

Supplemental:

Mises, *Human Action*, pp. 257-79, 357-79.

Rothbard, *Man, Economy, and State*, pp. 560-620.

Steindl, Josef, *Maturity and Stagnation in American Capitalism* (New York: Monthly Review Press, 1976), Part I.

Eichner, *The Megacorp and Oligopoly* (Cambridge: Cambridge University Press, 1976).

Kirzner, *Competition and Entrepreneurship* (Chicago: University of Chicago Press, 1973), pp. 1-29.

Kirzner, "Equilibrium Versus the Market Process," in *Foundations*, pp. 115-25.

Lachmann, "Methodological Individualism and the Market Process," in *Market Process*, pp. 149-65.

O'Driscoll, *Coordination*, pp. 16-34.

Armentano, D. T., "A Critique of Neoclassical and Austrian Monopoly Theory" in *New Directions*, pp. 94-110.

Topic V
Theory of Money and Monetary Institutions

Required reading:

Shand, *Capitalist Alternative*, pp. 158-73.

Rothbard, "The Austrian Theory of Money," in *Foundations*, pp. 160-84.

Keynes, *General Theory*, Chap. 17.

Moore, Basil, "Monetary Factors," in Alfred Eichner (ed.), *A Guide to Post-Keynesian Economics*.

Hyman Minsky, "The Financial Instability Hypothesis: A Restatement," in Philip Arestos and Thanos Skouras, *Post Keynesian Economic Theory* (Sussex, England, Wheatsheaf Books, 1985).

Davidson, "Money and the Real World," *Economic Journal* (1972).

Supplemental:

Mises, *Human Action*, pp. 398-432, 780-800.

Rothbard, *Man, Economy, and State*, pp. 661-79, 698-709.

Davidson, Paul, *Money and the Real World* (London: Macmillan, 1978).

Minsky, Hyman, *John Maynard Keynes* (New York: Columbia University Press, 1975).

Menger, *Principles of Economics*, pp. 257-85.

Mises, *Theory of Money and Credit*, pp. 29-37, 97-154.

Rothbard, "The Case for the 100 Percent Gold Dollar," in Leland B. Yeager (ed.), *In Search of a Monetary Constitution* (Cambridge: Harvard University Press, 1962), pp. 94-136.

Hayek, *Choice in Currency* (London: Institute for Economic Affairs, 1976).

Friedman, Milton, "Should There Be and Independent Monetary Authority," in Yeager, ed., *Monetary Constitution*, pp. 219-43.

Yeager, Leland B., "Essential Properties of a Medium of Exchange," in R. W. Clower, ed., *Monetary Theory* (New York: Penguin Books, 1969), pp. 37-60.

Yeager, ed., "Introduction," *Monetary Constitution*, pp. 1-25.

Nai-Pew Ong, "The Logic of Marx's Theory of Money," *Social Concept* (1983).

Topic VI
The Business Cycle and Macroeconomics

Required reading:

Shand, *Capitalist Alternative*, pp. 136-57.

Gerald P. O'Driscoll, Jr., and Sudha R. Shenoy, "Inflation, Recession, and Stagflation," in *Foundations*, pp. 185-211.

Harris, *Capital Accumulation*, Chapter 10.

Keynes, *General Theory*, Chaps. 12, 18, and 22.

Kalecki, *Capitalist Economy*, Chaps. 1, 6-11.

Supplemental:

Mises: *Human Action*, pp. 538-86.

Rothbard: *Man, Economy, and State*, pp. 745-51, 850-79.

Steindl, Josef, *Maturity and Stagnation in American Capitalism* (New York: Monthly Review Press, 1976), Part II.

Roy Harrod, *Towards a Dynamic Economics* (London: Macmillan, 1948).

Mises et al, *The Austrian Theory of the Trade Cycle and Other Essays* (New York: Center for Libertarian Studies, 1978).

Rothbard, *America's Great Depression* (Kansas City: Sheed and Ward, 1975), pp. 11-38.

Hayek, *Monetary Theory of the Trade Cycle* (New York: Augustus Kelly, 1966), pp. 139-92.

Hayek, *Prices and Production*, pp. 69-104.

Robbins, Lionel, *The Great Depression* (Freeport, New York: Books for Libraries Press, 1971), pp. 30-54.

O'Driscoll, *Coordination*, pp. 92-134.

Topic VII.
Socialist and Capitalist Economic Systems

Required reading:

Shand, *Capitalist Alternative*, pp. 186-98.

Hayek, "The Use of Knowledge in Society," in *Individualism and Economic Order* (Chicago: Henry Regnery, 1972), pp. 77-91.

_____, *The Road to Serfdom*, condensed version (Boulder, Colorado: Economic Institute for Research and Education) pp. 3-37.

Don Lavoie, "Between Institutionalism and Formalism: The Rise and Fall of the Austrian School's Calculation Argument: 1920-1950."

Dobb, *Welfare Economics and the Economics of Socialism* (Cambridge, U.K.: Cambridge University Press, 1969), Part II.

Nuti, Mario, "Socialism on Earth," *Cambridge Journal of Economics*, 5 (1981).

Bruce McFarlane, "Economic Planning: Past Trends and New Prospects," *Contributions to Political Economy* (1984).

Supplemental:

Mises: *Human Action*, pp. 697-715.

Hayek, "Two Pages of Fiction: The Impossibility of Socialist Calculation," in *Essence*, pp. 53-61.

Rothbard, "Ludwig von Mises and Economic Calculation Under Socialism," in *von Mises*, pp. 67-77.

Steele, David Ramsey, "Posing the Problem: The Impossibility of Economic Calculation under Socialism," *The Journal of Libertarian Studies* (Winter 1981), pp. 7-22.

Lavoie, Don, "A Critique of the Standard Account of the Socialist Calculation Debate," *The Journal of Libertarian Studies* (Winter 1981), pp. 41-87.

Mises, *Socialism: An Economic and Sociological Analysis* (London: Jonathan Cape, 1936), pp. 211-20.

Mises, "Economic Calculation in the Socialist Commonwealth," in Hayek, ed., *Collectivest Economic Planning* (Clifton, New Jersey: Augustus M. Kelly, 1975), pp. 87-130.

Hayek, "Socialist Calculation," in *Individualism and the Economic Order*, pp. 119-208.

Hayek, "The New Confusion About Planning," in *New Studies in Philosophy, Politics, Economics and the History of Ideas* (Chicago: University of Chicago Press, 1978), pp. 232-46.

Hoff, Trygve J. B., *Economic Calculation in the Socialist Society* (Indianapolis: Liberty Press, 1981).

O'Driscoll, *Coordination*, pp. 1-15.

Lange, Oscar, "On the Economic Theory of Socialism," *Review of Economic Studies* (1936).

Nuti, "Hidden and Repressed Inflation in Soviet-type Economies: Definitions, Measurements, and Stabilization," *Contributions to Political Economy* (1986).

10

Topic VIII
Policy Questions and Competing Paradigms

Required reading:

Shand, *Capitalist Alternative*, pp. 174-85, 199-223.

Hayek, "The Pretence of Knowledge," Nobel Memorial Lecture, in *Essence*, pp. 265-77.

Harris: *Capital Accumulation*, Chapter 11.

Keynes, *General Theory*, Chap. 24.

Kalecki, Michal, *Capitalist Economy* Chaps. 12, 13.

Robinson, *Economic Heresies* (New York: Basic Books, 1973), Chaps. 5, 6.

Supplemental:

Mises: *Human Action*, pp. 399-406, 780-803.

Rothbard: *Man, Economy, and State*, pp. 679-93, 751-64.

Kaldor, Nicholas, "Professor Hayek and the Concertina Effect," *Economica* (1942).

Hutchison, "Friedrich Engels and Marxian Political Economy," "The Limitations of General Theories in Macroeconomics," and "On the Aims and Methods of Economic Theorizing," in *The Politics and Philosophy of Economics: Marxians, Keynesians, and Austrians* (New York: New York University Press, 1984).

Bausor, Randall, "The Rational-Expectations Hypothesis and the Epistemics of Time," *Cambridge Journal of Economics*, 7, (1983).

Mises, "Stones into Bread, The Keynesian Miracle," in Henry Hazlitt ed., *The Critiques of Keynesian Economics* (New York: Arlington House, 1977), pp. 305-15. Hereafter, *Critics*.

Hayek, *A Tiger by the Tail*, Sudha R. Shenoy compiler (San Francisco: Cato Institute, 1979).

Hayek, "The Economics of Abundance," in Hazlitt ed. *Critics*, pp. 126-30.

Leijonhufvud, Axel, *Keynes and the Classics* (London: Institute for Economic Affairs, 1969).

11

Yeager, "The Keynesian Diversion," *Western Economic Journal* (June, 1973), pp. 150-63.

Coddington, Alan, "Keynesian Economics: In Search of First Principles," *Journal of Economic Literature* (December, 1979), pp. 1258-73.

Mises, *Theory of Money and Credit*, pp. 399-406.

O'Driscoll, "Spontaneous Order and Coordination of Economic Activities," in *New Directions*, pp. 111-42.

O'Driscoll, "Rational Expectations, Politics, and Stagflation," in Mario J. Rizzo, ed. *Essays on Disequilibrium and Expectations* (New York: Lexington Books, 1980).

Hayek, *Full Employment at any Price?*, pp. 11-29, 43-6.

Friedman, Milton, *Inflation and Unemployment* (London: Institute for Economic Affairs, 1977).

Thomas M. Humphrey, "On Nonneutral Relative Price Effects in Monetarist Thought: Some Austrian Misconceptions," *Economic Review*, Federal Reserve Bank of Richmond, May/June 1984, pp. 13-19.

Fritz Machlup, "The Rationality of 'Rational' Expectations," *Kredit und Kapital*, Jahrg. 16, 1983, pp. 172-83.

Kaldor, *The Scourge of Monetarism* (Oxford: Oxford University Press, 1982).

Ken Coutts, et al, "The Economic Consequences of Mrs. Thatcher," *Cambridge Journal of Economics* (1981)

Mott, "Mr. Keynes and the Neoclassics," *Social Concept* (1984).

Amit Bhadvri and Josef Steindl, "The Rise of Monetarism as a Social Doctrine," in Philip Arestos and Thanos Skouras, *Post Keynesian Economic Theory* (Sussex, England, Wheatsheaf Books, 1985).

Darity, William, Jr., "Kalecki, Luxemburg, and Imperialism," *Journal of Post Keynesian Economics*, Winter, 1979-80.

Duke University

Economics 150.1

The History of Economic Thought: From Aristotle to the Present

Spring, 1990
Craufurd D. Goodwin

Lecture Schedule

Date	Topic
January 12	Introduction
January 15	Application of the History and Philosophy of Science to the History of Economics, Economics as rhetoric
January 17	Greeks and Scholastics
January 22	Mercantilists
January 24	Physiocrats
January 29	Precursors of Classical Economics
January 31	A. Smith
February 5, 7	A. Smith
February 12, 14	Diminishing Returns: Malthus
February 19, 21	Ricardo
February 26, 28	J. S. Mill and The Classical Tradition
March 2	Mid-term Test
March 5, 7	Attacks on Classicism--Marx, Utopian Socialists, Henry George, The Historical School

Spring Break (March 9-18)

March 19, 21, 26, 28	Marginalism
April 2, 4	American Institutionalism
April 9, 11	From Marshall to Keynes
April 16, 18	Keynes
April 23, 25	Recent Develoments

Questions for Discussion

Economics 150

January 19	Organizational Session	
January 26	Was there really any economics in Greek, Scholastic or Mercantilist thought? Was it science or something else? Justify your answer. Give examples of economic thought which you think were scientific and which were not.	Letwin Allen Coats
February 2	The 1750-1776 period was characterized by "brilliant people groping unsuccessfully for a new science." Comment.	Letwin Chalk
February 9	Was A. Smith the founder of modern economics? Why?	Heilbroner Barber
February 16	Do you think Malthus was a real economic scientist? or maybe just a prophet or propagandist for class interest?	Barber
February 23	What was the nature of Ricardo's contribution to economics? Was it "The Ricardian Vice" or his emphasis on diminishing returns?	Barber
March 2	Mid-term Test	
March 9	Did the critics of classical economics find their mark? Why did they not prevail?	
	SPRING BREAK	
March 23	Did neo-classical theory contribute rigor to economics or rigor mortis?	
March 30	What was the essence of the developments in economics in 1870-1890? Was economics at last a science? or perhaps a psuedo-science?	Bronfenbrenner
April 6	Did American Institutionalism deserve to survive? Did it?	Gordon
April 13	Was Marshall achieving some kind of accommodation between classical and neo-classical economics?	
April 20	In what respect was Keynesian theory a revolution? Was it permanent?	

Economics 150
Spring Semester, 1970

Course Outline and Reading Assignment

Textbooks:

W. J. Barber, <u>A History of Economic Thought</u>, Penguin, Baltimore 1977

R. H. Heilbroner, <u>The Worldly Philosophers</u>, Simon and Schuster, New York 1980

Supplementary Class Materials

Note: Citations preceded by the letter R are contained in a bound volume available in the reserve room. Remaining references, except of course the chapters in Barber and Heilbroner, are contained in the <u>Supplementary Class Materials</u> volume. An asterisk indicates that the article is the basis for the discussion section.

1. Introduction - January 12

    D. F. Gordon, "The Role of the History of Economic Thought in the Understanding of Modern Economic Theory", <u>American Economic Review</u>, Papers and Proceedings, Vol. 55, 1965, pp. 119-127.

    K. Boulding, "After Samuelson, Who Needs Adam Smith?" <u>HOPE</u> 3:2, Fall 1971, pp. 225-237.

    E. H. Phelps Brown, "The underdevelopment of Economics", <u>Economic Journal</u>, March 1972, pp. 1-10.

    A. W. Coats, "Research Priorities in the History of Economics", <u>HOPE</u> 1:1, Spring 1969, pp. 9-18.

    A. W. Coats, "The first decade of HOPE (1968-79)", <u>HOPE</u> 15:3, Fall 1983, pp. 303-320.

2. Applications of the History of Philosophy of Science to the History of Economics - January 15

    C. Goodwin, "Some Notes on the Philosophy of Sciences and the History of Economics", <u>Mimeo</u>, pp. 1-13.

    M. Blaug, "Kuhn versus Lakatos or Paradigms versus Research Programmes in the history of economics", <u>HOPE</u> 7:4, Winter 1975, pp. 399-433.

    *C. Goodwin, "Toward a Theory of the History of Economics", <u>HOPE</u> 12:4, Winter 1980, pp. 610-619.

D. N. McCloskey, "The Rhetoric of Economics", *Journal of Economic Literature*, Vol. 21, No. 2, June 1983.

3. **Greeks, Scholastics and Mercantilists** - January 17, 22

   Aristotle, "Politics and Ethics", in A. E. Monroe (ed.) *Early Economic Thought*, Harvard U.P., Cambridge, 1930, pp. 3-29.

   St. Thomas Aquinas, "Summa Theologica", in Monroe, *ibid.*, pp. 53-77.

   B. W. Dempsey, "Just Price in a Functional Economy", in J. J. Spengler and W. R. Allen (eds.) *Essays in Economic Thought*, Rand McNally, Chicago, 1960.

   T. Mun, "England's Treasure by Forraign Trade", in Monroe, *op. cit.*, pp. 171-197.

   *W. R. Allen, "Modern Defenders of Mercantilist Theory", *HOPE* 2:2, Fall 1970, pp. 381-397.

   *A. W. Coats, "The interpretation of Mercantilist Economics", *HOPE* 5:2, Fall 1973, pp. 485-495.

   *W. Letwin, "Science and Objectivity in the Seventeenth Century", in *The Origin of Scientific Economics*, Methuen, London 1963, pp. 79-98.

4. **Physiocrats and Precursors of Classical Economics** - January 24, 29

   W. Petty, "A Treatise on Taxes and Contributions", in Monroe, *op. cit.*, pp. 201-206.

   B. Mandeville, "The Fable of The Bees", in S. E. Patterson (ed.), *Readings in the History of Economic Thought*, McGraw-Hill, New York 1930, pp. 2-18.

   D. Hume, "On the Balance of Trade", in Monroe, *op. cit.*, pp. 323-338.

   F. Quesnay, "Tableau Economique", in Monroe, *op. cit.*, pp. 341-348.

   *A. Chalk, "Natural Law and the Rise of Economic Liberalism in England", in I. Rima (ed.) *Readings in the History of Economic Theory*, Holt, Rinehart and Winston, New York, 1970, pp. 32-47.

   *W. Letwin, "Economic Theories during the Eighteenth Century", in Letwin, *op. cit.*, pp. 207-228.

5. **Smith** - January 31, February 5, 7

    *Heilbroner, chapter 3

    *Barber, chapter 1

    A. Smith, "The Wealth of Nations", in R. D. Collison Black (ed.), Readings in the Development of Economic Analysis: 1776-1848, Charles & Abbot, Devon 1971, pp. 11-52.

    *D. P. O'Brien, "The Longevity of Adam Smith's Vision", Scottish Journal of Political Economy, vol. 23, June 1976, pp. 133-151.

6. **Diminishing Returns: Malthus and Ricardo** - February 12, 14, 19, 21

    *Heilbroner, chapter 4

    *Barber, chapters 2 and 3

    T. R. Malthus, "An Essay on the Principle of Population", in Black, op. cit., pp. 77-90.

    J. B. Say, "A Treatise on Political Economy", in Black, op. cit., pp. 111-124.

    D. Ricardo, "The Principles of Political Economy and Taxation", in Black, op. cit., pp. 161-175.

    *F. Fetter, "The Rise and Decline of Ricardian Economics", HOPE 1:1, Spring 1969, pp. 67-84.

7. **J. S. Mill and the Classical Tradition** - February 26, 28

    J. S. Mill, "Of the Stationary State", in Principles of Political Economy, Book IV, Chapter VI, Kelley, New York 1964, pp. 746-751

    Barber, chapter 4

    *P. Deane, "The Scope and Methodology of Classical Political Economy", in The Evolution of Economic Ideas, Cambridge U.P., Cambridge 1978, pp. 71-92.

8. **The Utopian Socialists and Marx** - March 5

    Heilbroner, chapters 5 and 6

    Barber, chapter 5

K. Marx, "Das Kapital", in Patterson, op. cit.,
   pp. 640-666

   K. Marx, Various Quotations from Marx, Mimeo, pp. 1-6.

   *M. Bronfenbrenner, "The Vicissitudes of Marxian Econom-
   ics", HOPE 2:2, Fall 1970, pp. 205-224.

9. **Attacks from other quarters -- Henry George, the Historical School and the Fabians** - March 7

   *Heilbroner, chapter 7

   H. George, "The Single Tax", in Progress and Poverty, 1879.

   G. von Schmoller, "Political Economy and Its Method", (1894) in K. W. Kapp and L. L. Kapp (eds.) Readings in Economics, Barnes & Nobel, New York 1949, pp. 217-228.

   *G. J. Stigler, "Bernard Shaw, Sidney Webb and the Theory of Fabian Socialism", in Essays in History of Economics, Chicago U.P., Chicago 1965, pp. 268-286.

10. **The Marginalists** - March 19-28

    W. S. Jevons, "Theory of Political Economy", in Patterson, op. cit., pp. 324-345.

    T. W. Hutchison, "The 'Marginal Revolution' and the De-
    cline and Fall of English Classical Political Economy", HOPE 4:2, Fall 1972, pp. 442-468.

    *M. Blaug, "Was there a Marginal Revolution?" HOPE 4:2, Fall 1972, pp. 269-80.

    D. Winch, "Marginalism and the Boundaries of Economic Science", HOPE 4:2, Fall 1972, pp. 325-327.

11. **American Institutionalism** - April 2, 4

    Heilbroner, chapter 8

    T. Veblen, The Theory of the Leisure Class, Modern Library, New York 1934, pp. 22-53, 68-83, 140-155, 167-187.

    K. P. Saxena, "Views of the Institutional Economists on the Nature and Scope of Economics", Indian Economic Journal, 15, April-June 1968, pp. 624-634.

*R. A. Gordon, "Institutional Elements in Contemporary Economics", in J. Dorfman et al., Institutional Economics, U.C.P., Berkeley 1963, pp. 123-147.

12. From Marshall to Keynes - April 9, 11

    A. Marshall, Principles of Economics, Macmillan, London 1962, prefaces, contents, pp. 276-291.

    Barber, chapters 6, 7 and 8

    G. L. S. Shackle, "Economic Hard Times and the Riches of Ideas", in The Years of High Theory: Invention and Tradition in Economic Thought 1926-39, Cambridge U.P., Cambridge, 1967, pp.1-12.

    Heilbroner, chapter 9

    Ronald H. Coase, "Alfred Marshall's mother and father", HOPE 16:4, Winter 1984, pp. 519-527.

13. "The General Theory" and Thereafter - April 16, 18

    J. M. Keynes, "Preface", in The General Theory of Employment, Interest and Money, Macmillan, Royal Economic Society, London 1973, Vol. VII, pp. xxi-xxiii; xxxi-xxxv.

    J. M. Keynes, "The General Theory of Employment", Quarterly Journal of Economics, Feb. 1937, Vol. LI, pp. 209-223.

    R. L. Heilbroner, "Modern Economics as a Chapter in HET", HOPE 11:2, Summer 1979, pp. 192-198.

    A. Leijonhufvud, "Life among the ECON", Western Economic Journal, Vol. XI, No. 3, September 1973, pp. 327-337.

    Robert M. Solow, "What do we know that Francis Amasa Walker didn't?", HOPE 19:2, Summer 1987, pp. 183-189.

University of Sydney

P. D. GROENEWEGEN

DEPARTMENT OF ECONOMICS

ECONOMICS III - 1990

HISTORY OF ECONOMIC THOUGHT:
COURSE OUTLINE AND ESSAY LIST

This course deals with the evolution of economic ideas from the early eighteenth century to the present day, with emphasis on the intellectual and social background that influenced the more important contributions. After a discussion on mercantilism and physiocracy, the work of Adam Smith and Ricardo are studied in detail. Subsequently in first semester, nineteenth century economics is studied with special reference to the early criticisms of Ricardo and the work of John Stuart Mill. Marx, the marginal revolution and the experience during the twentieth century such as developments in neo-classical theory, the Keynesian revolution, and post-war developments in the theory of growth, distribution and economic policy are discussed in second semester.

Lectures are held on Mondays and Wednesdays at 11.00 a.m. in Lecture Room 3. The lecturers in the course are Peter Groenewegen, Louis Haddad and Flora Gill. Peter Groenewegen is lecture-in-charge of the course.

COURSE WORK

One essay in second semester of approximately 4,500 words in length. This will account for 50% of the final result. There is one three-hour examination paper at the end of the year which will count for the other 50% of the final result.

A list of essay topics and further details about the presentation of essays is included with this course outline.

READING AND TEXTBOOKS

This course is essentially a reading course, and students are urged to read as widely as possible from the large number of original texts and commentators which are available, especially in the Fisher Library. Students should also consult the specialist journal in the field, History of Political Economy, and the references to other journal literature provided in the Index of Economic Journals and in the Journal of Economic Literature. More immediately relevant books in the subsequent reading list are distinguishable by an *.

TEXT BOOKS

W.J. Barber, A History of Economic Thought (Penguin, 1977).

P. Deane, The Evolution of Economic Ideas (Cambridge, University Press, 1978.

Useful introductory material for an overview of the subject can be obtained from reading:

Phyllis Dean, The State and the Economic System, Oxford University Press, 1989.

Useful surveys of the recent literature on the history of economic thought are:

Pre-Classical Economic Thought, edited S. Todd Lowry, Kluwer, Dordrecht, 1987.

Classical Political Economy, edited W. Thweatt, Kluwer, Dordrecht, 1988.

Neo-classical Economic Theory 1870 to 1930, edited W.J. Samuels and K. Hennings, Kluwer, Dordrecht, 1990.

Additional References

E. Roll, History of Economic Thought

O.H. Taylor, A History of Economic Thought

J.A. Schumpeter, A History of Economic Analysis

I. Rima, Development of Economic Analysis

B.B. Seligman, Main Currents in Modern Economics

M. Blaug, Economic Theory in Retrospect

G. Routh, The Origin of Economic Ideas

I.I. Rubin, History of Economic Thought

COURSE WORK REQUIREMENT

Coursework consists of one, 4,500 words essay during the year. The completion of the essay is a pre-requisite for satisfactory completion of the course and will count for 50% of the final result.

Because the essay counts for such a large proportion of the total result, students should take care to follow the procedure laid down in connection with essays, which is listed below.

The essay is due on Monday, 8th October 1990, immediately after the second semester break. Essays should preferably be typewritten, double spaced, on one side of the paper only with an adequate margin (5 cms) for comments. Each essay should be accompanied by a synopsis and bibliography. Sources should be adequately documented in footnotes to the text, following the accepted principles for such documentation in academic journals. Excessively lengthy and LATE essays will be penalised.

ESSAY TOPICS

Write a critical review of ONE of the following economic works. In writing this review remember that the course of study is the History of Economic Thought so that you should make sure you place the work in its proper historical perspective, that is, either in terms of the development of the thought of the author, or in terms of the author's contemporaries and predecessors. The books for review are as follows:

1. Thomas Mun, England's Treasure by Forraign Trade (1664) various reprints available.

2. 'Some Thoughts on the Interest of Money in General' (1738) ascribed to Sir William Pulteney, reprinted Sydney, 1982.*

3. Thomas Robert Malthus, An Inquiry into the Nature and Progress of Rent (1815), various reprints available.

4. Robert Torrens, The Economists Refuted (1808) and other Early Economic Writings, reprinted Sydney, 1984.*

5. Thomas Chalmers, On Political Economy in Connection with the Moral State and Moral Prospect of Society, (1832).

6. W.T. thornton, On Labour, (1869).

7. J.E. Cairnes, Some leading Principles of Political Economy Newly Expounded, (1874).

8. W.S. Jevons, Money, (1975).

9. K. Marx, Wages, Price and Profit, (1865).

10. John Nevile Keynes, The Scope and Method of Political Economy, (1890).

11. Alfred Marshall, Money, Credit and Commerce (1923).

12. John Maynard Keynes, The Means to Property (1933).

* Copies of these reprints can be purchased from Miss Val Jones (Professor Groenewegen's Secretary) in Room 345.

If students wish to attempt a topic for an essay other than those listed, they should obtain permission from the lecturer-in-charge of the course no later than the end of the first week after Easter, that is, Monday, 23rd April.

Preliminary research material for all these essays can be obtained from the list of basic references given on the previous page and this can be expanded by consulting the Index of Economic Journals and the abstracts in the Journal of Economic Literature on the History of Economic Thought (Ref. 031). Students should also look up the author in Palgrave's Dictionary of Political Economy, New palgrave Dictionary of Economics and the Encyclopaedia of the Social Sciences (check both editions) which provide useful bibliographical information. History of Political Economy, Vol. 15, no. 4, Winter 1983, has a cumulative index of the first 15 years of this journal, classified by subject.

SEMESTER 1 - CLASSICAL POLITICAL ECONOMY
(Lecturer first 9 weeks: Peter Groenewegen
         last   5 weeks: Louis Haddad.

TOPIC 1: Introduction

The first eight lectures provide a basic introduction to the study of the history of economic thought in general, and to the rise of classical political economy in particular. The first two of these lectures provide an insight into the subject itself, with particular reference to the course for this year, including some explanations of what is expected in the essay, and in the form of reading during the year. These lectures also discuss reasons for the study of the subject, including reasons why the history of this subject is especially instructive for students of economics. There will also be a brief discussion on the history of the subject.

The third and fourth lectures present a brief account of some of the basic features of Mercantilism and discusses the manner in which economics emerged as a science during the 17th and 18th centuries. The last four lectures illustrates this final theme by examining in more detail the work of some major seventeenth and eighteenth century economists up to and including the early 1750s.

Lectures 1 and 2 - Introduction to the History of Economic Thought

    Reading

    * J.A. Schumpeter, History of Economic Analysis, London, 1954), Part I.

    * M.H. Dobb, Theories of Value and Distribution Since Adam Smith, Ch. 1.

    T.W. Hutchison, Knowledge and Ignorance in Economics, (Oxford: Basil Blackwell, 1977, ch. 3.).

T.W. Hutchison, On Revolutions and Progress in Economic Knowledge, Cambridge University Press, 1978, chs. 6, 9, 11.

* Phyllis Deane, The Evolution of Economic Ideas, Cambridge University Press, 1978, Introduction.

Lectures 3 and 4 - Mercantilism and the Emergence of Economics

Reading

* C. Wilson, Mercantilism, published for the Historical Association by Routledge & Kegan Paul, 1958.

D.C. Coleman (ed.), Revisions on Mercantilism, Methuen, 1969, chs. 1-5.

* J.A. Schumpeter, Economic Doctrine & Method, London, George Allen and Unwin, 1954, ch. I.

Harold J. Laski, The Rise of European Liberalism, Allen and Unwin, 1936, chapters II and III.

O.H. Taylor, A History of Economic Thought, New York, McGraw Hill, 1960, chapter 1, pp. 1-12.

* Phyllis Deane, op.cit., chapter 1.

T.W. Hutchison, Before Adam Smith, The Emergence of Political Economy, 1661-1776, Oxford, Blackwell, 1988.
* (worth dipping into).

* Peter Groenewegen, 'New Light on the Origins of Modern Economics', Economic Record 65(189) June 1989, pp. 136-49.

Lecture 5 - Sir William Petty (1623-1687)

Reading

* C.H. Hull (ed.), The Economic Writings of Sir William Petty, Vol. I, Introduction and from Petty's Works read Treatise of Taxes and Contributions (1662), Political Arithmetik (1676) and Quantalumcunque Concerning Money (1682).

A. Roncaglia, Petty. The Origins of Political Economy (Cardiff, University College Press, 1985.

* A. Aspromourgos, 'Political Economy and the Social Division of Labour: the Economics of Sir William Petty', Scottish Journal of Political Economy, 33, February, 1986, pp. 28-45.

* A. Aspromourgos, 'The Life of William Petty in Relation to his Economics', History of Political Economy, 20(3), Fall 1988.

Lecture 6 - John Locke (1632-1704)

Reading

* John Locke, A Second Treatise of Civil Government (1690) esp. chapters 4-5.

* John Locke, Some Considerations of the Consequences of the Lowering of Interest and Raising the Value of Money (1691) - various editions available.

Letwin, Origins, ..., op.cit., chapter 6.

K. Marx, Theories of Surplus Value, Part I, pp. 354-56.

K. Vaughan, John Locke, London, 1980.

Lecture 7 - Richard Cantillon (1690-1734)

Reading:

Richard Cantillon, Essay on the Nature of Commerce in General (1730), edited by H. Higgs for Royal Economic Society, London, 1931. This edition reprints two interpretative essays on Cantillon, one by W.S. Jevons and one by H. Higgs which are well worth reading.

* Essay, Part I, Part II, chapters 1-3.

* A Murphy, Richard Cantillon, Economist and Entrepreneur, Oxford, Clarendon Press, 1986, esp. ch. 13.

* A. Aspromourgos, 'The Theory of Production and Distribution in Cantillon's Essai', Oxford Economic Papers (41) 1989, pp. 356-73.

Lecture 8 - David Hume (1711-1776)

Reading:

* David Hume, Writings on Economics, edited with an Introduction by Eugene Rotwin (London, 1955) esp. 'Of Money', 'Of Interest', 'Of the Balance of Trade', 'Of the Jealousy of Trade'.

W.O. Taylor, Francis Hutcheson and David Hume as Predecessors of Adam Smith, Duke University Press, 1965, Part I, ch. 3, Part II.

E.A.J. Johnson, Predecessors of Adam Smith, Kelly, New York, 1960, chapter 9.

TOPIC 2: The Zenith of 18th Century, Classical Political Economy:
         The Physiocrats and A. Smith (7 lectures)

These seven lectures discuss the two basic systems of political economy developed in the eighteen century. The system of the Physiocrats developed by Francois Quesnay in the 1750s and 1760s, the system developed by Turgot with particular reference to his theory of development in the Reflections, and the system of Adam Smith. Four lectures are devoted to the Physiocrats; three to Adam Smith; this is not because the Physiocrats are more important than Smith; it is because their works are less accessible and not as well covered in the secondary literature. The first of the four lectures presents a picture of the Physiocrats as a school, some of the historical background and a guide to the commentaries. The next two lectures deal with the work of Quesnay - first his general economic system, second an analysis of the Tableau economique. The fourth lecture presents Turgot - the bridge between Physiocracy and modern classical economics and especially Smith. The last three lectures deal with Adam Smith's economics in the Wealth of Nations, with emphasis on the material in Books I and II.

Lecture 9 - Introduction to Physiocracy (1756-1776)

   Reading

   R.L. Meek, The Economics of Physiocracy, London, 1962. Introduction.

   * Charles Gide and Charles Rist, A History of Economic Doctrines, London, second edition, chapter 1.

   and, for a general introduction to the study of classical economics:

   * P. Garegnani, 'Value and Distribution in the Classical Economists and Marx', Oxford Economic Papers, Vol. 36, 1984, pp. 291-325.

   P.D. Groenewegen, 'Turgot, Beccaria and Smith', in Peter Groenewegen and Joseph Halevi (ed.), Italian Economics Past and Present, Sydney: Frederick May Foundation of Italian Studies, 1983.

Lectures 10-11: Francois Quesnay (1694-1714)

   Reading:

   R.L. Meek, The Economics of Physiocracy, op.cit., translations from Quesnay writings esp. Parts II, III of translations, and Essays 1, 4 in Part Two.

   P.D. Groenewegen, introduction to Francois Quesnay, Farmers (1756) and Turgot, Sur la grande et la petite culture (1766),

Sydney: Department of Economics, University of Sydney,
Reprints of Economic Classics, Series 2, no. 2, 1983.

* W.A. Eltis, 'Francois Quesnay: A Re-interpretation', Oxford
Economic Papers, Vol. 27, no. 2, July, 1975, pp. 167-200;
no. 3, November 1975, pp. 327-351. Reprinted in Walter Eltis,
The Classical Theory of Economic Growth, chapters 1 and 2.

K. Marx, Theories of Surplus Value, Part I, op.cit., pp. 48-67 and pp. 299-334.

* G. Vaggi, The Economics of Francois Quesnay, Durham,
Duke University Press, 1987, esp. chs. 1, 5.

Lecture 12 - A.R.J. Turgot (1727-1781)

Reading:

* Turgot, Reflections on the Formation and Distribution of
Wealth (1766), various editions available.

P.D. Groenewegen, 'A Re-appraisal of Turgot''s Theory of
Value, Exchange and Price Determination', History of Political
Economy, Vol. 2, no. 1.

* P.D. Groenewegen, 'A re-interpretation of Turgot's Theory
of Capital and Interest', Economic Journal, Vol. 81, June 1971.

R.L. Meek, 'Turgot, Smith and the Four Stages Theory',
History of Political Economy, Vol. 3, no. 1, Spring 1971.

P.D. Groenewegen, 'Turgot's Place in the History of Economic
Thought', History of Political Economy, Vol. 15, no. 4, 1983,
pp. 585-616.

Lectures 13-15: Adam Smith (1723-1790)

Reading:

* A. Smith, An Inquiry into the Nature and Causes of the
Wealth of Nations, 1776, Books I and II. (Various editions
available, the best are those by Cannan and the new definitive
edition included in the collected works of Adam Smith
and published by Oxford University Press in 1976.)

S. Hollander, Classical Economics, Oxford, Blackwell, 1987,
chapters 4, 7, 12.

* Phyllis Deane, op.cit., chapters 2, 3.

W. J. Barber, op.cit., chapter 1.

M.H. Dobb, Theories of Value and Distribution, chapter 2.

D.D. Raphael, Adam Smith, Oxford University Press, 1985.

William Letwin, 'Was Adam Smith a Liberal?' and Donald Winch, 'Adam Smith and the Liberal Tradition', in Traditions of Liberalism, edited K. Haakonassen, Sydney, C.I.S., 1988, pp. 65-104.

TOPIC 3:   From Smith to Ricardo: Population and Gluts (1 lecture)

In this lecture two major developments in economics will be discussed which occurred between the publication of the final edition of the Wealth of Nations in 1789 and the publication of the first edition of Ricardo's Principles of Political Economy in 1817. These are the publication of Malthus' Essay on the Principle of Population (first edition, 1798) which provided much of the background for the assumptions on which Ricardo constructed his analysis of distribution and growth, in the nineteenth century. This period also marks that of the French Revolution and the Napoleonic Wars, and in this way led to the development of Mr. Mill's "Principle", the English produced version of Say's Law.

Lecture 16:   Malthus on Population and Mr. Mill's "Principle"

Reading:

* T.R. Malthus, Essay on the Principle of Population (various editions available - but the first edition, which has been reprinted on numerous occasions is worth reading in toto).

Donald Winch, Malthus, Past Masters, Oxford University Press, 1987, chs.3-5. esp.

M. Blaug, Economic Theory in Retrospect, first edition, 1964, chapters 3,5.

* James Mill, 'Commerce Defended' in D. Winch (ed.), Selected Economic Writings of James Mill, chapters 5 and 6.

S. Hollander, The Economics of David Ricardo, Heinemann, 1979, chapter 2.

TOPIC 4 :   David Ricardo (1772-1823)

In the lectures devoted to Ricardo, his system of value and distribution is examined in some detail. This work is not only important in its own right, but is crucial for the understanding for much of the economic debate disc ussed during next term. Ricardo's economics must therefore be especially carefully studied and assimilated by reading of his work.

Lectures 17-18

Reading:

* David Ricardo, Principles of Political Economy and Taxation, especially chapters 1-7 (various editions available)

N.B. The serious student should read at least the first seven chapters of the Principles together with the preface as contained in the definitive edition of Ricardo's Works and Correspondence edited by P. Sraffa in collaboration with Maurice Dobb, Vol. I.

Additional Reading:

* L.L. Pasinetti, 'A Mathematical Formulation of the Ricardian System', Review of Economic Studies, 1960, reprinted in L.L. Pasinetti, Growth and Income Distribution, chapter 1.

G.J. Stigler, 'The Ricardian Theory of Value and Distribution', Journal of Political Economy, 1952, reprinted in G.J. Stigler, Essays in the History of Economics, chapter 6.

P.D. Groenewegen, 'Three Notes on Ricardo's Theory of Value and Distribution', Australian Economic Papers, June 1972.

S. Hollander, Classical Economics, Oxford, Blackwell, 1987, chapters 5, 8, 13.

Phyllis Deane, op.cit., ch. 5.

W.J. Barber, op.cit., ch.3.

G. Caravale (ed.), The Legacy of Ricardo, Oxford, Blackwells, 1985.

TOPIC 5: Introduction (1 lecture)
(lectures by Mr. Louis Haddad)

A review of classical economics, the over-simplification and popularisation of Ricardo's ideas by James Mill, J.R. McCulloch and Thomas de Quincey.

Reading:

D. Winch (ed.), James Mill's Selected Economic Writings, 1966.

* I.H. Rima, Development of Economic Analysis, 1967, ch.9.

* T.W. Hutchison, On Revolution and Progress in Economic Knowledge, C.U.P., 1978, ch. 2.

J.R. McCulloch, Principles of Political Economy.

Thomas de Quincey, Dialogue of Three Templars on Political Economy.

TOPIC 6: Ricardo's Critics: The Subjective School (3 lectures)

These lectures deal with Senior, Bailey, Lloyd, Longfield and other forerunners of Marginalism.

Reading:

Nassau Senior, An Outline of the Science of Political Economy, London, 1836.

Samuel Bailey, A Critical Dissertation of the Nature, Measure and Causes of Value, London, 1825, L.S.E., Reprint, 1932.

M. Longfield, Lectures on Political Economy, Dublin, 1834.

* W F. Lloyd, A Lecture on the Notion of Value, 1833.

* R.M. Romano, 'William Foster Lloyd, a Non-Ricardian', History of Political Economy, Vol. 9, no. 3, 1977.

S. Hollander, Classical Economics, ch. 16.

* T W. Hutchison, op.cit., ch. 3.

Marian Bowley, Nassau Senior and Classical Economics.

* Maurice Dobb, Theories of Value and Distribution Since Adam Smith, C.U.P., 1973, ch. 4.

* G.J. Stigler, 'The Development of Utility Theory', J.P.E., 1950, reprinted in his Essays in the History of Economics, 1965.

TOPIC 7: The Ricardian Socialists (2 lectures)

These lectures deal with the Ricardian socialists: Hodgskin, Bray, Thompson, Gray and Owen.

Reading:

Thomas Hodgskin, Labour Defended Against the Claims of Capital, London, 1825.

William Thompson, An Inquiry into the Principles of the Distribution of Wealth, 1824.

E. Lowenthal, The Ricardian Socialists, 1911.

E. Halevy, Thomas Hodgskin, London, 1956.

Robert Owen, A New View of Society, 1813.

* M. Beer, A History of British Socialism, Part III, ch. 21.

* K. Marx, Theories of Surplus Value, Part III, ch. 21.

* Gide and Rist, History of Economic Doctrines, Book II, chs. 3 and 5.

* E.K. Hunt, 'Value theory in the Writings of Classical Economists, Thomas Hodgskin and Karl Marx', in History of Political Economy, Vol. 9, no. 3, 1977.

TOPIC 8: J.S. Mill 1806-1873 (4 lectures)

Reading:

* J.S. Mill, Essays on some Unsettled Questions in Political Economy, 1844.

J.S. Mill, Principles of Political Economy, 1848 (specific references will be given in lectures).

P. Schwartz, The New Political Economy of J.S. Mill, 1972.

* Maurice Dobb, op.cit., ch. 5.

* A.C. Pigou, 'Mill and the Wages Fund', The Economic Journal, Vol. 57, 1947.

* John Hicks, Classics and Moderns, Oxford University Press, 1985.

S. Hollander, The Economics of John Stuart Mill, Oxford, 1985.

S. Hollander, Classical Economics, chapters 6, 9, 14.

SECOND SEMESTER
(Lecturers: L. Haddad (first four weeks)
F. Gill (last nine weeks).

TOPIC 9: K. Marx (1818-1893) (6 lectures)
(Lectures by Louis Haddad)

Reading:

K. Marx, Theories of Surplus Value, Part II.

K. Marx, Capital, 3 vols., (specific references will be given in lectures).

E. Mandel, The Formation of the Economic Thought of Karl Marx, M.R.P. 1971.

M. Desai, Marxian Economics, Blackwell, 1979.

* Joan Robinson, Essays on Marxian Economics (2nd ed.), 1966.

* Claudio Napoleoni, Smith, Ricardo, Marx, Blackwell, 1975, ch. 5.

* Ben Fine, Marx's Capital, Macmillan, 1975.

* M. Morishima, Marx's Economics, C.U.P., 1973.

* Maurice Dobb, op.cit., ch. 6.

S. Hollander, Classical Economics, ch. 15.

TOPIC 10: The Emergence of the Marginal Revolution (2 lectures)

Reading:

* R.D.C. Black, A.W. Coats and C.D.W. Goodwin (eds.), The Marginal Revolution in Economics, Duke University Press, 1973.

* Maurice Dobb, op.cit., ch. 7.

* Philip Mirowski, 'Physics and the Marginalist Revolution', Cambridge Journal of Economics, Dec. 1984.

R.M. Fisher, The Logic of Economic Discovery: Neoclassical Economics and the Marginal Revolution, Wheatsheaf Books, 1986.

D.A. Walker, 'Walras's Theory of Tatonement', Journal of Political Economy, 95(4) August, 1987.

TOPIC 11: The Development of Modern Economics 1870 and After
(lectures given by Flora Gill)

Introduction (1 lecture)

An outline of the structure of the lectures given during the final part of the course. The central theme, the general approach and the specific chapters of economic thought dealt with. (Dr. Gill has indicated she will provide some amendments to this part of the reading list at the start of second semester).

TOPIC 12: From Classical to Neo-classical Economics (1 lecture)

A brief sketch of the historical evolution and a juxtoposition of the structure of classical and neo-classical economics in terms of the central question, the fundamental assumption about the economic process, the conception employed and the skeleton of their internal logic.

Reading:

* Vivian Walsh and Harvey Gram, Classical and Neoclassical Theories of General Equilibrium, Oxford University Press, 1980, chs. 1, 6

* C. Napoleoni, Economic Thought in Twentieth Century, Martin Robertson, 1963, ch. 1.

* J.A. Schumpeter, History of Economic Analysis, part IV, ch. 6, sections 2 and 3.

* P. Deane, The Evolution of Economic Ideas, Cambridge University Press, 1978, ch. 3, 6.

For the broader socio-economic, political and intellectual background, you may consult the following sources:

J.A. Schumpeter, ibid., chs. 2 and 3. (You may wish to glance at ch. 4 as well.)

* Gareth S. Jones, Outcast London, Penguin Books, 1971, esp. pp. 1-16.

TOPIC 13: From Jevons, Menger and Walras to Marshall - or from "The First Wave" of the Marginal Revolution to the "Second Wave"
(2 lectures)

Reading:

* History of Political Economy, Vol. 4, no. 2, Fall 1972, especially article by R.S. Howey.
Walsh and Gram, ibid., chs. 4, 5 and 6.

* Walsh and Gram, ibid., chs. 4, 5 and 6.

* Mark Blaug, Economic Theory in Retrospect, ch. 8 (Jevons and other forerunners with only brief mention of menger), ch. 9. (marshall's utility and demand analysis), ch. 10. (Marshall's cost and supply analysis), ch. 13, Section 1 (on Walrasian general equilibrium.

To sharpen focus you may also consult:

* Schumpeter, ibid., Part IV, ch. 7, Section 3 (on the concept of general equilibrium), Section 6 on Marshall's partial equilibrium analysis) and Section 7 (on Walrasian equilibrium analysis).

Roy Weintraub, 'General Equilibrium Theory', in Sydney Weintraub (ed.), Modern Economic Thought, University of Pennsylvania Press, 1977, pp. 105-125.

* Deane, ch. 7.

TOPIC 14: The "Second Wave" of the Marginal Revolution and the emergence of a number of specific propositions about the distribution of income and welfare economics, and the Austrian Theory of Capital and Interest. (J.B. Clark, Wicksell and Wicksteed; Pareto and Pigou, Bohm Bawerk and Von Misses; Fisher
(2 lectures)

Reading:

* Walsh and Gram, ibid., chs. 8 and 9 (on neo-classical theory of resource allocation).

* Blaug, ibid., ch. 11 (on marginal productivity and factor prices), ch. 12 (on the Austrian school), ch. 13, Section 2 (on Paretian and Pigouvian welfare economics).

M. Dobb, Theories of Value and Distribution since Adam Smith, Cambridge University Press, 1973, ch. 7 (the Jevonian Revolution).

Schumpeter, ibid., Part IV, ch. 8, Section 2.

TOPIC 15: The Neo-classical Theory of Money.
(Marshall, Wicksell, Fisher). (1 lecture)

Reading:

* Blaug, ch. 13.

* Deane, chs. 4 and 11.

TOPIC 16: Ensuing Debates: The Importance of markets, and the Role of Money (P. Sraffa, A. Young, J. Chamberlain, Joan Robinson, D.H. Robertson and J.M. Keynes. (3 lectures)

Reading:

* P. Sraffa, 'The Law of Returns Under Competitive Conditions', Economic Journal, 1926, (cost controversy).

Joan Robinson, The Economics of Imperfect Competition, Macmillan 1969 (first edition, 1933), skim selectively.

* Blaug, pp. 412-17, 432-7 (imperfect competition).

J. Viner, 'Cost Curves and Supply Curves', reprinted in Boulding and Stigler, Readings in Price Theory, A.E.A., Allen and Unwin, 1953.

Economic Journal, March 1930, pp. 79-116.

D.H. Robertson, 'A Survey of Monetary Theory Controversy', in Manchester School of Economics and Social Studies, 1938.

J.R. Hicks, 'The Monetary Theory of D.H. Robertson', in Economica, 1942.

A.C. Pigou, 'The Value of Money', Quarterly Journal of Economics, XXXII (1917-1918).

G.L.S. Shackle, Years of High Theory, chs. 3-6.

Schumpeter, ibid., Part V, ch. 2, Section 2.

TOPIC 17: Economics between the Wars: The Keynesian Revolution, the Stokholm School and the Emergence of Business cycle theory (Keynes, Kalecki, Lindhal, Myrdal, Ohlin). (4 lectures)

Reading:

* J.M. Keynes, The General Theory of Employment, Interest and Money (1936). (At least chs. 1-3, 5, 11-13, 16, 18-21, 22.

* J.M. Keynes, 'The General Theory of Employment', Q.J.E., 1937.

* J.M. Keynes, Essays in Persuasion, II-2 (pp. 80-104), II-2 (pp. 186-212), IV-2 (pp. 312-322), IV-3 (323-338), V-2 (pp. 358-376).

* F.S. Lee, 'The Oxford Challenge to Marshallian Supply and Demand: The History of Oxford Economic Research Groups', Oxford Economic Papers , Vol. 33, Nov. 1981, No. 3, PP. 339-351.

* J.C. Andvig, 'Ragnar Frisch and Business Cycle Research During the Interwar Years', in HOPE, Vol. 13, no. 4, Winter 1981.

* Deane, Ch. 10, (neo-classical economics during the inter-war years) ch. 12 (the Keynesian Revolution).

* Bertil Ohlin, 'Stockholm and Cambridge: Four Papers n the Monetary Employment theory', in HOPE, Vol. 13, No. 2, Summer 1981.

* Otto Steiger, 'Bertil Ohlin 1899-1979', in HOPE, Vol. 13, no. 2, Summer 1981.

* M. Kalecki, Selected Essays on the Dynamics of the Capitalist Economy, Cambridge University Press, 1971, chs. 1, 3 and 24.

Schumpeter, ibid., Part V, chapter 4.

TOPIC 18: Methodological Issues; Between Philosophy of Science and Economics (2-3 lectures)

Reading:

* M. Blaug, (1980) The Methodology of Economics, pp. 1-128.

* Bruce Caldwell (1982), Beyond Positivism Economic Methodology in the Twentieth Century, ch. 5 (pp. 68-93), chs. 10-15 (pp. 211-252)

Bruce Caldwell (ed.) (1984), Appraisal and Criticism in Economics, Allen and Unwin.

* A.F. Chalmers (1976), What is This thing Called Science [SKIM]

* Flora Gill (1981), 'Some Methodological Implications of the Marginal Revolution', Australian Economic Papers, June 1981.

T.W. Hutchinson, Knowledge and Ignorance in Economics, Blackwell, 1977, ch. 4.

Homa Katouzian, Ideology and Method in Economics, McMillan, 1980, chs. 1, 2, 6.

Joan Robinson, Economic Heresies, Basic Books, 1971, 1973.

Joan Robinson, Contribution to Modern Economics, Blackwell, 1978, ch. 1.

THE UNIVERSITY OF SYDNEY

FACULTIES OF ECONOMICS, ARTS, ETC.

Economics III
Economics III Additional
Economics III Supplementary
Economics III Advanced

Paper

History of Economic Thought

November, 1989.　　　　　　　　　　　　　　Time Allowed: Three Hours.

Answer FOUR questions, AT LEAST ONE from each section.

Answer each question in a separate book.

SECTION A

1. Prior to the emergence of Economics as a separate science (circa 1750) there were several crucial contributions by individual economists which assisted this process. In the context of a discussion of the causes of the emergence of economics as a science, evaluate the work of <u>one</u> of those authors with whose work you are familiar.

2. Critically evaluate the four stages theory as developed by Turgot, particularly with respect to the final two stages discussed in his <u>Reflections</u>, making sure to comment on the impact, if any, his stadial process theory may have had on his economic theory.

3. Compare and contrast the growth models of François Quesnay and Adam Smith, highlighting the major differences as well as the similarities.

4. Either

    a) What are the differences between Smith and Ricardo on the measure of value with special reference to the different aims they had on the measure they evolved.

    Or

    b) "The <u>Principles of Political Economy and Taxation</u> is, in so far as its core is concerned, nothing but the earlier <u>Essay on the Profits of Stock</u> writ large." Discuss.

..2

SECTION B

5. Explain why the early developers of the principle of marginal utility (Senior, Longfield, Lloyd and Whateley) failed to construct a coherent theory of value based on this principle.

6. Evaluate the role of J.S. Mill in the transition from Classical, Political Economy to Modern Economics, with particular reference to value and distribution.

7. Either
    a) Discuss the contribution of Friedrich Engels to Marxian Political Economy.

    Or
    b) Compare and contrast Ricardo's growth model with that of Marx.

8. Does the term Marginal Revolution describe adequately what took place in the development of economic thought from 1862 to 1874?

SECTION C

9. "With the elevation of the static frame of analysis to centre stage, the break with the classical past occurred during the last quarter of the nineteenth century. This shift of focus from the dynamic to the static was inevitable, given the prime role accorded to marginal analysis and individual utility." Discuss.

10. Illustrating with example(s) of your own choice, discuss the evolution of economic thought in terms of the contribution of the purely internal intellectual development, as well as of the economic and political currents and intellectual climate in the society at large.

11. Discuss the impact of logical positivism on economic method. In your answer evaluate the latter in the light of some of the more recent developments in the philosophy of science.

12. Present the essence of the moment by Walsh and Gram dealing with the relative roles of marginalism and the demand side of the Marginal Revolution. Do you agree with that argument? Give reasons for your answer.

University of Puget Sound
ECONOMICS 321
History of Economic Thought
Fall 1989

U

Instructor: D. Wade Hands
Class: 12:00-1:50 T Th
Office: MC 013M
Phone: X3592 (office), 845-7166 (home)
Office Hours: 1:00-2:00 M W F; 3:00-5:00 M W

Course Purpose:

To acquaint the student with the major theories and theorists in the history of economic thought. The course will focus on the economists who have been instrumental in the development of the principal "schools" of economic thought both orthodox and heterodox.

Course Requirements:

The student will be required to complete the reading assignments prior to the relevant lectures. There will be four essay exams (3 + final) to test the student's broad understanding of the course material. In addition to the exams, the student will be expected to write a short essay (approximately 4 pages) on each of the major figures discussed during the semester. The specific topics of these seven papers will be chosen by the instructor. If the student wishes to write a traditional term paper on a particular topic in the history of economic thought, the term paper may be substituted for one of the exams.

Grades:

Grades will be computed on the basis of the following weighting system and scale:

Exam 1 -- 20%	92 - 100%	A
Exam 2 -- 20%	90 - 91%	A-
Exam 3 -- 20%	88 - 89%	B+
Final -- 20%	82 - 87%	B
Papers -- 20%	80 - 81%	B-
	70 - 79%	C
	60 - 69%	D

Books To Be Purchased:

Heilbroner, Robert L., The Worldly Philosophers, 3rd ed., (New York: Touchstone, 1980)

Keynes, John M., The General Theory of Employment, Interest, and Money, (New York: Harcourt, Brace, Jovanovich, 1936)

Marshall, Alfred, Principles of Economics, 9th ed. (1949)

ECON321 -- Page 2

Books To Be Purchased (continued):

Marx, Karl, Wage, Labor, and Capital/Value, Price, and Profit (International)

Mill, J. S., Principles of Political Economy, (Penguin)

Ricardo, David, The Principles of Political Economy and Taxation, (New York: Dutton, 1911)

Smith, Adam, Selections from the Wealth of Nations, George Stigler (ed.), (Arlington Heights, IL: Harlan Davidson, 1957)

Reserve Readings (in Library):

In addition to the required texts the following books will be placed on reserve in the Library.

Breit, W. and Ransom, R. L. The Academic Scribblers, revised ed., (Dryden, 1982)

Jaffe, W., Essays on Walras (Cambridge, CUP, 1983)

Sweezy, P., The Theory of Capitalist Development (Monthly Review: 1942)

ECON321 -- Page 3

Course Outline

* indicates reserve reading
** indicates paper to be handed out in class

I. Mercantilism and Physiocracy

        Heilbroner: Introduction (Ch 1), The Economic Revolution (Ch 2)
        **Meek: Introduction to Physiocracy
        **Bell: Mercantilism (Ch 4)

II. Classical Economics

    A. Adam Smith

        Heilbroner: The Wonderful World of Adam Smith (Ch 3)
        Smith: Book I (pp. 1-47), Book IV (pp. 62-88)

    B. Ricardian Economics

        Heilbroner: Malthus and Ricardo (Ch 4)
        **Malthus: "Mathematics of Population and Food"
        Ricardo: Chapters I-VII, XVIII, XXVII, XXX, and Introduction

EXAM 1

    C. J. S. Mill and the Philosophic Radicals

        Heilbroner: Utopian Socialists (Ch 5)
        Mill: Introduction, Book IV (pp. 55-117), Book V (pp. 277-303), Book II (pp. 349-367)

    D. Marx

        Heilbroner: Marx (Ch 6)
        Marx: "Wage-Labor and Capital" and "Value, Price and Profit"
        **Marx: "Preface to the Critiquie of Political Economy"
        *Sweezey, Chapters I-IV, VII-X

EXAM 2

ECON321 -- Page 4

III. Neoclassical Economics

    A.   Jevons and Menger and Walras

          **Jevons: "The Theory of Political Economy" (1871)
          **Hayek: "Menger"
          *Jaffe: "Reflections" (Ch 15), "Jevons, Menger, and Walras De-Homogenized" (Ch 17)

    B.   Alfred Marshall

          **Keynes: "Alfred Marshall"
          Marshall: Book III (Chs 3 and 4), Book IV (Chs 1 and 3), Book V (Chs 2, 3, 5 and 8), Appendix I

IV. Thorstein Veblen and the American Heterodoxy

       Heilbroner: The Savage Society of Thorstein Veblen (Ch 8)
       *Breit, W. and Ransom, R. L.: "Thorstein Veblen" in The Academic Scribblers, 1982, 19-28
       **Ayres, C. E.: "The Legacy of Thorstein Veblen" in Institutional Economics, 1963
       **Veblen: The Theory of Business Enterprise (1904), Ch I-IV, X

EXAM 3

V. Keynes and Macroeconomics

       Heilbroner: The Heresies of Keynes (Ch 9)
       **Stewart: Chapters 1-3
       Keynes: Chapters 2, 3, 8-10, 13, 14, 16, 18, 19, 21, 23, 24

VI. Modern Topics

       (Readings assigned as time remaining permits)

FINAL EXAM

Hands   Fall 1989

ECONOMICS 321
History of Economic Thought
Exam #1

Answer any four of the following six questions.

1. Adam Smith is very critical of Mercantilist politics. What are these policies and what are Smith's criticisms?

2. The following quote is from Ricardo's Principles:

    "It follows then, that the interest of the landlord is always opposed to the interest of every other class in the community."

    Give a detailed Ricardian defense of this statement.

3. Explain the Physiocratic model and discuss its policy implications.

4. Summarize Adam Smith's theory of economic growth (i.e. what causes the wealth of nations?).

5. In Ricardo's value theory different capital to labor ratios (different ratios of fixed to circulating capital) create problems for the labor theory of value. Explain this problem.

6. Explain Ricardo's long run wage theory with special reference to Malthusian population theory.

ECON 321
History of Economic Thought
Fall 1989

Exam #2

Answer **any four** of the following **six** questions.

1. Discuss the utilitarian philosophy of Jeremy Bentham and how it influenced J. S. Mills economics.

2. Discuss Marx's Theory of history.

3. Explain the theory of profit in Marx's work with particular attention to the following quote from Marx:

   "To explain the general nature of profits, you must start from the theorem that, on the average, commodities are <u>sold</u> <u>at</u> <u>their</u> <u>real</u> <u>values</u>, and that profits are derived from selling them at their values...If you can not explain profit upon this supposition, you can not explain it at all!"

4. Discuss in detail J. S. Mills' view of the <u>stationary state</u> with particular attention to how his view differed or agreed with Ricardo's view.

5. Compare and contrast Ricardo's theory of <u>wages</u> with Marx's theory of <u>wages</u>.

6. In Vol. III of <u>Capital</u> Marx states:

   "The real barrier to capitalist production is capital itself."

   Give a detailed Marxian defense of this argument.

Hands   Fall 1989

ECONOMICS 321
History of Thought
Exam #3

Answer **any four** of the following questions.

1. Compare and contrast Veblen's view of late 19th century capitalism with Marx's view of capitalism.

2. Discuss in detail <u>Marshall's interpretation</u> of Jevons and Ricardo (i.e. what did Marshall think was right with these theories and what did he think was wrong?).

3. Discuss Marshall's stable equilibrium of supply and demand (i.e. how do markets work for Marshall?).

4. On pg. 394 of <u>The Principles</u>, Marshall says, "it might even be for the advantage of the community that government should levy taxes on commodities which obey the law of diminishing return, and devote part of the proceeds to bounties on commodities which obey the law of increasing return."

   <u>Explain</u> Marshall's defense of this quote.

5. Neoclassical economists all had basically the same theory of the <u>demand</u> for goods. Discuss this theory in detail.

6. Compare and contrast the <u>questions</u> asked by classical economists (Smith-Ricardo), neoclassical economists (Jevons-Marshall), and institutionalist economics (Veblen). [Note this is not about how their "theories" are alike or different but rather how the "thing" they were trying to explain was alike or different.]

Hands
Fall 1989

ECON 321
History of Economic Thought

Answer any _three_ of the following _five_ questions.

1. What determines the <u>rate of interest</u> in the economy according to Keynes' <u>General Theory</u>? Discuss.

2. According to Keynes' <u>General Theory</u> what determines the aggregate level of employment in a market economy? Explain.

3. What is right and/or wrong with the "classical" theory of <u>employment</u> according to Keynes' <u>General Theory</u>? Discuss.

4. Keynes discusses the "Fate of Midas" in a number of places in the <u>General Theory</u>. What does he mean by this? Explain.

5. Compare and contrast the general economic philosophy of J. M. Keynes with that of Adam Smith and Karl Marx.

ECON 321
History of Economic Thought
D. Wade Hands

Paper #1

Adam Smith discusses "natural prices" many places in the <u>Wealth of Nations</u>. Answer the following questions regarding his discussion.

    a) What does Adam Smith mean by "natural prices"? (Use quotes with references.)
    b) How do Smith's "natural prices" relate to the equilibrium prices of modern supply and demand analysis?

Paper #2

According to Adam Smith's "adding-up" theory of price/value, an increase in the price of labor would increase the price of all commodities. Ricardo argues that this is incorrect. What does Ricardo say will happen when wages rise? (Use quotes with references.)

Paper #3

Summarize J. S. Mill's view of the stationary state. How is it different from Ricardo's view of the stationary state.

Paper #4

Explain Marx's distinction between the "value of labor power" and the "value produced by labor power."

Paper #5

In the <u>Principles of Economics</u>, Alfred Marshall discusses a <u>stable</u> equilibrium of Supply and Demand. Explain this, i.e. how does Marshall characterize a stable equilibrium (use quotes from Marshall to support your argument, you may want to draw diagrams).

Paper #6

In <u>The Theory of Business Enterprise</u>, Veblen emphasizes the distinction between "Business" and "Industry." Discuss how Veblen uses these two terms (support your argument with quotes).

Paper #7

There is only one diagram in J. M. Keynes' <u>General Theory of Employment, Interest and Money</u>. <u>Explain it</u> (what does it say, what point is Keynes making, how does it relate to the "classical" theory, his theory, etc.?).

RL/3   **University of Cambridge**   U

<u>Prelim. to Part II, Papers 1, 2</u>   Michaelmas Term 1988
G. C. Harcourt

                                       Wednesday 9, Friday 9
                                       (first four weeks only)

                History of Economic Thought 'Circus'

This course of 12 lectures by a group of persons* is designed as an introduction to the history of ideas in the discipline. While reading the works of the 'Greats' is a 'must', the following books may also be found useful and stimulating:

* We hope it will be <u>persons</u>. Last year, with one exeption, it was a circus with a clown only, GCH.

Roger Backhouse, <u>A History of Modern Economic Analysis</u> (Blackwell, 1985).

A.K. Dasgupta, <u>Epochs of Economic Theory</u> (Blackwell, 1985).

Phyllis Deane, <u>The Evolution of Economic Ideas</u> (CUP, 1978).

Robert Heilbronner, <u>The Worldly Philosophers</u>, (New York, 1978).

M.H. Dobb, <u>Theories of Value and Distribution Since Adam Smith</u>, (CUP, 1973).

Samuel Hollander, <u>Classical Economics</u> (Blackwell, 1987)

<u>Topics</u>

1.   Classical Political Economy: Smith, Ricardo, Malthus.

<u>Reading</u>

        Adam Smith, <u>The Wealth of Nations</u>.

        David Ricardo, <u>The Principles of Economics and Taxation</u>, Sraffa with
            Dobb edition, Vol. I.

        Robert Thomas Malthus, <u>Principles of Political Economy</u>.

        Walter Eltis, <u>The Classical theory of Economic Growth</u>, (Macmillan, 1984) Chs. 3-6.

        J.C. Weldon, "The classical theory of distribution", in A. Asimakopulos (ed.) <u>Theories of Income Distribution</u> (Kluwer, 1988).

2. Marx

Reading

> Capital, 3 Vols.
>
> Anthony Brewer, A Guide to Marx's Capital, (CUP, 1984).
>
> M.C. Howard & J.E. King, The Political Economy of Marx, (Longman, 2nd ed., 1985).
>
> W. Eltis, Chs. 7, 8.
>
> David Levine, "Marx's theory of income distribution", in Asimakopulos (ed.) Theories of Income distribution

3. Neoclassical Economics:

1) Jevons, Menger, Walras.

Reading

> W.S. Jevons, The Theory of Political Economy, London Macmillan, 2nd ed. 1879, 1st ed. 1871.
>
> Karl Menger, Principles of Economics, Free Press 1950.
>
> Leon Walras, Elements of Pure Economics, Trans. William Jaffe. London, Allen and Unwin, 1954.

2) Marshall

Reading

> Alfred Marshall, Principles of Economics Vol. I Macmillan 9th ed. (Variorum) 1961.
>
> J.M. Keynes, "Alfred Marshall" Essays in Biography, Vol. X of the Keynes Volumes.
>
> J.K. Whitaker "The Distribution Theory of Marshall's Principles" in Asimakopulos (ed.) Theories of Income Distribution.

4. Reactions against neoclassical theory.

1) The imperfect competition and monopolistic competition "revolutions".

Reading

> John Maloney, Marshall, Orthodoxy and the Professionalisation of Economics (C.U.P. 1985)
>
> Piero Sraffa, "The Laws of returns under competitive conditions", Economic Journal, Econ. J. 1926.
>
> "Symposium on increasing returns and the representative firm', Economic Journal, 1930.

Joan Robinson, The Economics of Imperfect Competition, (Macmillan 1933).

Edward Chamberlin, The Theory of Monopolistic Competition (Harvard U.P. 1933).

G.L.S. Shackle. The Years of High Theory, (CUP 1967), Chs. 3, 4, 5.

2) The Keynesian "revolution", Cambridge Monetary Thought and the Marshallian tradition.

Reading

J.M.. Keynes, "Alfred Marshall", Essays in Biography, (Vol. X of Keynes Volumes).

R.F. Harrod, "Mr. Keynes and traditional Theory" in Seymour Harris (ed.), The New Economics, (1947).

P. Sraffa, "Dr Hayek on Money and Capital", Economic Journal, 1932.

J.M. Keynes, A Tract on Monetary Reform, 1923.

J.M. Keynes, Treatise on Money, 2 Vols, 1930.

J.M. Keynes, The General Theory of Employment, Interest and Money 1936.

Joan Robinson, Introduction to the Theory of Employment (1936).

G.L.S. Shackle. The Years of High Theory, Chs. 11,12.

Richard Kahn, The Making of Keynes' General Theory, (CUP 1984).

3) The modern Cambridge tradition: Michal Kalecki, Joan Robinson, Richard Kahn, Nicholas Kaldor and Piero Sraffa.

Reading

M. Kalecki, Selected Essays on the Dynamics of the Capitalist Economy 1933-70, (CUP 1971).

Joan Robinson, The Accumulation of Capital, (Macmillan 1956)

Nicholas Kaldor, Economics without Equilibrium, (M.E. Sharpe 1985).

Piero Sraffa, Production of Commodities by Means of Commodities, (CUP 1960).

Peter Kriesler, Kalecki's Micro Analysis, (CUP, 1987)

Further reading and topics will be given as the 'circus' is assembled. I hope to get some of the present 'greats' of the Faculty to appear and talk about their favourite economists and/or episodes in economic theory.

G.C.H.

U

University of Cambridge

RL/2

Prelims, Papers 1 and 2   Lent Term 1990 Thursday at 10.00 a.m.
G.C. Harcourt Friday at 9.00 a.m.

Lectures on Post Keynesian and Growth Theory

Reading List

A.   Background on leading figures

Piero Sraffa; Luigi Pasinetti's article on 'Sraffa, Piero', in David L. Sills (ed.), International Encyclopaedia of the Social Sciences, Biographical Supplement, Vol. 18 (Free Press, 1979)

Michal Kalecki: Josef Steindl, 'A personal portrait of Michal Kalecki'. Journal of Post Keynesian Economics, Vol. III, 1981, 590-96

Joan Robinson: G.C. Harcourt, 'Joan Robinson', in The Social Science Imperialists. Selected Essays. G.C. Harcourt. Edited by Prue Kerr (Routledge and kegan Paul, 1982), 346-61

Nicholas Kaldor: Luigi Pasinetti's article on 'Kaldor, Nicholas' in David L. Sills (ed.), International Encyclopaedia of the Social Sciences, Biographical Supplement, Vol. 18 (Free Press, 1979).

G.C. Harcourt, "Nicholas Kaldor, 12 May 1908 - 30 September 1986", Economica, May 1988.

G.C. Harcourt, "On the Contributions of Joan Robinson and Piero Sraffa to Economic Theory", Controversies in Political Economy (Wheatsheaf Books), 90-112. (See also supplement to Economic Journal, 1986).

B.   The Classical and Marxian surplus approach

Krishna Bharadwaj, Classical Political Economy and Rise to Dominance of Supply and Demand Theories, R.C. Dutt lectures, 1976 (Orient Longman, 1978)

Vivian Walsh and Harvey Gram, Classical and Neoclassical Theories of General Equilibrium. (Oxford University Press, 1980)

(See also A & J Cohen, 'Classical and Neoclassical Theories of Distribution', Aust. Econ. Papers, June 1983)

Pierangelo Garegnani, 'Value and Distribution in the Classical Economists and Marx', Oxford Economi Paper, 1984, 291-325

C.   Theories of Distribution

Nicholas Kaldor, 'Alternative Theories of Distribution', Review of Economics Studies, xxiii, 1956, 83-100

Michal Kalecki, Selected Essays on the Dynamics of the Capitalist Economy, 1933-1970 (Cambridge University Press, 1971), Essays 5, 6, 7, 14

A. Asimakopulos, 'A Kaleckian Theory of Income Distribution', Canadian Journal of Economics, 8, 1975, 313-33; reprinted in A. Asimakopulos, Investment Employment & Income Distribution. Polity Press, 1988, Ch. 2

A. Asimakopulos, 'Themes in a post Keynesian Theory of Income Distribution', Journal of Post Keynesian Economics, 111, Winter 1980-81, 158-69

Joan Robinson, 'The Theory of Distribution', Collected Economic Papers, Vol. 11 (Blackwell, 1960), 145-158

Joan Robinson, "Growth and the Theory of Distribution". Collected Economic Papers, Vol. V (Blackwell, 1979), 71-75

M.C. Howard, Modern Theories of Income Distribution, (Macmillan) Chs. 5, 6, 7

A. Asimakopulos (ed), Theories of Income Distribution (Kluwer Academic Publishers 1988), especially Chs 1, 2, 6, 7.

D.   Micro Foundations

Michal Kalecki, Selected Essays....., Essay 5

Paolo Sylos-Labini, 'Prices and Income Distribution in Manufacturing Industry', Journal of Post Keynesian Economics, Fall 1979, 11, 3-25

G.C. Harcourt and Peter Kenyon, 'Pricing and the Investment Decision', in The Social Science Imperialists, Essay 8

Nicholas Kaldor, Economics without Equilibrium (Sharpe, 1985), Chapter 2

Peter Kenyon, 'pricing in Post-Keynesian Economics', Challenge, Vol. 21, July-August 1978, 43-8 (also in A.S. Eichner (ed.) A Guide to Post-Keynesian Economics (M.E. Sharpe, 1979)

Adrian Wood, A Theory of Profits (Cambridge University Press, 1975)

E.   Accumulation and Synthesis

Joan Robinson, The Accumulation of Capital, (Macmillan, 1956), especially Book II

Joan Robinson, Essays in the Theory of Economic Growth, (Macmillan 1962), especially pp. 34-59

G.C. Harcourt, 'Harcourt on Robinson' in H.W. Spiegel and W.J. Samuels (eds.), Contemporary Economists in perspective (J.A.I. Press, 1984), pp. 639-54, esp. pp. 644-47 (cpy of mimeo version in Marshall)

A. Asimakopulos, Investment, Employment and Income Distribution, (Polity Press, 1988).

Michal Kalecki, Selected Essays...., especially Essays 9, 10 and 15

Nicholas Kaldor, 'Equilibrium Theory and Growth Theory' in Michael Boskin (ed) Economics & Human Welfare, (Academics Press, 1979)

Nicholas Kaldor, 'Some Fallacies in the Interpretation of Kaldor', Review of Economic Studies, 37, 1970, 1-7

Nicholas Kaldor, Economics without Equilibrium (M E Sharpe, 1985)

G.C. Harcourt, The Social Science Imperialists, Essays 6,7

Bob Rowthorn, Demand, Real Wages and Economic Growth, Thames Papers in Political Economy, Autumn 1981

Peter Skott, Vicious Circles & Cumulative Causation, Thames Papers in Political Economy, Summer 1985

Donald J. Harris, 'Structural Change and Economic Growth: a review article'. Contributions to Political Economy, 1, 1982, 25-46

Malcolm C. Sawyer, Towards a Post-Kaleckian Macro-economics, Thames Papers in Political Economy, Autumn, 1982 (see also Sawyer, Macro-economics in Question (Wheatsheaf Books, 1982) especially Chs. 5, 6 and 7)

G.C. Harcourt, Post Keynesianism: Quite Wrong and/or Nothing New?, Thames Papers in Political Economy, Summer 1982. Reprinted in Arestis and Skouras (eds), Post-Keynesian Economic Theory (Wheatsheaf 1985)

O.F. Hamouda and G.C. Harcourt, "Post Keynesianism: from criticism to coherence?", Bulletin of Economic Research, january, 1988, 1-33.

Stephen A. Marglin, 'Growth Distribution, and Inflation: A Centennial Synthesis', (The 1983 Marshall Lectures), Cambridge Journal of Economics, June 1984, 115-44

Sheila Dow, "Post Keynesian monetary theory for an open economy", Journal of Post Keynesian Economics, Winter 1986-87, 237-57.

Philips Arestis, "Post-Keynesian Theory of Money, Credit and Finance", Thames Papers in Political Economy, Spring 1987.

Marc Jarsulic, Effective Demand and Income Distribution, (Polity Press 1988).

F. Capital Theory: The Cambridge Controversies

J.A. Kregel, Theory of Capital (Macmillan, 1976)

Avinash Dixit, 'The Accumulation of Capital Theory', Oxford Economic Papers, 29 March, 1977, 1-29 (review article of Bliss, Capital Theory and the Distribution of Income, 1975)

Donald J. Harris, 'Profits, Productivity and thrift: the neoclassical theory of capital and distribution revisited', Journal of Post Keynesian Economics, Spring 1981, 111, 359-82

G.C. Harcourt, Some Cambridge Controversies in the Theory of Capital, Cambridge University Press, 1972, Chs. 1,4

G.C. Harcourt, The Social Science Imperialists, Part V, Essays 16, 18

b:RLPrelimPaper1/Harcourt

H/1

Prelim. to Part II, Papers 1 and 2   Lent Term 1990, Thursday at 10.00 a.m.
                                           and Friday at 9.00 a.m.

G.C. Harcourt

Lectures on Post Keynesian and Growth Theory

A.   Overview: growth theory from Adam Smith via Hahn and Matthews to Solow's 1988 Nobel Prize lecture.

Reading

F.H. Hahn and R.C.O. Matthews, "The Theory of Economic Growth: A Survey", Economic Journal, December 1964, Part 1.

F.H. Hahn, "Neoclassical Growth Theory", The New Palgrave Dictionary of Economics (Eatwell et al, ed) Macmillan 1987, vol. III, 625-33.

A.K. Sen (ed.), Growth Economics, (Penguin 1970), Introduction.

Hywell Jones, An Introduction to Modern Theories of Economic Growth (Nelson, 1975), Chaps. 1, 2.

Joan Robinson, Essays in the Theory of Economic Growth, (Macmillan, 1962). Essay 2

Walter Eltis, The Classical Theory of Economic Growth, (MacMillan, 1984), Ch.9.

Robert M. Solow, "Growth Theory and After", American Economic Review, June 1988.

B.   Classical growth theory: David Ricardo

Reading

L.L. Pasinetti, "A Mathematical Formulation of the Ricardian System", Review of Economic Studies, 1960.

N. Kaldor, "Alternative Theories of Distribution", Review of Economic Studies, 1955-56, Section on Ricardo.

Walter Eltis, The Classical Theory of Economic Growth, Ch.6

Paul A. Samuelson, "Mathematical Vindication of Ricardo on Machinery", Journal of Political Economy, 1988, 274-82.

C.   Introduction to Marxian Growth Theory

Reading

Donald J. Harris, Capital Accumulation and Income Distribution, Stanford University Press, 1978 p. 249-62.

Claudio Sardoni, "Multi-Sectoral Models of Balanced Growth and the Marxian Schemes of Expanded Reproduction", Australian Economic Papers, December 1981.

K. Marx, Capital, Vols I and II.

Walter Eltis, The Classical Theory of Economic Growth, Chs. 7 and 8.

D. Post General Theory Growth Theory: (a) Harrod and Domar

Reading

A.K. Sen, (ed.) Introduction and Readings 1 and 2.

(If you cannot get access to Sen, Harrod's paper is in the Economic Journal 1939, pp. 14-33 and Domar's paper is in Econometrica, 1946, pp. 137-47).

(b) Joan Robinson

Reading

A.K. Sen (ed.) Reading 5 (it is pp. 34-59 of Joan Robinson, Essays in the Theory of Economic Growth (1962)

A. Asimakopulos 'A Robinsonian growth model in one-sector notation' Australian Economic Papers, 1969, 1970.

G.C. Harcourt, Some Cambridge Controversies in the Theory of Capital (Cambridge U.P., 1972), pp.232-40.

G.C. Harcourt, "Harcourt on Robinson", in Spiegel and Samuels (eds.) Contemporary Economists in Perspective (JAI Press, 1984) esp. pp. 643-47.

R.F. Kahn, Reading 6 in Sen (ed.) or Oxford Economic Papers 1959, 143-56.

(c) Neoclassical Growth Theory: Swan and Solow

Reading

"Economic Growth and Capital Accumulation", Economic Record, Nov. 1956, 333-43

R.M. Solow, Reading 7 in Sen (ed.) or Quarterly Journal of Economics 1956, pp. 65-94. (Solow is exposited in many textbooks. Swan, who in some ways is more profound, is not in the textbooks).

F.H. Hahn, "Neoclassical Growth Theory", The New Palgrave Dictionary of Economics, Vol III, 625-33.

R.M. Solow, "Growth Theory: An Exposition, (Oxford University Press, 1969).

Hywel Jones, An Introduction to Modern Theories of Economic Growth, Ch. 5. (Nelson, 1975)

(d) Post Keynesian and Marxian Growth Theory (The themes of section (d) will be taken up in more detail in lectures in the Lent Term).

Reading

Donald J Harris, Capital Accumulation and Income Distribution. pp. 262-84 (you may find Harris's paper in the American Economic Review, May 1975 easier to follow).

Bob Rowthorn, Demand, Real Wages and Economic Growth, Thames Papers in Politial Economy, Autumn 1981.

G.C. Harcourt, Post Keynesianism: Quite Wrong and/or Nothing New? Thames Papers in Political Economy, Summer 1982, pp. 7-9, 14-15. Reprinted as Ch. 6 in P. Arestis and T. Skouras (eds.), Post-Keynesian Economic Theory, A Challenge to Neo-Classical Economics (Wheatsheaf 1985).

O.F. Hamouda and G.C. Harcourt, "Post Keynesianism: From Criticism to Coherence?", Bulletin of Economic Research, January 1988, pp. 1-33.

Joan Robinson, "Michal Kalecki on the Economics of Capitalism", Oxford Bulletin of Economics and Statistics, special issue, 1977, pp. 7-17.

D. Canning, "Increasing returns in industry and the role of agriculture in growth", Oxford Economic Papers, September 1988.

Please note that the reading is much 'harder' than the level at which the lectures will be pitched.

b;RLPrelimPaper1/harcourt

U&G

University of Cambridge

RL/3

CAPITAL AND GROWTH THEORY IN THE CAMBRIDGE TRADITION

Part II   Lent Term 1990   G C Harcourt

Tuesday at 2.00 p.m.

Reference marked * are regarded as the most important readings, I shall give <u>six to eight</u> lectures on the following topics.

I   Overview: the issues

Reading

G.C. Harcourt, The Social Science Imperialists: Selected Essays, Edited by Prue Kerr (Routledge and Kegan Paul, 1962), Essays 18 and 19.
*A.K. Sen, "On Some Debates in Capital Theory", Economica, 1974.
*Bob Rowthorn, "Neo-classicism, Neo-Ricardianism and Marxism", New Left Review, 1974.
Edwin Burmeister, Capital Theory and Dynamics, (C.U.P., 1980), ch. 4.
*P. Garegnani, 'Value and Distribution in the Classical Economists and Marx', Oxford Economic Papers, 1984.
*Avi J. Cohen, "Prices, capital and the one-commodity model in neoclassical and classical theories", mimeo, 1986. (in Marshall)
Avi J. Cohen, "Samuelson and the 93% Scarcity Theory of Value", mimeo, 1987. (in Marshall).

II   Capital measured in a unit independent of distribution and prices.

Reading

*Joan Robinson, "The Production Function and the Theory of Capital", R.E. Studs., 1953-54; reprinted in G.C. Harcourt and N.F. Laing (eds.), Capital and Growth, (Penguin, 1971).
*D.G. Champernowne, "The Production Function and the Theory of Capital: A Comment", R.E. Studs., 1953-54; reprinted in G.C. Harcourt and N.F. Laing (eds.).
T.W. Swan, "Notes on Capital", Ec. Record, 1956, reprinted in G.C. Harcourt and N.F. Laing (eds.).
*G.C. Harcourt, Some Cambridge Controversies in the Theory of Capital, (C.U.P.), Ch.1.
*Piero Sraffa, Production of Commodities by Means of Commodities, (C.U.P.), pp. 34-8, reprinted in G.C. Harcourt and N.F. Laing (eds.).

III   Solow on the rate of return

Reading

*R.M. Solow, Capital Theory and the Rate of Return, (North-Holland, 1963), Chapter 1, reprinted in G.C. Harcourt and N.F. Laing (eds.).
*Joan Robinson, "Solow on the Rate of Return", Economic Journal, 1964 reprinted in Col. Econ. Papers, Vol. III (Blackwell, 1965) and G.C. Harcourt and N.F. Laing (eds.).
*G.C. Harcourt, Some Cambridge Controversies....., Ch.3.
A. Dixit, "The Accumulation of Capital Theory", Oxford Economic Papers, 1977.

IV Reswitching and Capital-Reversing

   Reading

   *Paul A. Samuelson, "Parable and Realism in Capital Theory: The Surrogate Production Function", R.E. Studs., 1962, reprinted in G.C. Harcourt and N.F. Laing (eds.).
   D. Levhari, "A Non-substitution Theorem and Switching of Techniques", Quarterly Journal of Economics, 1965.
   *P. Garegnani, "Heterogeneous capital, the production function and the theory of capital", R.E. Studs., 1970.
   *Paul A. Samuelson, "A Summing Up", Quarterly Journal of Economics, 1966, reprinted in G.C. Harcourt and N.F. Laing (eds.).
   A. Bhaduri, "On the significance of recent controversies on capital theory: A Marxian view", Econ. J., 1969, reprinted in G.C. Harcourt and N.F. Laing (eds.).
   *G.C. Harcourt, Some Cambridge Controversies..., Ch. 4
   *G.C. Harcourt, The Social Science Imperialists, Essay 17, (also in Oxford Economic Papers, 1976).
   *L.L. Pasinetti, "Switches of Techniques and the 'Rate of Return' in Capital Theory", Econ. J., 1969, reprinted in G.C. Harcourt and N.F. Laing (eds.).
   C.R.S. Doughtery, "On the Rate of Return and the Rate of Profit", Econ.J., 1972.

V The End of The Affair

   Reading

   *Joan Robinson, History versus Equilibrium, Thames Papers in Political Economy, 1974, reprinted in Collected Economic Papers, Vol. V, (Blackwell, 1974).
   *Joan Robinson, "The Meaning of Capital" in Collected Economic Papers, Vol. V.
   *Joan Robinson, "The Unimportance of Reswitching", Quarterly Journal of Economics, 1975 reprinted in Collected Economic Papers, Vol. V.
   C.J. Bliss, Capital Theory and the Distribution of Income, (North-Holland, 1975).
   *A. Dixit, "The Accumulation of Capital Theory", Oxford Economic Papers, 1977.
   F.H. Hahn, "The Neo-Ricardians", Cambridge J. Econ., 1982, reprinted in F.H. Hahn, Equilibrium and Macroeconomics, (Blackwell, 1984).
   *Stephen Marglin, Growth, Distribution and Prices (Harvard University Press, 1984), Chs 19, 20, 21.

VI The Capital Theory Critique and the Foundations of Monetary Theory

   *Colin Rogers, Money, Interest and Capital (Cambridge U.P. 1989), Chapters 1,2,3,7.11.

University of Cambridge
Faculty of Economics and Politics

Switchboard: (0223) 335200
Direct line:

Austin Robinson Building
Sidgwick Avenue
Cambridge CB3 9DD

8-90

From: Dr G C Harcourt

M Phil in Economics
Subject 3: Macroeconomics

Thursdays, 12.00-1.00, Lecture Room 1   Dr G C Harcourt

Keynes: from the Treatise to the General Theory

Reading

CW	Vol 13, Vol 14, Vol 29	
J M Keynes	The Treatise and The General Theory	
T K Rymes	Keynes's Lectures, 1932-1935	Macmillan, 1989
E J Amadeo	Keynes's Principle of Effective Demand,	Edward Elgar, 1989
R F Kahn	The Making of Keynes's General Theory	CUP, 1984
R F Kahn	The Economics of the Short Period	Macmillan, 1989
P Clarke	The Keynesian Revolution in the Making, 1924-1936	Oxford, 1988
G C Harcourt	"Theoretical Methods and Unfinished Business" in D A Reese (ed) The Legacy of Keynes	Harper & Row, 1987

Post Keynesian Economics

Reading

O F Hamouda & G C Harcourt	"Post Keynesian Economics: From Criticism to Coherence?"	Bulletin of Economic Research, Jan 1988
P Reynolds	Political Economy: A Synthesis of Kaleckian and Post Keynesian Economics	Wheatsheaf, 1987
C Rogers	Money, Interest and Capital	CUP, 1989
M Jarsulic	Effective Demand and Income Distribution	Polity, 1988
A Asimakopulos	Investment, Employment and Income Distribution	Polity, 1989
C Torr	Equilibrium, Expectations and Information	Polity, 1988

Indiana University
Kniesner's Guide to Doctoral Dissertations
THOMAS J. KNIESNER

1. Sections of the Dissertation

The following describes the issues to address in each chapter.

(1) Chapter 1. Introduction
The introduction chapter should been written last, should be the most literary of all the chapters (a real attention grabber), should foreshadow what is to come, and should answer the following two questions:
   (i) What is the general area of research and why is it important to economists and policymakers?
   (ii) What is the specific research question that interests you and why is it important to economists and policymakers? Make sure that the "punchline" appears as the last sentence of the first paragraph.

(2) Chapter 2. The Literature
This chapter should set the stage for your original research to follow by convincing the reader that you are building on the current state of knowledge rather than rediscovering the wheel. It should answer the following two questions:
   (i) What do we know about the topic of your research issue from the existing economic literature? (Explain the findings from the key articles and books on the topic.)
   (ii) What do we not know about your research issue from the existing literature?

(3) Chapter 3. Conceptual Framework
This chapter explains the economic tools (expressed in equations or graphs) that you will use to test the economic hypothesis or to measure the economic phenomenon that is the focal point of your dissertation. It should answer the following questions:
   (i) What is the theoretical tool(s) or model(s) you will use to guide your analysis of the research question described in Chapter 1. above? (Carefully explain your graphs and equations.)
   (ii) What economic hypothesis or hypotheses will you be examining or economic phenomena will you be quantifying? More specifically, what is the dependent variable in your analysis and what are the independent variable? Simply put, what are you trying to explain and with what are you trying to explain it?

(4) Chapter 4. Results
It is here that you present your findings. In the context of displaying your "wares" be sure to touch on how your hypothesis or hypotheses were tested or your economic phenomena were measured. The reader should come away with a clear understanding of the data that you used as well as the statistical techniques involved in processing the data.

(5) Chapter 5. Conclusion
This is where you tie things up, and in a highly literary way remind the reader what he or she should remember about the dissertation just read.

(6) Appendixes (as needed)
The purpose of an appendix is to collect technical information that will be important to someone who really wants to understand your work, but that technical information is too long to put into the main body or a footnote.
   Your dissertation should definitely have an appendix with the formal definitions of the variables and summary statistics that include (i) means, (ii) standard deviations, (iii) minimum values, and (iv) maximum values of the variables.
   Example appendixes appear at the end of this document.

(7) **References**
Put your references in a list using the bibliographical style in Turabian's book on dissertation style. Be sure that everything you cite in the body of your dissertation is contained in the references section. List only things in the references section that you actually use and cite in the body of your dissertation.

2. Typing Details

Here are some details to incorporate in the final typed copy of your dissertation.

(1) **University Regulations**
Adhere to the details in "A Guide to the Preparation of Theses and Dissertations," which is put out by the Graduate School and available from the Director of Graduate Studies.

(2) **Equations**
Equations are numbered consecutively with numbers in parentheses flush to the right-hand margin. An example is

$$E = MC^2 \qquad (1)$$

(3) **Figures and Tables**
Should be numbered consecutively throughout the text of the dissertation.

(4) **Footnotes**
Number consecutively throughout the dissertation and place them at the bottoms of the pages on which they appear.

3. Stylistics

Here are some simple rules to follow concerning writing style. I also highly recommend that you read two books by Donald N. McCloskey, (1) <u>The Rhetoric of Economics</u> and (2) <u>The Writing of Economics</u>.

(1) **Active vs. Passive Voice**
At least 75 per cent of your sentences should be in the active voice. Research is dull enough reading without making it duller yet. Brighten the dialogue by writing predominantly in the active voice.

(2) **Direct Quotes**
Minimize the use of quoted material. It makes for choppy reading because of the change in writing styles and gives the reader the impression that you are too dumb to think for yourself and to write your own dialogue. *Rule of Thumb:* only use a quote if the thought and way of saying it is <u>exceptionally brilliant</u>. (Example: "My blood, ejaculated the vexed coachman.")

(3) **Equations**
Be sure to punctuate sentences that contain equations; just because a sentence contains some algebra doesn't mean you can stop punctuating it.

(4) **First Person Singular**
Write in the first person singular, rather than first person plural or third person. We is reserved for when you have a coauthor or are writing a children's

book, and "this author" became obsolete when Walter Winchell died. In other words, your sentences should say something like "In my dissertation, I ...."

(5) Footnotes
Do NOT use reference footnotes. All references should be in the text in one of two forms appearing in the examples below.

Jones (1986) and Green (1949, p. 55) both argue ....

It is well known that demand curves are downward sloping (Jones, 1985; J. Smith, 1986; and Brown, 1986a).

Minimize the use of information footnotes. If it is important enough to say it is probably important enough to put into the main body of the text, and if it is not important enough to say in the main body it probably doesn't need to be said at all. Footnotes should largely be used to explain important, but distracting, technical details.

(6) Headings
Use three levels of headings to organize your material. The first level is centered and contains mixed upper and lower case letters. The second level of heading begins flush with the left-hand margin and also contains mixed upper and lower case letters. The third level of heading is an underlined sentence that starts a paragraph. The first real sentence of the paragraph then follows. Here is an example

2. The Literature

In this chapter I ....

A. Microeconomic Analyses

Microeconomic analyses of the substitution hypothesis focus on ....

<u>1. Studies of the United States.</u> Arguably the most important books written on ....

Finally, do not to have a heading with nothing under it but another heading. A heading ALWAYS has some dialogue under it.

(7) Latin
The following Latin abbreviations are <u>off limits</u>: etc., op. cit., ibid., viz., e.g., and i.e. (Use their English equivalents.)

(8) Quotation Marks
Only put quotes around a term if you wish to indicate <u>unfamiliar</u> usage.

(9) Nonsexist Dialogue
Use sexless terms or pronouns. (Example: letter carrier instead of mailman or police officer instead of policeman.) Avoid sentences that contain the phrase "he or she .....", however, and be sure to use good English in the sense that nouns and verbs agree. A handy trick is to use <u>the</u> instead of <u>his or her</u>.

(10) That vs. Which
Learn the difference between that and which, and then go on a "which" hunt to change most of your whiches to thats. That begins a <u>conditional</u> statement and which begins an <u>unconditional</u> statement. Here are some examples

Would you please remove the books that are on the table?

Love, which is one of life's great emotions, makes one feel all warm inside.

(11) Two-Word Adjectives
Two-word adjectives are hyphenated and two-word nouns are not. Here is an example

A well-known economist is ....

The downward-sloping demand curve is ....

Exception: do not hyphenate a two-word adjective when the first word ends in ly.

(12) United States vs. U.S.
Use United States when you are using it as a noun and U.S. when you are using it as an adjective. Here are some examples

Michigan is part of the United States.

IBM is a U.S. corporation.

(13) Visual Aids
Figures and tables should be self explanatory. The reader should be able to understand a table or a figure without reading the main body of your dissertation. Use visual aids liberally.

EXAMPLE

APPENDIX I

CLEARING AND PAYMENT CONVENTIONS
OF THE TREASURY SECURITIES MARKET

The standard clearing convention of the Treasury securities market is that bills or bonds purchased must be exchanged for funds the following day. The daily Treasury return data provided to me by Mark Flannery reports prices for bills and bonds deliverable two business days later. Thus, a Friday announcement return (corresponding to a Thursday announcement) requires financing from the following Monday to the day after. A Monday announcement return (corresponding to a Friday announcement) also requires only one day of financing, that is, from the next Tuesday to Wednesday.

EXAMPLE

APPENDIX II

CALCULATION OF THE UNADJUSTED
RETURNS OF TREASURY SECURITIES

The purpose of this section is to explain exactly how the daily return for the Treasury bills and bonds were calculated. The calculations were made by Mark Flannery, who supplied me with the daily returns.

The raw data for the Treasury bills is the average of bid and asked discount yield on the outstanding security closest to the constant maturity described by the series. Government securities dealers buy at a price corresponding to the bid discount yield and sell at a price corresponding to the asked discount yield. To explain what is meant by "the outstanding security closest to the constant maturity described by the series," I give the following example of what security is used for the calculation of the daily returns for what I label a 3-month T-bill. That is, for the period when the announcements were made on Friday, a bill with 87 remaining days to maturity is used. For the Thursday announcements, a bill with 88 remaining days to maturity is used. These raw data are collected from the Federal Reserve Bank of New York's daily report "Composite Closing Quotations for U.S. Government Securities." The prices quoted are for bills to be delivered two business days after the day the Federal Reserve collects the quotes. The collected yield was converted to a bill price with the

formula:
$$(100 - P)(360 / DSM) = YAV, \qquad (8)$$
where YAV is the average of bid and discount yields and DSM is the number of calendar days from the time the bill was delivered to the maturity date. Finally, the daily returns for the Treasury bills were computed as:

$$\text{daily return} = [P(t) - P(t-1)] / P(t-1). \qquad (9)$$

The daily return for Treasury bonds is similar:

$$\text{daily return} = [P(t) - P(t-1)] / P(t-1)$$
$$+ [C/P(t-1)] [n/365], \qquad (10)$$

where C is the coupon rate for the bond and n is the number of calendar days between settlement dates.

APPENDIX III - SUMMARY STATISTICS

Variable	Mean	Standard Deviation	Mininum Value	Maximum Value
Period I - November 4, 1977 to October 5, 1979 (105 Observations)				
UM	-0.447619	1.513535	-5.00000	3.60000
EM	0.720952	1.197409	-3.00000	4.00000
d[1MTB]	-0.515652	1.029891	-6.54900	1.80652
d[3MTB]	-0.721466	2.534111	-12.64142	7.64284
d[6MTB]	-0.852372	3.702127	-13.75414	7.84190
d[7YB]	-2.691677	16.745672	-46.83132	44.92697
d[30YB]	-4.391193	25.250280	-69.49662	51.84200
d[SP500]	6.347393	65.424930	-157.55754	207.73391
d[WGM]	-0.000455	0.004186	-0.01389	0.01159
d[SWF]	0.000015	0.008529	-0.03218	0.02439
d[JAY]	-0.001275	0.006236	-0.02918	0.01715
d[UKP]	-0.000198	0.004318	-0.01230	0.01478
Period II - October 11, 1979 to October 12, 1982 (155 Observations)				
UM	0.220645	2.192303	-4.80000	8.90000
EM	0.178065	1.351828	-4.20000	6.50000
d[1MTB]	-0.755773	3.503227	-12.58993	12.65973
d[3MTB]	-1.490954	9.526670	-32.97593	23.04186
d[6MTB]	-3.038385	18.576201	-61.37919	42.01453
d[7YB]	-11.772091	96.979402	-348.95406	252.22290
d[30YB]	-25.077634	138.705840	-431.39669	387.89256
d[SP500]	-19.668918	107.885065	-304.00663	270.97205
d[WGM]	-0.000994	0.008164	-0.02171	0.02282
d[SWF]	-0.000460	0.008790	-0.02165	0.02198
d[JAY]	0.000061	0.008066	-0.02279	0.02147
d[UKP]	-0.000438	0.006770	-0.02569	0.01668
Period III - October 18, 1982 - January 3, 1984 (62 Observations)				
UM	0.396774	2.006217	-3.30000	4.90000
EM	0.700000	1.684549	-3.00000	6.80000
d[1MTB]	-0.356585	0.822506	-3.37628	0.85161
d[3MTB]	-0.341790	2.709872	-6.98822	5.51410
d[6MTB]	-0.655195	6.076504	-16.70726	10.79762
d[7YB]	-5.300406	54.816535	-139.97298	114.83598
d[30YB]	-2.214615	93.419241	-210.89142	188.97718
d[SP500]	-11.679285	122.003036	-404.65458	321.02268
d[WGM]	-0.001170	0.006238	-0.01474	0.00923
d[SWF]	-0.000937	0.007273	-0.02008	0.01327
d[JAY]	-0.000194	0.007405	-0.02003	0.01596
d[UKP]	-0.000435	0.007027	-0.02380	0.01188

Example

Wolfe, B.L. and J.R. Behrman [1982] "Determinants of Child Mortality, Health, and Nutrition in a Developing Country", Journal of Development Economics, 11:163-193.

Wolfe, B.L. and J.R. Behrman [1984]

Wolfe, B.L. and J.R. Behrman [1986] "Child Quantity and Quality in a Developing Country: Family Background, Endogenous Tastes, and Biological Supply Factors", Economic Development and Cultural Change, 34:703-720.

World Bank [1980] Health Sector Policy Paper, pp.5-43.

World Bank [1987] Philippines: A Framework for Economic Recovery. Washington D.C.: The World Bank.

World Bank [1987a] World Development Report 1987. New York: Oxford University Press.

World Bank [1988] World Development Report 1988. New York: Oxford University Press.

World Bank [1989] World Development Report 1989. New York: Oxford University Press.

World Health Organization [1985] The Quantity and Quality of Breast Milk. Geneva: World Health Organization.

Worthington-Roberts, B. and S.R. Williams [1989] Nutrition in Pregnancy and Lactation. St. Louis: Times Mirror/Mosby.

Ybanez-Gonzalo, S. and R. Evenson [1978] "The Production and Consumption of Nutrients in Laguna Households: An Exploratory Analysis", The Philippine Economic Journal, 17:136-153.

U&G

THE UNIVERSITY OF NEW SOUTH WALES

SCHOOL OF ECONOMICS

15.173 ECONOMIC METHODOLOGY

SESSION 2, 1990

JOHN LODEWIJKS

ABOUT THE SUBJECT:

This subject covers the methodology of classical and modern economics (including views on the application of the philosophy of science literature to economics) and of applied econometrics.

Themes considered will include some of the major issues in macro theory, classical and neoclassical value and distribution theory and equilibrium analysis.

Dr. John Lodewijks is the lecturer-in-charge and can be found in JG 312 (ext. 3386). Dr. Eric Sowey can be found in JG 252 (ext. 3319).

ASSESSMENT:

Assessment will consist of a final exam (50%), two seminar papers (40%) and seminar participation (10%). The two seminar papers should be approximately 2000 words each.

TEXT:

Bruce Caldwell (ed), **Appraisal and Criticism in Economics**, 1984.

The following two books are also highly recommended:

Mark Blaug, **The Methodology of Economics**, 1980.
Arjo Klamer, **Conversations with Economists**, 1983, (published in the U.K. under the title **The New Classical Macroeconomics**, 1984).

THE VALUE OF A SEMINAR:

Especially valuable skills you can acquire as a student are the capacities (a) to read critically, (b) to gather information and analyze and present it in oral and written form and (c) to contribute effectively to an organized discussion. These skills can be developed in preparing for and participating in a seminar.

Unlike a lecture class, a seminar necessarily requires regular attendance and active participation. You will be asked specifically to lead the discussion during the session, but in addition you will be expected to take a constructive and informed part in the discussion at every meeting.

You should prepare yourself for each meeting by reading and thinking about the material and having ready both observations and questions that occur to you.

A SHORT LIST OF BOOKS ON ECONOMIC METHODOLOGY:

It will be be useful to refer to these books regularly during the session.

B. Caldwell, **Beyond Positivism**, 1982.

L. Boland, **The Foundations of Economic Method**, 1982.

F. Hahn and M. Hollis (ed), **Philosophy and Economic Theory**, 1979.

D.M. Hausman (ed), **The Philosophy of Economics**, 1984.

W. Marr and B. Raj (eds), **How Economists Explain**, 1983.

F. Machlup, **Methodology of Economics and other Social Sciences**, 1978.

S.R. Krupp (ed), **The Structure of Economic Science**, 1966.

T.C. Koopmans, **Three Essays on the State of Economic Science**, 1957.

J.C. Pitt (ed), **Philosophy in Economics**, 1981.

H. Katouzian, **Ideology and Method in Economics**, 1980.

G.L. Johnson, **Research Methodology for Economists**, 1986.

H.K.H. Woo, **What's Wrong with Formalization in Economics?** 1986

Methodus, Bulletin of the International Network for Economic Method, first issue December 1989.

A.W. Coats, The Methodology of Economics, **Kyklos**, 1982, pp. 310-321 and Economic Methodology, **Kyklos**, 1986, pp.109-115

LECTURE PROGRAM

Weeks 1 - 3

Methodological Discussions in Economics: An Introduction

1. What economic methodology is about: (i) Mill, Keynes, Robbins, Friedman, Blaug (ii) Science, hypothesis testing, positivism, conventionalism, instrumentalism, rhetoric, assumptions, rational economic man, positive-normative distinctions.

Reading:

I.M.T. Stewart, **Reasoning and Method in Economics**, 1979.

Mark Blaug, **The Methodology of Economics**, 1980. Ch. 1-5,15.

_____, 1980, Economic Methodology in One Easy Lesson, in M. Blaug, **Economic History and the History of Economics**, Wheatsheaf Sussex 1986 pp.265-279

D. M. Hausman, Economic Methodology in a Nutshell, **Journal of Economic Perspectives**, 3 (2), Spring 1989 pp.115-127

Bruce Caldwell, (ed) **Appraisal and Criticism in Economics**, Ch. 1-2.

2. Application of the Philosophy of Science to Economics - Popper, Kuhn and Lakatos.

Reading:

M. Blaug, *Kuhn versus Lakatos, or Paradigms versus Research Programmes in the History of Economics*, **HOPE**, 7:4 1975 pp. 399-433.

C. Goodwin, *Toward a Theory of the History of Economics*, **HOPE**, 12:4 1980 pp. 610-619.

Additional References:

Thomas S. Kuhn, **The Structure of Scientific Revolutions**, 1970.

Imre Lakatos and Alan Musgrave (eds), **Criticism and the Growth of Knowledge**, 1970.

Imre Lakatos, **The Methodology of Scientific Research Programmes**, Vol. I 1978.

B. J. Heijdra & A. D. Lowenberg, *The Neoclassical Economic Research Program: Some Lakatosian and Other Considerations*, **Australian Economic Papers**, Vol. 27 No. 51 December 1988 pp. 272-284

3. Is there a 'crisis' in economics? Do economists really matter? How can methodologists help?

Reading:

D. Colander and A.W. Coats (eds.) **The Spread of Economic Ideas**, Cambridge University Press 1989. Chapters by Clower and Colander

G. Stigler, *Do Economists Matter?*, **Southern Economic Journal**, 42:3 1976 pp. 347-354.

A.W. Coats, *Research Priorities in the History of Economics*, **HOPE**, 1:1 1969 pp. 9-18.

Weeks 4 - 6

Microeconomic Theory

1. Introduction

Reading:

Martin Shubik, *A Curmudgeon's Guide to Microeconomics*, **Journal of Economic Literature**, 8, June 1970 pp. 405-434.

2. English Classical Political Economy and the Marginal Revolution.

Reading:

Collison-Black, R.D. et. al. **The Marginal Revolution in Economics**, 1972 (articles by Blaug, Hutchison, Meek, Shackle and Coats).

M. Blaug, **Economic Theory in Retrospect**, 1985, *Ricardo's System, The Marginal Revolution*, and *General Equilibrium and Welfare Economics*.

P. Deane, **The Evolution of Economic Ideas**, 1978, Ch. 5 - 8.

Additional References:

M. Hollis and E. Nell, **Rational Economic Man**, 1975.

T.W. Hutchison, **A Review of Economic Doctrines: 1870-1929**, 1953.

G.L.S. Shackle, **The Years of High Theory**, 1967.

V. Walsh and H. Gramm, **Classical and Neoclassical Theories of General Equilibrium**, 1980.

Vivian Walsh, **Introduction to Contemporary Microeconomics**, 1970 (A fascinating "history" of micro theory from cardinal utility to modern axiomatic approaches).

Stanley Wong, **The Foundation of Paul Samuelson's Revealed Preference Theory**, 1978.

Elster, Jon, **Explaining Technical change: A Case Study in the Philosophy of Science**, Cambridge: CUP 1983 Part II

3. The Appraisal of General-Equilibrium Analysis.

Reading:

E.R. Weintraub, *Appraising General Equilibrium Analysis*, **Economics and Philosophy**, 1:1, April, 1985.

Additional References:

E.R. Weintraub, **General Equilibrium Analysis: Studies in Appraisal**, 1985.

_____, **General Equilibrium Theory**, 1974.

_____, **Microfoundations**, 1979.

_____, *The NeoWalrasian Program is Empirically Progressive*, in N. De Marchi, **The Popperian Legacy in Economics**, Cambridge University Press 1988 pp. 213-230.

_____, **Stabilizing Economic Knowledge**, Cambridge University Press. forthcoming, Chapters 3,4,9 & 10

Frank Hahn, *On the Notion of Equilibrium in Economics*, 1973; *The Winter of Our Discontent*, 1973; and *General Equilibrium Theory*, 1981, all reprinted in **Equilibrium and Macroeconomics** Blackwell: Oxford 1984.

D.M. Hausman, **Capital, Profits and Prices** 1981, Ch. 6-7.

_____, *Are General-Equilibrium Theories Explanatory?*, in his **The Philosophy of Economics**, 1984 pp. 344-359.

W.J. Samuels, *Roy Weintraub's* **Microfoundations**: *The State of High Theory*, **Journal of Economic Issues**, 13:4, December 1979 pp. 1019-1028.

A. Rosenberg, **Microeconomic Laws: A Philosophical Analysis** 1976.

Janos Kornai, **Anti-equilibrium**, 1971, Ch. 1-3, 25.

N. Kaldor, **Further Essays on Economic Theory**, 1978 Ch. 7 *The Irrelevance of Equilibrium Economics*, and Ch. 8 *What is Wrong with Economic Theory*. There is now a book by Kaldor entitled **Economics Without Equilibrium**, Sharpe, New York 1985. Also of interest is Kaldor's *Limitations of the* **General Theory**, Keynes Lecture in Economics 1982, Oxford University Press, and *Keynesian Economics after Fifty Years*, in David Worswick and James Trevithick (ed) **Keynes and the Modern World**, Cambridge University Press 1983.

J. Robinson, *History versus Equilibrium*, in her **Collected Economic Papers**, Vol. 5, 1979, pp. 48-58.

Negishi, T. **Economic Theories in a non-Walrasian Tradition**, Cambridge 1985. See also the review of this and Weintraub (1985) by Larry Boland in **HOPE**, 19.4, 1987, pp.659-666.

M. Shubik, *The General Equilibrium Model is Incomplete* ... **Kyklos** Vol. 28 1975 pp. 545-573

B. Heijdra and A. D. Lowenberg, "The Neoclassical Economic Research Program" **Australian Economic Papers** 27 (51) December 1988 pp.272-284.

L. Boland, **Methodology for a New Microeconomics**, 1985.

Roemer, J. **Analytical Foundations of Marxian Economic Theory**, Cambridge: CUP 1981

For those interested in the historical development of models of general equilibrium see Don Walker "A Primer on Walrasian Theories of Economic Behaviour" American **History of Economics Society Bulletin**, 11.(1). Spring 1989 pp.1-24 and Roy Weintruab "On the Existence of a Competitive Equilibrium: 1930-54" **Journal of Economic Literature**, 21, March 1983 pp. 1-39.

Weeks 7 - 10

Macroeconomic Theory

1. Macroeconomics from the 1930's through to the present. Topics include macro textbook "histories", classical macro, business cycle research, Keynes,

Hansen seminar, Cowles versus NBER, Klein's macroeconometric models and contemporary developments.

2. The methodology of Arthur M. Okun.

3. The new classical macroeconomics and real business cycle theory.

Reading:

A. Klamer, **Conversations with Economists**, 1983.

A. Leijonhufvud, *Schools, 'Revolutions' and Research Programmes in Economic Theory*, in S.J. Latsis (ed), **Method and Appraisal in Economics**, 1976, pp. 65-108.

B. Caldwell, 1984 (Cross, Weintraub, Dow and Brown)

Lodewijks, J. 1988. *Arthur Okun and the Lucasian Critique* **Australian Economic Papers**, 27 (51) pp.253-271; *Arthur M. Okun : Economics for Policymaking*, **Journal of Economic Surveys**, 2(3) 1988 pp.245-264; *Arthur Okun's Contribution To the Macroeconomic policy debates*, **Economic Analysis and policy** 19(2) Sept. 1989 pp.141-166; *Macroeconometric Models and the Methodology of Macroeconomics*, **American History of Economics Society Bulletin**, 11(1) Spring 1989 pp.33-58.

Additional References:

S.C. Dow, **Macroeconomic Thought: A Methodological Approach**, 1985.

R. Lucas, *Methods and Problems in Business Cycle Theory*, in **Studies in Business-Cycle Theory**, 1981, pp.271-296.

A. Klamer, *Levels of Discourse in New Classical Economics*, and R.Maddock, *Rational Expectations Macrotheory*, in **HOPE**, 16:2, 1984, pp.263-309.

R. Maddock and M. Carter, *A Child's Guide to Rational Expectations*, **Journal of Economic Literature**, March 1982, pp.39-51.

S.J. Kamath, 1987, *A Rational Reconstruction of the Rational Expectations Revolution*, in **History of Economics Society**, 14th Annual Meeting, Harvard, June

G. Barrett, *Equilibrium Business Cycle theory in Historical Perspective*, **HETSA Bulletin**, 10. Summer 1988 pp.24-29

J. Rotemberg, *The New Keynesian Microfoundations*, **NBER Macroeconomics Annual** 1987 pp. 69-116

C.I. Plosser, *Understanding Real Business Cycles*, and N.G. Mankiw, *Real Business Cycles: A New Keynesian Perspective*, in **Journal Of Economic Perspectives**, 3(3) Summer 1989 pp. 51-90

A.S. Blinder, *The Fall and Rise of Keynesian Economics*, Invited Paper, 1988 Australian Economics Congress, Canberra.

R.H. Nelson, *The Economics Profession and the Making of Public Policy*, **Journal of Economic Literature**, Vol. 25 March 1987 pp. 49-91.

H. Aaron, *Politics and the Professors Revisited*, **AER** 79 (2) May 1989 pp. 1-15

WEEKS 11 - 13

ECONOMETRICS

1. The Promise of Econometrics

G. Stigler, *The Politics of Political Economists*, **QJE**, 73, 1959, 522-532.

W. Leeman, *The Status of Facts in Economic Thought*, **J. of Philosophy**, 48, 1951, 401-413.

I.M. Stewart, *Sense and Nonsense in Econometrics*, Ch. 9 in his **Reasoning and Method in Economics**, McGraw-Hill, 1979.

M.K. Evans, *Econometric Models*, pp. 161-189 in W.F. Butler, R.A. Kavesh and R.B. Platt (eds) **Methods and Techniques of Business Forecasting**, Prentice-Hall, 1974

L.R. Klein, *Whither Econometrics?*, **J.A.S.A.**, 66, 1971, 415-421.

G.C. Archibald, *Refutation or Comparison?*, **British J. for the Philosophy of Science**, 17, 1966, 279-296.

V.J. Tarascio and B. Caldwell, *Theory Choice in Economics: Philosophy and Practice*, **J. Economic Issues**, 13, 1979, 983-1006.

2. The Problems of Econometrics

T. Mayer, *Economics as a Hard Science: Realistic Goal or Wishful Thinking?*, **Economic Inquiry**, 18, 1980, 165-178.

J. Kmenta, *Summary of the Discussion*, pp. 262-284 in K. Brunner (ed), **Problems and Issues in Current Econometric Practice**, Ohio State Univ. Press, 1972.

H.T. Shapiro, *Is Verification Possible?*, The Evaluation of Large Econometric Models, **American Journal Agricultural Economics**, May 1973, 250-258. With discussion, 271-279.

A.M. Okun, *Uses of Models for Policy Formulation*, Ch. 8 in G. Fromm and L.R. Klein (eds), **The Brookings Model - Perspectives and Future Developments**, North-Holland, 1975.

3. The Performance of Econometrics

L. Thurow, *Econometrics: An Icebreaker Caught in the Ice*, Ch. 4 in his **Dangerous Currents: The State of Economics**, O.U.P. 1983.

C.K. Wilber, *Empirical Verification and Theory Selection*, **J. Economic Issues**, 13, 1979, 973-982.

W. Leontief, *Theoretical Assumptions and Nonobserved Facts*, **AER**, March 1971, 1-7.

G.D.N. Worswick, *Is Progress in Economic Science Possible?*, **Economic Journal**, 82, 1972, 73-86.

D.A. Belsley and E. Kuh, *Comment* (on a paper by Zellner), **J.A.S.A.**, 74, 1979 643-645.

E.E. Leamer, *Let's Take the Con Out of Econometrics*, **AER**, March 1983, 31-43. Reprinted in Caldwell, 1984. See also *Interpreting Leamer* by C. Glymour and *Self-Interpretation* by E. Leamer in **Economics and Philosophy**, Vol. 1 1985 pp.290-302.

M.H. Peston, *Economics and Quantitative Economics: A Defence*, **Omega**, 2, 1974, 147-156.

D.F. Hendry, *Econometrics - Alchemy or Science?*, **Economica**, 47, 1980, 387-406.

Week 14

Epilogue

Reading:

R.L. Heilbroner, *Modern Economics as a Chapter in HET*, **HOPE**, 11:2, 1979, pp.192-198.

A. Leijonhufvud, *Life among the Econ*, **Western Economic Journal**, 11:3, September 1973, pp.327-337.

SEMINAR PROGRAM

Week 2

(A) **Is there a 'crisis' in Economics?**

References:

T.W. Hutchison, **Knowledge and Ignorance in Economics**, 1977, Introduction, chapter 4.

E.H. Phelps Brown, *The Underdevelopment of Economics*, **Economic Journal**, March 1972, pp.1-10.

G.D.N. Worswick, *Is Progress in Economic Science Possible?*, **Economic Journal**, 1972, pp.73-86.

W. Leontief, *Theoretical Assumptions and Non-observed Facts*, **AER**, 1971, pp.1-7. (Update in **Journal of Economic Perspectives** 2 (4) Fall 1988 pp.159-164).

D. Bell and I. Kristol (ed), **The Crisis in Economic Theory**, 1981.

T. Morgan, *Theory versus Empiricism in Academic Economics*, **Journal of Economic Perspectives**, Vol.2 No.4 Fall 1988 pp.159-164.

(B) **A Critical Appraisal of Mark Blaug, The Methodology of Economics**, 1980, chs 6-14.

References:

D. Hands, *Blaug's Economic Methodology*, **Philosophy of the Social Sciences**, 14, 1984, pp.115-125. See also Caldwell's review in **Southern Economic Journal**, July 1981, pp.242-245 and Blaug's review of Caldwell pp.30-36 in P. Wiles and G. Routh, **Economics in Disarray**, Blackwell, Oxford 1984.

Week 3 - **The Sociology of Knowledge Approach to Economics**

References:

D. Colander and A. Klamer, 1987, *The Making of an Economist*, **Economic Perspectives**, Vol.1. No.2, Fall pp.95-111

D. Colander and A.W. Coats, **The Spread of Economic Ideas**, op. cit., Part IV

P.E. Earl. 1983. *A Behavioral Theory of Economist's Behavior*, in A.S. Eichner (ed), **Why Economics is not yet a Science**, Macmillan, London pp.90-125

C.A. Garner, 1979, *Academic Publication, Market Signaling, and Scientific Research Decisions*, **Economic Inquiry**, 17, Oct., pp.575-584

H.G. Grubel and L.A. Boland, 1986, *On the Efficient Use of Mathematics in Economics*, **Kyklos**, 39, pp.419-442

H. Katouzian, 1980, *Big Science versus Great Science*, **Ideology and Method in Economics**, Macmillan, London, Chap.5

R. Whitley, 1984, **The Intellectual and Social Organization of the Sciences**, Clarendon, Oxford, particularly Ch. 6. See also by the same author *The Rise of Modern Finance Theory* and *The Structure and Context of Economics as a Scientific Field* in **Research in the History of Economic thought and Methodology**, Vol. 4 1986 pp.147-209. Also useful is the paper by Tarascio in the same issue.

A.W. Coats, *The Sociology of Knowledge and the History of Economics*, in **Research in the History of Economic Thought and Methodology**, Vol. 2 1984 pp.211-234

R. Leonard, *To Advance Human Welfare: Economics and the Ford Foundation*, in **Proceedings** of the 16th Annual History of Economics Society Meeting, Richmond, Virginia June 1989 Vol I.

T.W. Schultz, *Distortions of Economic Research*, in W.H. Kruskal (ed.) **The Social Sciences: Their Nature and Uses**, University of Chicago press, Chicago 1982 pp.121-133

Week 4 - **Friedman's Methodology of Positive Economics**

References:

B. Caldwell (ed), **Appraisal and Criticism in Economics**, 1984, Chs 3,4,5.

M. Blaug, **The Methodology of Economics**, 1980, Ch.12.

A. Hirsch and N. de Marchi, *American Pragmatic Instrumentalism and the Methodology of Positive Economics*, **Mimeo**, 1984. Also their article *Making a Case when Theory is Unfalsifiable: Friedman's Monetary History*, **Economics and Philosophy**, 2:1.

R.H. Coase, **How Should Economists Choose?**, 1982.

W.L. Marr and B. Raj (eds), **How Economists Explain**, 1983, Chs 5-7.

B. Caldwell, **Beyond Positivism**, 1982, Chs 8-9.

A. Rosenberg, **Microeconomic Laws**, 1976, Ch.7.

_____, *Friedman's Methodology for Economics: A Critical Examination*, **Philosophy of the Social Sciences** 2, 1972, pp.15-29.

D. Hammond, 1987, *Realism in Friedman's* **Essays in Positive Economics**, **mimeo**; *Wesley Mitchell as Harbinger of Friedman's Method*, **mimeo**; and *How Different are Hicks and Friedman on Method?*, **Oxford Economic Papers**, June 1988.

Week 5 - **A Critical Appraisal of G. Tullock and R.B. McKenzie, The New World of Economics, 1985.**

Reference:

L.H. Officer and L. Stiefel, *The New World of Economics*, **Journal of Economic Issues** 10.1 1976, pp. 149-158.

G. Becker, *Economic Analysis and Human Behaviour*, in L. Levy-Garboua, **Sociological Economics**, 1979, pp. 7-24.

G. Becker, **A Treatise on the Family**, Harvard University press, Cambridge, 1981

R.B. McKenzie, **The Limits of Economic Science**, 1983, Chs. 1-3.

A. M. Diamond, *Unusual Applications of price theory*, **American economist**, 32 (1) Spring 1988 pp. 78-79

Week 6 - **Classical and Neoclassical Value Theory: Much the Same or Radically Different?**

References:

S. Hollander, **The Economics of Smith** (1973), **Ricardo** (1979) and **Mill** (1985). Summarized in part in *Smith and Ricardo: Aspects of the Nineteenth Century Legacy*, **American Economic Review**, 67:1, Feb. 1977, pp. 37-41. See the reviews by O'Brien, **Oxford Economic Papers**, 33:3, 1981 (replies and rejoinders in Vol.34 No.1), Peach, **Economic Journal**, March, 1981, Stigler, **Journal of Economic Literature**, March, 1981, Thweatt **H.O.P.E.**, 12:4, 1980, and Coats, **The Manchester School ...**, No.3, Sept. 1987. There is also now available Hollander's, **Classical Economics** Oxford: Blackwell, 1987.

P. Mirowski, **More Heat than Light**, Cambridge University Press, New York 1990 chapters 5-7

D.P. O'Brien, **The Classical Economists**, 1975, pp. 53-74, 272-293.

J.R. Hicks, *'Revolutions' in Economics*, in Spiro J. Latsis, **Method and Appraisal in Economics**, 1976.

D.M. Hausman, **Capital, Profits and Prices**, 1981, Chs. 1-3.

E.K. Hunt and J.G. Schwartz, **A Critique of Economic Theory**, 1972, chs. 1-2.

R.V. Eagly, **The Structure of Classical Economic Theory**, 1974, Ch. 7.

P. Mirowski, 1984, *Physics and the Marginalist Revolution*, **Cambridge Journal of Economics**, Dec. pp.361-379.

R. Fisher, 1986, **The Logic Of Economic Discovery: Neoclassical Economics and the Marginal Revolution**, Wheatsheaf.

Week 7 - **A Critical Appraisal of E.R. Weintraub, General Equilibrium Analysis: Studies in Appraisal, 1985.**

References:

A. Rosenberrg, 1986, *Lakatosian Consolations for Economics*, **Economics and Philosophy**, 2, pp. 127-139 (Reply and Rejoinder in Vol.3, pp.139-144)

A.Salanti, 1987, *Roy Weintraub's* **Studies in Appraisal**, **History of Economics Society** Annual Meeting, June. Vol.4

E.R. Weintraub, 1985, *Joan Robinson's Critique of Equilibrium: An Appraisal*, **AER**, May, pp.146-149

Week 8 - **Chicago Economics - Tight Prior Equilibrium?**

References:

M.W. Reder, *Chicago Economics: Permanence and Change*, **Journal of Economic Literature**, March 1982, pp. 1-38. Reprinted in Caldwell 1984.

W.J. Samuels (ed), **The Chicago School of Political Economy**, 1976.

H.L. Miller, *On the Chicago School of Economics*, **Journal of Political Economy**, February 1962, pp. 64-69.

G. Stigler, **Memoirs of an Unregulated Economist**, New York: Basic 1988. Chapters 8, 10 & 13

Week 9 - Since a public holiday falls on the Monday of this week, we will have the **Lecture on Thursday** and skip a seminar.

Week 10 - **The Rhetoric of Economics?**

References:

A. Klamer, **Conversations with Economists**, 1983.

D.N. McCloskey, *The Rhetoric of Economics*, **Journal of Economic Literature**, June 1983, pp. 481-517. Reprinted in Caldwell 1984. There is also now a book by McCloskey, **The Rhetoric of Economics**, Wisconsin 1985. See the review of the article by Caldwell and Coats, **Journal of Economic Literature**, June, 1984.

A. Rosenberg, *"Economics is Too Important to be left to the Rhetoricians"*, **Economics and Philosophy**, Vol.4 No.1, 1988 pp.129-149 & 173-175.

P. Mirowski, 1987, *Shall I Compare thee to a Minkowski-Ricardo-Leontief-Metzler Matrix of the Mosak-Hicks Type?*, **Economics and Philosophy** 3 pp.67-96

A. Klamer, D. McCloskey and R. Solow, **The Consequences of Economic Rhetoric**, Cambridge University Press, Cambridge 1988. Particularly chapters 1, 3, 6, 7 & 11.

Week 11 - **Alternative Approaches to Macroeconomics?**

Reference:

S.C. Dow, **Macroeconomic Thought: A Methodological Approach**, 1985. An early version of the book is in Dow's *Schools of thought in Macroeconomics: The Method is the Message*, **Australian Economic**

Papers, June 1983, pp. 30-46. See also the articles by Dow, Weintraub, and Brown in Caldwell 1984 and the reviews of Dow in **Research in the History of Economic Thought and Methodology**, 6, 1989 by Lodewijks and Shapiro.

Week 12 - **Discussion of G.C. Archibald, Refutation or Comparison?** (1966).

Week 13 - **Discussion of T. Mayer, Economics as a Hard Science: Realistic Goal or Wishful Thinking?** (1980).

Week 14 - **Discussion of L. Thurow** (1983) **and G.D.N. Worswick** (1972).
See Week 9 reading list.

THE UNIVERSITY OF NEW SOUTH WALES
SCHOOL OF ECONOMICS
SESSION 2, 1988

15.173 ECONOMIC METHODOLOGY

Time allowed - 3 hours
There are seven (7) questions in total.
Answer any four (4) questions
All questions are of equal value
No examination materials may be taken into the examination room
This paper may be retained by the candidate

1. "Methodological pluralism ... seems to be tantamount to the abandonment of all standards, indeed the abandonment of methodology itself as a discipline of study. If all methodological views are equally legitimate, it is difficult to see what sort of theorizing is ever excluded. Can we really say nothing to appraise competing research programmes except that "anything goes" in methodology? Are there no minimum standards which we may demand of any species of economics claiming to be scientific? **Methodological pluralism**, I would contend, is a sham, an excuse for never making any final judgements about competing theories."

Mark Blaug (1984)

Bruce Caldwell in his Beyond Positivism has advocated that economic methodologists should follow a program of "methodological pluralism" because he believes that "no universally applicable, logically compelling method of theory appraisal exists". Clearly Blaug does not agree. Where do you stand on this issue? What role do you then see the economic methodologist playing? How would you go about appraising theories?

2. Outline and discuss the assault on neoclassical economic theory provided by either Keynes or the Cambridge Capital debates. What has been the response of the mainstream to these assaults and what methodological lessons do we learn from either episode?

3. "In discussion of economic science, "Chicago" stands for an approach that takes seriously the use of economic theory as a tool for analyzing a startlingly wide range of concrete problems, rather than as an abstract mathematical structure of great beauty but little power; for an approach that insists on the empirical testing of theoretical generalizations and that rejects alike facts without theory and theory without facts".

Milton Friedman

Discuss the distinctive features of the "Chicago" School approach to economics and try to account for its pervasive influence on modern economics.

4. "In short, macroeconomics has yet to come of age. The closeness of macroeconomists to policy problems makes them often impatient of the abstractions of the theorist. Their finger is always on the trigger. There is something in the nature of this sort of enquiry which leads people to take shortcuts, make exaggerated claims, and attach far too much significance to prediction at the expense of understanding. The result has been surveyed by Klamer."

Frank Hahn (1986)

Discuss Hahn's statement. Do you agree? In answering this question compare and contrast the development of micro-and macroeconomics.

5. "What is it that has so enthused a whole younger generation of economists about the rational expectations assumption? The answer is plain. Make that assumption, and a whole set of problems in dynamic analysis that were previously messy or downright intractable can be made to yield interesting, suggestive and testable solutions. I imagine that a similar excitement was felt many years ago by economists using the principles of optimization and the marginal calculus for the first time."

Patrick Minford (1986)

Discuss. Do you see any parallels between the rational expectations "revolution" of today and the Marginal "revolution" of the 1870s?

OR

" the ascendancy of new classicism in academia was instead a triumph of a priori theorizing over empiricism, of intellectual aesthetics over observation, and, in some measure, of conservative ideology over liberalism."

Alan Blinder (1988)

How can the fall of Keynesian economics, and its apparent resurrection, at least according to Blinder, be explained?

6. "One might say that the biggest challenge facing econometrics is to persuade its enemies that it has some virtues, without at the same time persuading its friends that it has no limitations."

Carl Christ (1967)

What criticisms might enemies of the econometric approach make about the subject today, i.e. in 1988?

Assess each criticism you mention for its methodological significance to economics. Is each one in your opinion a valid criticism?

7. "If economics is a science ... it is evidently a science whose powers of prediction and control are limited, largely because the phenomena it seeks to explain are subject to persistent change and often for reasons that may lie outside the traditional boundaries of the discipline."

Phyllis Deane (1983)

Discuss the proposition in this quotation from the perspective of the econometrician.

Give examples from the literature of macro- and/or microeconomics that illustrate the points of your discussion.

THE UNIVERSITY OF NEW SOUTH WALES
SCHOOL OF ECONOMICS
SESSION 2, 1987

15.173 ECONOMIC METHODOLOGY

1. "In the long run, the economic scholar works for the only coin worth having - our own applause."

    P. A. Samuelson (1961)

    Discuss how the incentive structure in the profession influences the nature and direction of research in economics.

    OR

    "Has it not really been one of the great sources of weakness in economics that people have been content with plausible speculations, attractively presented, instead of insisting upon putting their ideas to the final test of correspondence with facts as they are known and working out modifications or realigning the whole discussion when the speculations and the facts seem out of balance?"

    W. C. Mitchell (1910)

    Discuss. Use the work of particular economists to support your statements.

2. Roy Weintraub has alleged that GE reasoning is central to all economic analysis which lays claim to being scientific. Why does he regard GE analysis as the centerpiece of the discipline of economics? How might one appraise work in this tradition? What are the difficulties?

3. Is there a 'Chicago' school?

    If so, describe and analyze its distinctive methodological approach to the study of economics. What has been its influence and impact on modern economics?

4. "... a theory is only overthrown by a better theory, never merely by contradictory facts."

    J. B. Conant, On Understanding Science. 1947

    What line of thought would an economist see behind this conclusion?

    If Conant's conclusion applied to economics, what role can econometrics have in the evolution of economic principles?

    Looking at the field of macroeconomics since 1950, do you think Conant is right?

5. "... the most powerful policy advocacy of economists often involves the marshalling of information that makes a case forcefully. However, it is usually simple data, rather than sophisticated econometric studies, that are most influential. Responsible officials are frequently skeptical of empirical analyses that they cannot understand and evaluate themselves and may well dismiss them. In general, (economists) hoping to have a significant influence on policy must design arguments that directly persuade ....".

    R.H. Nelson, The economics profession and the making of public policy. 1987

    Why might a policy proposal supported by an apt econometric analysis not be persuasive even if the "responsible officials" understood the analysis?

    Should economists nevertheless use "sophisticated econometric studies" to lay the foundation for their policy advice?

    Do you think skepticism towards the results of a well conducted applied econometric study is justified?

6. Present a methodological appraisal of the Rational Expectations 'Revolution' in economics.

7. Why and how has macroeconomic thought developed differently from microeconomics? Use a number of specific case studies to illustrate your views.

Orientation to Economic Research

G

T. Mayer Econ. 280 Winter 1989
University of California, Davis
Readings

TEXTS

George Ladd, "Imagination in Research". For the methodology "section" also: M. Blaugh, The Methodology of Economics

RECOMMENDED READINGS

Methodology

B. Caldwell, Beyond Positivism

M. Friedman, Essays in Positive Economics, Ch. 1.

L. Boland " A Critique of Friedman's Critics", JEL, June, 1979

A. Musgrave, "'Unreal Assumptions' in Economic Theory: The F Twist Untwisted," Kyklos, 1981, # 3.

D. McClosky, The Rhetoric of Economics (For a brief version see his paper with the same title in the June 1983 JEL)

R. Cross, " The Duhem-Quine Thesis, Lakatos and the Appraisal of Theories..." E.J. June 1982.

Note: watch for papers in Philosophy and Economics

General Background

Beveridge, I. The Art of Scientific Research

A. Klamer, Conversations with Economists

E. Prewill, " How CEO's Manage their Time", Fortune, Jan. 18, 1988 (to top of p. 96 only)

G. Frank " Goal Ambiguity and Conflicting Standards..." Human Organization Winter 1958

R. Penaskovik, "Facing Up to the Publication Gun," Scholarly Publishing,, January 1985.

Luey, Beth, Handbook for Academic Authors

G. Stigler, "Do Economists Matter?" Journal of Economic Issues, Jan. 1976

M. Mahoney, Scientists as Subjects

P. Medawar, Advice to a Young Scientist

Locating Literature

D. Ekwurzel and B. Saffran, " Online Information Retrieval for Economists," JEL, Dec. 1985

Uses of Data and Empirical testing

J. Morton, " A Student's Guide to American Federal Government Statistics," JEL, June 1972.

A. Kamark, Economics and Reality

O. Morgenstern, On the Accuracy of Economic Observations

M. Friedman A Theory of the Consumption Function

T. Mayer Permanent Income, Wealth and Consumption

Writing

A. Vandermeulen, " How to Fabricate an Article," American Economist

D. McClosky, " Economical Writing," Economic Inquiry, April 1985

H. Becker, Writing for Social Scientists

W. Salant, " Writing and Reading in Economics," JPE July/August, 1969

R. Minghell and E Lane "Writing and the Economic Researcher," Agricultural Economics Research , Jan. 1973.

Note: I will place a file with some light pieces on writing on reserve.

Economics 7000
History of Economic Thought
Fall 1989

University of Colorado
SYLLABUS

G
Professor Mott
Office: Econ 102
Hours: MTW 2:30-3:30 p.m.

"(I)t seems that economic science has not yet solved its first problem--what determines the price of a commodity?"

Joan Robinson, An Essay on Marxian Economics, p. 79

This course is designed to cover certain topics in the history of economic thought. This of course is a very broad subject, and so to handle it during one semester we will have to confine ourselves to dealing with only one or two areas of concern in depth, touching lightly on a few others, and ignoring many topics, which hopefully if they are of concern to people will be able to be treated independently with the help of the material we study here and in other courses. We will start by considering some fundamental issues in philosophy of science and in defining the subject matter and concerns of economics, and then we will investigate the history of thought concerning the working of a capitalist economy, mainly by examining differing schools of thought on the determination of value, distribution, growth, and fluctuations in such an economy. The pace of the course and the depth into which we go on any particular topic will be uneven because of the magnitude of our task. The reading list given below is long and has been chosen with the purpose of covering certain points as economically (believe it or not) as possible (the secondary sources) and of giving you a flavor of the work of certain thinkers (the primary sources). My advice is to read as much as you can without worrying about whether or not you understand it. Some understanding hopefully will come in class and as you do your written assignments; this will come more easily if you have at least looked at the reading assigned.

The assignments requires to receive a grade in the course are three essays plus a final exam. Each essay and the exam count 1/4 of your grade. The essays are not to exceed ten (8 1/2 x 11 inch) pages, including references, and in fact any other extra pages will be thrown away prior to grading. Lateness in the essays will be tolerated but penalized (1/3 of a letter grade off if handed in one week late; 2/3 of a letter off if over one week late). The questions to be answered in the essays are:

#1   Compare and contrast the positivist and the idealist points of view in philosophy. Give the strengths and weaknesses of each. (Due two class days after we finish Topic I.)

#2   What does it take for the labor theory to be an adequate conception of the determination of value in a capitalist economy? (Due two class days after we finish Topic IV.)

#3   What does it take for the utility theory to be an adequate conception of the determination of value in a capitalist economy? (Due on the last day of class.)

All but one of the following books should be available for purchase in the bookstore:

Maurice Dobb, Theories of Value and Distribution Since Adam Smith
Robert Heilbroner, The Essential Adam Smith
David Ricardo, The Principles of Political Economy and Taxation
Piero Sraffa, The Production of Commodities by Means of Commodities
Robert Tucker, The Marx-Engels Reader
George Zinke, The Problem of Malthus: Must Progress End in Overpopulation?

George Zinke's book is out of print but the University of Colorado Press has given me all of its stock, so I can give you a copy of the book.

The divisions of the course and the reading assignments are as follows:

1.   Philosophy and Economics
     Axel Leijonhufvud, "Life Among the Econ"
     Robert Kuttner, "The Poverty of Economics"
     Frederick Copleston, A History of Philosophy, Vol. IV, Introduction
     Daniel Hausman, The Philosophy of Economics, Introduction
     Karl Popper, "Science: Conjectures and Refutations"
     Brian Loasby, "Logic, Evidence, and Belief"

Warren Samuels, "An Essay on the Nature and Significance of the Normative Nature of Economics"
Herbert Marcuse, Reason and Revolution, Preface and pp. 3-29, 91-120, 323-329
David Levine, Economic Theory, Prologue

2. Some Pre-Classical Economics
    Ronald Meek, The Economics of Physiocracy, Introduction and the "Tableau Economique": the "Analysis"
    Shigeto Tsuru, "On Reproduction Schemes"
    Joseph Schumpeter, History of Economic Analysis, Park II, Chap. 7
    Thomas Mun, "England's Treasure by Foreign Trade"
    J.M. Keynes, The General Theory, Chap. 23
    Joan Robinson, "The New Mercantilism"
    Paul Krugman, "Is Free Trade Passé?"

3. Classical Economics
    David Hume, three extracts of Political Discourses
    Dobb, Chaps. 2, 3, 4, 5
    Heilbroner, pp. 57-78, 149-247
    Bernard Mandeville, The Fable of the Bees, Preface and "The Grumbling Hive"
    Lucio Colletti, "Rousseau as Critic of Civil Society" and "Mandeville, Rousseau, and Smith"
    George Gilder, "The Heroes of Growth"
    Zinke, the whole book
    Ricardo, Preface and Chaps. 1-8, 19-21, 26, 30-31
    Sraffa, Preface and Chaps. 1-4, 6, and p. 93

4. Marx
    Dobb, Chap. 6
    Tucker, Introduction and pp. 3-6, 53-65, 143-145, 203-217, 294-465
    Paul Sweezy, The Theory of Capitalist Development, Chaps. 5, 6, 7
    Albert Einstein, "Why Socialism?"
    Josef Steindl, Maturity and Stagnation in American Capitalism, Chap. 14

5. Neoclassical Economics
    Dobb, Chap. 7
    Stanley Jevons, The Theory of Political Economy, Chaps. 1, 2, 3
    Carl Menger, Principles of Economics, Chap. 3
    Eugen von Böhm-Bawerk, Capital and Interest, Vol. II, Book II, Chap. 2, and Book IV, Chap. 1
    Leon Walras, Elements of Pure Economics, Chaps. 1, 3, 10, 11, 12, 16, 18, 20, 35
    William Jaffe, "Menger, Jevons, and Walras Dehomogenized"
    Alfred Marshall, Principles of Economics, Book I, Book V, Chaps. 1-5, 15, Appendix I
    Encyclopedia of Social Science, "Alfred Marshall"
    Peter Dooley, "Alfred Marshall: Fitting the Theory to the Facts"

6. Critiques of the Preceding Theories
    Thorstein Veblen, "The Limitations of Marginal Utility"
    Rona Wilensky, "The Theory of Demand in Marshall and Hicks:
    Levine, Economic Studies, Chaps. 6, 7, and Chap. 8, pp. 249-266
    _____, "Aspects of the Classical Theory of Markets"
    Paul Samuelson, Economics, Appendix to Chap. 30
    Robinson, "The Measure of Capital: The End of the Controversy"
    _____, "Marx and Keynes"
    _____, "Kalecki and Keynes"
    _____, "Marx, Marshall, and Keynes"
    Dobb, Chaps. 8, 9
    Keynes, Chaps. 1, 2, 16
    Friedrich Hayek, "The Use of Knowledge in Society"
    Gerald O'Driscoll, Introduction to the condensed version of The Road to Serfdom

Econ. 7000
Mott
Fall 1989

FINAL EXAM

Answer one question from Part A and one question from Part B. Put each answer in a separate blue book.

Part A

1. Increasing returns to scale serve as a support for Adam Smith's theory of the growth of the wealth of nations, but they also could serve as a support for mercantilism. Discuss, and explain why Smith disagreed with mercantilism.

2. What are the strengths and weaknesses of the partial equilibrium method of Alfred Marshall? What are the strengths and weaknesses of the general equilibrium method of Léon Walras?

Part B

3. The issue of effective demand destroys both the classical and neoclassical value theories. Do you agree or not? Discuss.

4. Classical and neoclassical economics both reduce economics to a natural science rather than treating it as a social science. Do you agree or not? Discuss.

University of Pittsburgh

MARK PERLMAN
Economic Thought I: The History of Economic Thought and Society until 1870

Coverage: The development of economic thought from its patristic origins (Plato, Aristotle, the Church Fathers including Aquinas) through the XVII, XVIII, and first 70 years of the XIX centuries.

The principal divisions are: (a) the Patristic Legacy, (b) Mercantilism and Its Concurrent Philosophical Developments -- Thomas Hobbes and his "successor,", (c) Four System Builders -- Cantillon, Quesnay, Steuart, and Adam Smith, (d) the Era of the Dominance of English Classical Economics including the tensions between the Malthus-Tory advocates of balanced socio-economic growth and the Ricardian advocates of market-controlled economic growth, and (e) The Question of Method and Methodology in the Study of the History of Economic Thought.

Student Responsibilities: There are three weekly lectures. Attendance at the lectures is obligatory; more than 3 hours of unexcused absence will adversely affect the final grade. In-term examinations will be during the lecture hours of 14 October and 4 November. There will also be a two hour final examination, currently scheduled for 10:00 to 11:50 p.m. on Friday, 15 December.
Required reading assignments are greater for Economics 207 than for Economics 107.

Papers: Except for those taking the course as part of the Honors Program, all students are to write a term paper (discussed below). It is due at the beginning of class 27 November.

Honors students are to write three short essay papers, due on 6 October, 23 October and 27 November. If feasible, the honors students' papers will be discussed in a group, meeting separately three times during the course. Written papers are due on or before the specified dates and in conventional typed form (that is, with words properly spelled, the traditional rules of syntax observed, and with footnotes and references in a standard mode).

Textbook and Reading Assignments: The assigned textbooks are:

Henry William Spiegel. The Growth of Economic Thought, Durham, N. C.: Duke University Press, 1971.
and either
Mark Blaug. Economic Theory in Retrospect. Fourth edition. Cambridge, New York: Cambridge University Press, 1985.
or
Robert B. Ekelund, Jr & Robert F. Hebert. A Historyu of Economic Theory and Method. New York: McGraw-Hill, 1983, 2nd ed.

The assigned reading consists of required materials (indicated by a preceding asterisk). There are also recommended supplementary materials; the latter include original sources (identified by preceding double asterisks). All of these materials, except for the textbooks, can be found in the Economics library or in my own office seminar room (enter 4D02, Forbes Quad).

Course Outline

I   The Patristic Approaches
    A. Hierarchy, democratic openness: Plato & Aristotle

    B. The medieval Roman Church views
        1. Some of the questions
        2. Thomas Aquinas's answers
        3. Nicole Oresme
        4. Assertion, problem, and practice: de Roover's contribution

II Mercantilism
    A. Its historical origins

    B. The earlier phase, the tract writers and their objectives

    C. Secularism, political theory, and the "scientific" mind
        1. Hobbes' Leviathan
        2. The ecclesiastical answer: Bishop Joseph Butler
        3. Efforts at the introduction of an empirical answer
            a. Anthony Ashley Cooper
            b. Bernard de Mandeville
            c. The Scots: Hume and Smith [Theory of Moral Sentiments]

III Four system builders

    A. Cantillon

    B. Quesnay

    C. Steuart

    D. Smith [The Wealth of Nations]

IV British Classical Economics

    A. The radical philosophers, their origins and their impact

    B. Malthus's Essay on Population

    C. The Ricardian strand

    D. The Senior synthesis compared to Say and McCulloch

    E. John Stuart Mill

    F. Karl Marx

    G. State of the "art," pre-1870.

V   Method and methodology in the study of economics

Lecture Schedule

	Date	Topic
1.	30 August	Orientation lecture, distribution of assignments
2.	1 September	The earlier Patristic Approach: Plato & Aristotle
3.	4	No class: Labor Day
4.	6	The Roman Church Fathers and medieval philosophy
5.	8	Doctrine: problems, practices and policy
6.	11	The scholastic approach and its uses
7.	13	The political origins of mercantilism
8	15	Mercantilism as a social policy
9.	18	Mun, Misselden, and Malynes
10.	20	Child, Barbon, and North
11.	22	Steuart's and other mercantilist systems
12.	25	Mercantilism assayed
13.	27	XVI and XVII British history & philosophy
14.	29	Hobbes' *Leviathan* and the problems it posed
15.	2 October	The ecclesiastical answer
16.	4	Sentimental Morality and its critics, including de Mandeville's *Fable of the Bees*
17.	6	Smith's *Theory of Moral Sentiments*
18.	9	No class: Jewish holiday
19.	11	Cantillon's system
20.	13	First Examination
21.	16	French history in the XVI and XVIII
22.	18	Quesnay's system [Physiocracy]
23.	20	British history in the late XVII and XVIII
24.	23	Smith's *Wealth of Nations*
25.	25	Smith's *Wealth of Nations*
26.	27	Smith Assessed: Was there "An Adam Smith Problem?"
27.	30	Comparing four systems: Steuart, Cantillon, the Physiocrats, and Smith
28.	1 November	Second Examination
29.	3	Bentham's Utilitarianism and his other work
30.	6	Malthus's *Essay on Population*
31.	8	Ricardo's *Principles* . . .
32.	10	Malthus's *Principles* . . .
33.	13	J. B. Say and Ricardo's immediate successors
34.	15	Nassau Senior
35.	17	John Stuart Mill
36.	20	Open
37.	22	Thanksgiving Holiday

3

38.	24	Thanksgiving Holiday
39.	27	Marx's classical economics
40.	29	Marx's method and theory of history
41.	1 December	Surveying pre-1870 classical economics
42.	4	Method and Methodology
43.	6	Open
44.	8	Last Class

###

HONORS STUDENTS' ESSAYS

<u>General</u>. Each essay should be about 2,500 words.

<u>Essay I</u> (due 18 September) deals with the Patristic tradition. Discuss the differences in method between Plato and Aristotle, on the one hand, and the conflict between the medieval realists and the medieval nominalists. Identify, after consulting an encyclopedia, how Abelard and Thomas Aquinas sought to "bridge" the gap.

<u>Essay II</u> (due 27 October) deals with mercantilism and is to be written after you have read Robert B. Ekelund, Jr. and Robert D. Tollison. <u>Mercantilism as a rent-seeking society: Economic regulation in historical perspective</u>. College Station, Texas: Texas A & M University Press, 1981.

The task is to compare their view with Hecksher's and Viner's.

<u>Essay III</u> (due 27 November)

The task is to identify your own perception of classical economics and explain how and/or why the utilitarian economics of John Stuart Mill and the materialistic economics of Karl Marx both fit into the same school.

###

TERM PAPERS
(for all but the Honors students)

General. Each paper should be about 22 double-spaced pages (i.e. about 6000 words). This assignment will be fulfilled only when a passing grade for it is awarded; a passing grade will not be awarded if the paper is in an illiterate form (there are spelling, literature, and scholarly conventions).

The paper is due no later than the beginning of the class period on 28 November.

The paper is to be an effort to put a history of thought question into scholarly perspective. The first step is to select the question: I suggest any of the following.

1. Just what is usury? What has just price got to do with usury, and in what senses do they stem from completely different philosophic sources? Is this distinction the basis for de Roover's approach to the medieval Patristic writers? Is a prime interest rate of 15 percent usurious? Discuss.

2. How do Hecksher's, Viner's and Keynes's views of mercantilism differ?

3. Using von Hornick's defense of mercantilism (c.f. Alexander Gray & A. E. Thompson. The Development of Economic Doctrine. New York: Longman, 1980, 2nd ed., pp. 80-82), how do you view the economic problems of a typical modern (e.g. Brazil) country?

4. Aside from the impact of Smith's Wealth of Nations, what he meant to say has been commonly misperceived. Just what was he trying to argue in terms of long haul economic development? He was clearly not opposed to governmental intervention; but what was he really opposed to? To what degree was he in favor of limiting individualism? Discuss fully.

5. Identify and discuss Ricardo's writings on money and currency.

6. Identify and discuss the evolution of Ricardo's views regarding the role of capital substitution on social organization and economic distribution.

7. Lord Robbins thought that Senior's work contained the prototype statement of English classical economics. In what senses were his views different from Ricardo's and more like Malthus's?

8. In what sense is John Stuart Mill's Principles the apotheosis of the English classical tradition? In what ways does it really repudiate the Ricardian emphasis in that tradition? Was he, in terms of his interests, much of a follower of the economics as distinct from the demographic side of Malthus?

5

9. Schumpeter and others suggest that economics through the time of Adam Smith's Wealth of Nations was, except for a few notable exceptions, tied to moral philosophy, and that afterwards it developed a professional independence and offered political leadership a set of functional rather than principally a philosophical or meta-philosophical value-system kind of advice. What were the issues that characterized the new economics offerings?

The second step (by 22 October) is to notify me of your choice.

The third step is to read a minimum of four discussions of your topic. They are to be cited in your footnotes and/or your references.

The fourth step is to organize how you will put the question, how you will organize the parts of the answer, and report same to me by giving me an outline. Wait for my approval before you start writing.

The fifth and sixth steps are to write a draft and revise it. Hand in the latter to me on or before the due date (and time).

READING ASSIGNMENTS

Undergraduates' required reading includes all material preceded by an asterisk. Graduate students intending to present the history of thought as a Ph.D. field should read in addition to the undergraduate assignments the additional listed material and they should peruse carefully (i.e. look over) the material preceded by two asterisks. Graduate students taking the course for reasons other than presentation as a Ph.D. field should look over the listed material, even if they do not try to take notes on it.

Unit I (to be completed by 7 September)

*Spiegel. Chapters 1 (pp. 14ff.), 2, & 3.
*Robert B.Ekelund, Jr. and Robert F. Hebert. A History of Theory and Method. New York: McGraw-Hill, 1983, 2nd edition. Chapter 2.
*Raymond A. de Roover. "Ancient and Medieval Thought," in the International Encyclopedia of the Social Sciences, vol. 4, pp. 430-44.

Barry Gordon. Economic Analysis before Adam Smith: Hesiod to Lessius. New York: Barnes & Noble, 1975.
S. Todd Lowry. "Recent Literature on Ancient Greek Economic Thought," Jour. of Econ. Lit., XVII (1979), 65-86.
Raymond A. de Roover. Business, banking, and economic thought in the later medieval and early modern Europe. Chicago: University of Chicago Press, 1974.
Jacob Viner. Religious thought and economic society: Four chapters of an unfinished work. Durham, N.C.: Duke University Press, 1978.

Unit II (to be completed by 25 September)

*Spiegel. Chapters 4, 5, 6, & 7.
*Blaug. Chapter 1.
*Alexander Gray & A. E. Thompson. The development of economic doctrine. London & New York: Longman, 1980, 2nd ed. Chapter III.
*Paul Studenski, The income of nations. Part One: History. New York: New York University Press, 1961. Pp. 13-16.

Eli F. Heckscher, "Mercantilism," Ency. of Social Sciences, vol. 10, pp. 333-39.
Jacob Viner, "Mercantilist Thought," Int. Ency. of Social Sciences, vol. 4, pp. 435-43.
_____. Studies in the theory of international trade. New York & London: Harper, 1937. Chapters 1 and 2.
Edgar S. Furniss, The position of the laborer in a system of nationalism: A study in the labor theories of the later English mercantilists.
William Letwin. The origins of scientific economics. London: Methuen, 1963. Chapters 1, 2, and 7.

7

Tony Aspromourgos. "The life of William Petty in relation to his economics: a tercentenary interpretation," Hist. Pol. Econ. (20 (Fall 1988), pp. 337-356.
E. A. J. Johnson. Predecessors of Adam Smith: The growth of British Economic Thought. New York: Prentice-Hall, 1937. Chapter I, II, III, IV, and V.
**Thomas Mun. A discourse of trade, [1621].
**Gerard de Malynes. The maintenance of free trade, [1622].
**Edward Misselden. Free trade or the meanes to make trade florish wherein the causes of the decay of trade in this kingdom are discovered. [1622].
**Gerard de Malynes. The center of the circle of commerce or a refutation of a treatise, intituled "The Circle of Commerce," or "The Balance of Trade," lately published by E. M.. [1623]

Unit III (to be completed by 4 October)

*Overton, H. Taylor. A history of economic thought. New York: McGraw-Hill, 1960. Chapters 1 & 2.
*Bernard de Mandeville. The fable of the bees. Read "The grumbling hive: or, knaves turn'd honest," [1705] and also the "Remarks" on lines 167, 173, 200, 201, 307, & 367.
*Adam Smith. The Theory of Moral Sentiments, Par I -- Sections I, II; Part II -- Section 1 (chapters 1, 2, 3); Part II -- Chapters 1, 2, 7; Part V.

Thomas Hobbes. the Leviathan or the matter, forme and power of a commonwealth ecclesiasticall and civil. Read chapters 13, 14, 15, 18, 19, & 21.
L. A. Selby-Bigge. British moralists being a selection of writers .... Read in this order the selections by T. Hobbes, J. Butler, A. A. Cooper, F. Hutcheson, A. Smith, and B. de Mandeville.

Unit IV (to be completed by 30 October)

*Spiegel, chapters 8, 9, 10, & 11.
*Blaug, chapter 2.
*Edwin G. West, "Richard Cantillon and Adam Smith: A Reappraisal," in Warren J. Samuels [ed.] Research in the History of Economic Thought and Methodology, vol. 3. Greenwich, CT: JAI Press, 1983, pp. 27-50.
*Joseph Schumpeter. History of economic analysis. New York: Oxford, 1954, pp. 186-93.
*Anthony Brewer. "Cantillon and mercantilism," Hist. of Pol. Econ. 20 (Fall 1988), pp. 447-460.

Ekelund & Hebert, chapters 4 & 5.
Richard Cantillon, Essai sur la nature du commerce en general as translated in the August Kelley edition [1964]. Read the essays by W. S. Jevons and H. Higgs.
Ronald L. Meek, The economics of Physiocracy, Part II -- "Essays."
David Hume, Economic writings, edited with an Introduction by Eugene Rotwein; read Rotwein's Introduction.

8

[Sir] James Steuart, An inquiry into the principles of political economy. Read the Andrew S. skinner edition [1966] and the biographical and analytical Introductions (pp. xxi-xxxiv) as well as Books 1 and 2.

**Adam Smith, The Wealth of Nations, Glasgow -- R. H. Campbell & A. S. Skinner edition [1976]. Read their "General Introduction" and Book I -- chaps. 1, 2, 3, 5, 6, 7, 8, 9, 10, & 11a; Book II -- chaps. 1, 3, & 5; Book III -- chap. 1; Book IV -- chaps. 4.1, 4.2, 4.3, 5, 7, 8; Book V -- chap. 2.

Unit V (to be completed by 17 November)

*Spiegel, chapters 12, 13, 14, & 15.
*Blaug, chapters 3, 4, & 5.

Elie Halevy, The growth of philosophical radicalism [trans. by Mary Morris]. Par I -- chapter 3; Part II -- chapter 3.

**Thomas R. Malthus, An essay on the principle of population [1798], chapters 1 & 2.
** _____, Principles of political economy. Book I -- chapters 1, 2, 3, 6.
**David Ricardo, On the principles of political economy and taxation, chapters 1, 2, 4, 5, 6, 7, & 18.
**Nassau Senior, An outline of the science of political economy.

Unit VI (to be completed by 27 November)

*Speigel, chapters 16, 17, 18, 19, 20.
*Blaug, chapters 6 & 7.
*Ekelund & Hebert, chapters 8, 9, 10, & 11.

**John Stuart Mill, Principles of political economy [Ashley edition], read the Ashley "Introduction" and Book I -- chapters 1, 2, 3, 4, 5, 6, 7, 10, 11, 12, & 13; Book II -- chapters 3, 4, 11, 12, 13, 14, 15, 16; Book III -- chapters 1, 2, 3, 4, 7, 8, 14, 17, 23; Book IV -- chapters 1, 2, 3, & 6; Book V -- chapters 1 & 11.
**Michael Wolfram [ed.] Political Economy: Marxist study courses. Chicago: Banner Press, 1976.

Unit VII (to be completed by 1 December)

*Mark Perlman, "Reflections on Methodology and Persuasion," in Jacob S. Dreyer [ed.], Breadth and depth in economics. Lexington: Heath, 1978, pp. 27-45.
* _____. "Perceptions of our Discipline: Three Magisterial Treatments of the Evolution of the History of Economic Thought." Processed.
*McCloskey, Donald N. "The Rhetoric of Economics," Jour. Econ. Lit., 21 (1983), 481-517.

Fritz Machlup. Methodology of economics and other social sciences. New York: Academic Press, 1978. Chapters, 1, 2, 4, 22, 25.

OLD EXAMINATIONS
First Hour Examinations

10 February 1986

1. Describe in detail Cournot's duopoly pricing proof. What inferences about the nature of competitive pricing can be drawn? What significance do you draw from the specifications of his assumptions? Given the "force" of the proof, the importance of his inferences, and the significance of his specifications, what usefulness does his work now have to (a) professional economists and (b) to businessmen?

2. Sketch out as completely as you can the contributions of William Stanley Jevons to modern economics. Identify the Utilitarian elements in his approach by contrasting them with the comparable elements in Menger's contributions.

3. Describe the Austrian School of Economics from the time of the elder Menger to the time of Hayek. What are the underlying consistent themes? Are there areas where the School has changed its position? Identify some of the principle shifts.

****

11 February 1987

Students may choose to write either Examination A or Examination B, but there is no opportunity for switching once the choice is made.

Examination A (notes, but not texts, may be used)

Answer both questions:

1. Identify five contributions associated with von Thünen's <u>The Isolated State</u>. Explain the significance of each.

2. Explain thoroughly and carefully Jevons' and Wicksteed's perceptions of the economic science, taking care to show the likely sources of their views. How did their view differ from that of Menger/von Boehm-Bawerk/von Wieser?

Examination B (closed book)

Answer two questions: one from each part

Part I

1. What was Cournot's theory of monopoly and oligopoly price? Where desireable
Yuse a geometric diagram.

2. What was the basic contribution of von Thünen to the theory of regional economics?

Part II

3. How did Jevons introduce the concept of marginalism in his work? Explain fully.

4. What was the logic of Böhm-Bawerk's theory of interest, how did it lead to his theory of the roundaboutness of production, and how was the "degree" of roundaboutness explained? Describe fully.

*****

5 February 1988

Answer three questions, one from each part.

Part I

1. Central to von Thünen's work was a theory of rent (location), how did it differ from Ricardo's?

2. Cournot's theories of (1) monopoly, (2) duopoly, and (3) of demand [D = f (p)] combine both logical and empirical elements. Summarize these theories and identify briefly what you think are the key logical and the critical empirical elements of each.

Part II

3. What did Jevons mean when using the phrase, "final degree of utility?" What beside diminishing "final degrees of utility" affect the amount of work that a laborer will offer to his employer? What would an increase in the price per hour do to affect a worker's willingness to work extra hours per day (or per week)? What would an increase in yearly pay do to a woman worker's willingness to give up a job and raise an (n + 1th) child?

4. Wicksteed asserted that he was Jevons's disciple. In what senses did the disciple "reinterpret" (go beyond in a different way) the master?

Part III

5. What were Carl Menger's perceptions of **subjectivity, imputed values of higher order goods, value** as distinct from **utility** or even **price**, and how did his system differ from Jevons'? Discuss.

6. In what sense was Böhm Bawerk's perception of time and <u>agio</u> different from what Wicksell offered in the way of a theory of interest and the role that it plays in the production process?

****
Second Hour Examinations

8 March 1987

Answer either three or four questions. Your grade will reflect an allowance for breadth as well as depth.

1. Write a brief essay on the concept of equilibrium and how it got into the mainstream of economic analysis after the "marginal revolution." What relationship do you see it having to the central roles of value and price in the post-classical treatment of the topic --- what had classical economics emphasized? How does the concept of the role of equilibrium sharpen the differences among the contributions of Menger and Jevons? Discuss.

2. Discuss Marshall's "objectives" for the teaching of economics as put forth in his Principle of Economics, taking care to stress what he wanted to synthesize in terms of the classical and various marginal contributions, what he wanted to stress in terms of the role of time in the productions process, and what he thought of the relative importance of empiricism and deduction.

Identify at least four of his more-or-less original contributions such as (1) two ways to perceive elasticity of demand, (2) consumer and/or producer surplus, (3) the short and long runs, (4) joint, complementary and substitute products, (5) the bit-at-a-time method, (6) quasi-rents, and (7) prime vs. supplementary costs.

3. Describe Pigou's Welfare Economics, taking care to show its relationship to the system which Marshall had sought to install at Cambridge. Discuss it fully.

4. What was the implication of the imperfect competition and/or monopolistic competition attack on the traditional Marshallian synthesis? How does the concept of marginal revenue change the mechanics of microeconomics?

> Writers at the time thought that his assertion of the overwhelming "truth" of increasing costs "had finished" Marshall: others have argued that it was his assumption of perfect knowledge. What do you think made Marshall passé?

5. How did Keynes seek to revolutionize the Cambridge perception of economic analysis? What did his Treatise on Money offer, and what did his General Theory offer that was new and what was new only to Cambridge? How did Keynes's 1937 QJE article differ from the 1936 book (or did it?)? Discuss.

****

4 March 1988

1. Write an essay on the neo-classical contributions of Alfred Marshall to economics. Cover briefly.

    a. How his perceptions of what economics is about differed from Menger's and Jevons' perceptions, and how this difference affected the rigor of his presentation.

    b. His technical assumptions.

    c. His contributions regarding consumer surplus, elasticity, and time.

2. Write an essay on the dissatisfactions with Marshallian competitive partial equilibrium analysis and what emerged.

*****

25 March 1987 (special exam)

Instructions: Answer each question:

This is an open-book examination: You have one week to turn in your answers. They should be in polished essay form.

1. What were Wicksell's contributions? Identify and discuss.

2. Discuss the differences between the positions taken by Maynard Keynes in his Treatise on Money and in his later General Theory. . .. What was the "contradiction" between Keynes' views in compensatory governmental investment programs and his views on uncertainty? Discuss.

3. What is the rationale for Marshallian partial equilibrium analysis and the one for general equilibrium analysis?

Final Examination

22 April 1986

Answer four questions, at least one from each part.

Part I

1. Write an essay on the role of mathematics in the evolution of modern economics, taking care to identify the arguments, pro and con, for its use as an expository and/or an analytical instrument(s).

2. Write a brief essay on the purposes of studying the history of economic thought. First, what is the delineation of economics? Second, where and why, in your view, has "Professionalism" (define the term) occurred? Third, discuss the variety of sources of ideas which have been incorporated into the "core area" of economics (delineate that area) and explain why some contributions have been more and some less "acceptable."

3. Write a brief essay on the development of macroeconomics in the development of the discipline.

Part II

4. What were the schema introduced into economics by any _four_ of these "groups":

   a. William Stanley Jevons and Philip Wicksteed
   b. John Bates Clark
   c. Alfred Marshall
   d. Leon Walras and Vilfredo Pareto
   e. John Maynard Keynes and/or the "Keynesians"
   f. Wesley Clair Mitchell
   g. Roy F. Harrod and Evsey Domar
   h. John von Neumann and Oskar Morgenstern
   i. Paul H. Douglas and Charles E. Cobb
   j. Knut Wicksell, Gunnar Myrdal and the Swedish group
   k. Karl Popper or some other [economic] methodologist

5. Using as exemplar material from three of the following:

   1. The Austrians
   2. The "neoclassical economists"
   3. The Lausanne general equilibrium writers
   4. The American Institutionalists
   5. The English "neo-Ricardians"

Identify what constitutes a school of economic thought -- does it include a reaction to a change in socio-economic problems, a change in assumptions and/or method, an advance in analytical process, or something else?

6. Write a brief essay on the evolution and ultimate disappearance of interest in (a) the "residual," (b) the wages-fund, <u>or</u> (c) "the greatest good for the greatest number."

Part III

7. Discuss the "rise" and "fall" of "Pigovian welfare economics" <u>or</u> imperfect competition.

8. How did modern national income accounting come to be established? What are the issues which separated one of its principal architects, Simon Kuznets, from the work done by his successors in the Department of Commerce? What was the contribution of Richard Stone, and what part did John D. Hicks's <u>The Social Framework</u> play?

*****

26 April 1988

Answer each question:

1. Schumpeter mentions that von Thünen and Cournot "wrote before their time." Indicate **fully and in detail** what was so prescient about their work.

2. How do you explain the <u>rise and fall</u> of Marshallian neo-classical economics. **Discuss fully.**

3. Discuss the impact of John Bates Clark and Irving Fisher on the development of American economic thought.

4. What is there to the American Institutional Economics of Thorstein Veblen, Wesley Clair Mitchell? **Discuss.**

5. Trace the development of macroeconomics from the time of Walras through the institutionalization of modern national income analysis.

Files of Past Examinations

First hour examinations:

1984

Answer each question:

1. Discuss the similarities of and the differences between the economic arguments advanced by Plato, Aristotle, and St. Thomas Aquinas. Focus on the concepts of hierarchy of occupation, inherited personal status, inherited social responsibilities, and the social role that market interactions were to play in maintaining social stability. What Stoic virtues were required to make the system work? And how were their systems intellectually conceived? [The idea is simultaneously to show that you have read widely, thought through what you have picked up, and can wrap the foregoing in an attractive intellectual package.]

2. Give three (or more) interpretations (taking care to identify their origins) of what mercantilism in the 16th and the 17th centuries was said to be about. Use the work of Thomas Mun to illustrate one or more of these interpretations. How did the Malynes vs. Misselden debate or Petty's contribution illustrate the transition of economic thinking from the Patristic tradition to "something more modern?" What was that "something more modern?" Discuss.

3. What was the convention-shattering contribution of Thomas Hobbes? How did each of the following try to answer Hobbes's argument: Joseph Butler, Anthony Ashley Cooper, Adam Smith (in the Theory of Moral Sentiments)? How does Mandeville's Fable of the Bees fit in? In what sense does this "debate" have methodological implications? What was the difference between Bacon's approach and the one advocated by Descartes? [The idea here is to show what you have grasped, and how you have integrated it.]

####

1985

Answer each question:

1. Discuss the similarities of and the differences between the analytical methods suggested by Plato, Aristotle, and St. Thomas Aquinas as they applied to economics. Focus on the role of social hierarchy of occupation, on inherited personal status, on inherited social responsibilities, as well as on the social role that market interactions were to play in maintaining social stability. What Stoic virtues were required to make the system work?

Also work into your discussion any evidence you are aware of relating to how the economic systems of their times actually worked.

2. What are some (perhaps three or four) of the interpretations (cite sources) of what mercantilism in the sixteeth to the eighteenth centuries was all about? Use the work of Thomas Mun or von Hornick to illustrate one

or more of these interpretations. How did the Malynes vs. Misselden debate or Petty's contribution illustrate the transition of economic thinking from the Patristic tradition to "something more modern?" What was that "something more modern?" Discuss.

3. What was logic of the Thomas Hobbes argument about interpersonal relations? What, if anything, was so special about it, such that it was perceived as something revolutionary in its implications? How did each of the following try to answer the Hobbes argument from the standpoint of economic market implications: Joseph Butler, Anthony Ashley Cooper, and Adam Smith (in the Theory of Moral Sentiments)? How does Mandeville's Fable of the Bees fit in? In what sense does this "debate" have methodological implications? What was the difference between the Hobbes-Bacon approach and the one advocated by either those pursuing the Acquinas or the Descartes legacies? [The idea here is to show what you have grasped, and how you have integrated it.]

####

Second hour examinations:

1984

Answer each question:

1. Outline the principal ideas in the Physiocratic legacy.

2. List and discuss the contributions of Richard Cantillon to economic analysis. In what sense, if any, does Cantillon's work bear greater resemblance to modern economics than the work of Steuart and even Adam Smith?

3. Discuss the following aspects of Adam Smith's work:

   a. Human nature and the "Adam Smith Problem."
   b. The sources and limits of economic growth.
   c. Market vs. natural price.
   d. The "Invisible Hand."
   e. Productive vs. unproductive labor.

####

1985

Answer each question:

1. Outline the organization and contributions of Sir James Steuart's An Inquiry into the Principles of Political Oeconomy.

2. Identify the contributions of Richard Cantillon and the Physiocrats to current economic analysis. Discuss in detail three of those contributions, at least one from either "source."

3. Discuss the following:

   a. The organization of the Wealth of Nations.
   b. Smith's theory of production, including the sources

c. Smith's concern with market **vs.** natural price.
   d. The significance and limitations of the "Invisible Hand," and the concept of **laissez-passer, laissez-faire** in his system.

////

1985 (alternate)

Answer each question

1. What was the Classical School's theory of value? From what sources did it derive?

2. What in your view is the role of David Ricardo in the development of the economics discipline? Discuss fully, taking care to identify the role that Malthus played in the development of Ricardo's approach.

3. Sir James Steuart's *summa* is offered in this course as a relatively complete treatment of the mercantilist view of economics. Smith's two principal books are offered as another comparable *summa*. Contrast the two views, taking care to describe them fully.

4. The Political Arithmeticians and Richard Cantillon could be considered to be the forerunners of one of the methodological divisions in modern economics. Identify fully their respective contributions and relate them to what you know of the methodological divisions in modern economic theory.

*****

Final Examinations:

1984

Answer four (4) questions, one from each part

PART A

1. Identify the role that utilitarianism played in the economics of the English Classical School.

2. What were the political issues which interested the principal English Classical School writers, and how did their analysis affect the policy positions they supported? Cite issues and people.

PART B

3. What was the labor theory of value? How did it tie to Locke's perceptions of the "unalienable" rights of man? How did it fit into the Smithian, Ricardian, and Marxian schemes of thought?

4. What were Nassau Senior's postulates relating to Classical Economics and what were their origins? What views did Senior have about the variety of monopolies, and what could be "done" about each?

PART C

5. Compare the economics of Richard Cantillon, a forerunner of the Classical tradition, and the economics of John Stuart Mill, the apotheosis of that tradition. Cite specific topics and compare their "answers."

6. What was Malthus's concern with economic gluts? What was the position taken by the more "orthodox" (i.e. Ricardo and the adherents of "Say's Law")? Does this "conflict of view" suggest that the dominant or Ricardian group had a theory of supply but not a theory of demand? If so, why did they eschew concern with demand -- what to them was so big a worry that "demand" paled in comparison? Was this point indicative of a social class foundation to Classical Economics, or do you think that it was more a functional (independent of class structure) reality? Discuss.

PART D

7. Professor Sir Moses Finley argues that there was little economic analysis in the Greek civilization because there were few if any markets. Using similar reasoning, there are those that argue that all pre-industrial societies lack economic analysis if there is no evidence of focus on price and quantity exchanges. What in your judgement represents the "absolute minimum" exchange conditions for concern with what you would define as economic analysis? And why?

8. From a methodological standpoint how does one explain the Malthusian Law of Population and what a later writer called "the Iron Law of Wages," the "law of diminishing returns," the principle of "Ricardian rent," and the destruction of the "Wages Fund theory?"

1985

Answer four questions, one from each part

Part A

1. What was the Classical School's theory of value? From what sources did it derive?

2. Compare the organization of James Mill's Elements of Political Economy and John Stuart Mill's Principles of Political Economy. What do you see as the principal differences between their views?

Part B

3. What in your view is the role of Adam Smith in the development of the economics discipline? Discuss fully, taking care to identify the principal differing assessments regarding this topic.

4. What in your view is the role of David Ricardo in the development of the economics discipline? Discuss fully, taking care to identify the role that Malthus played in the development of Ricardo's approach.

Part C

5. Wesley Clair Mitchell argues at one point that the study of economics can appropriately begin with Adam Smith's <u>Wealth of Nations</u> because what passes for today's economics discipline is largely a collection of idiosyncratic interpretations of reactions to the process of national industrialization and that anything that is relevant to today's discipline surfaced in Smith's book and/or has surfaced since. Given that we started the course with a discussion of Plato's and Aristotle's contributions and then went on to a discussion of medieval and mercantilist thought, it is clear that the course designer did not "buy" Mitchell's assessment. What did you get out of the discussion of pre-Smithian writers which did not surface in Smith's 1776 book or in the classical period? Discuss.

6. Sir James Steuart's <u>summa</u> is offered in this course as a relatively complete treatment of the mercantilist view of economics. Smith's two principal books are offered as another comparable <u>summa</u>. Contrast the two views, taking care to describe them fully.

Part D

7. The Political Arithmeticians and Richard Cantillon could be considered to be the forerunners of one of the methodological divisions in modern economics. Identify fully their respective contributions and relate them to what you know of the methodological divisions in modern economic theory.

8. The importance of observation (as distinct from excogitated theorizing) is an old theme in economics, one stemming from the influence of Aristotle. In many ways Malthus "worked both sides of the street." Discuss fully Malthus's contributions and influence on the development of the economics discipline.

*****

University of Pittsburgh

U&G

MARK PERLMAN
HISTORY OF ECONOMIC THOUGHT II:
The Evolution of Professional Specialization,
1870-1955
(Economics 108/208)

1. The course is designed for students wishing to examine the underpinnings of the various schools of modern western economic thought and the relationships both direct and indirect of these schools. The previous course, Economics 108/208, deals with the pre-1870 period. This whole sequence (107/108 and 207/208) covers the background spectrum of current professional thought. Economics 107/108 can be taken in two forms; in one, the writing program is organized for University Honors students; the other is designed for Economics Department undergraduate majors and has a different set of writing requirements. Economics 207/208, although primarily designed for those taking the History of Thought as a doctoral sub-field for the Ph.D., should be useful for any economics graduate student wanting to understand the origins. the developmental history, and the surfacing of the dynamics of the economics discipline.

2. The course offers an overview of the development of modern western economics, particularly as it has emerged in the last century. It focusses on four lines of inquiry: (1) the marginalist tradition and its XIX critics; (2) the neo-classical traditions, particularly as they evolved until 1950, and their critics; (3) several efforts at formulating general equilibrium analyses; and (4) the American traditions of "theoretical" and empirical economics. Students completing the course on the 108 level should have achieved a comprehensive grasp of the bases of modern economic thought. Those who undertake the 208 level will also have read considerable secondary interpretive material and will have sampled many selections of the original writings; these students will be prepared in good part for the second half of the doctoral comprehensive examination in the history of economic thought.

3. Lectures will be for both Economics 108 and 208. Thus, each week, students will have three contact hours with the lecturer. **Attendance is required.**

4. Two in-term one-hour examinations are required as well as a final two-hour examination. They will be on 2 February and 19 March. The final examination will be given on **Saturday, 29 April from 12:00 until 1:50 p.m.**

5. Grades are based on all of the written work -- exams (60 percent) and essays (40 percent).

OUTLINE OF THE COURSE

I. The Legacy from Classical Economics

II. Two overlooked now "mainstream" writers

    A. von Thuenen
    B. Cournot

III. Two marginalist traditions and their sequelae

    A. Jevonian Utilitarianism
    B. Austrian Subjectivism
    C. The Swedish offshoot
    D. The first Cambridge School
    E. A digression into the economics of socialism
    F. The second Cambridge School
    G. The London School of Economics and uncertainty

IV. The third marginalist tradition and general equilibrium analysis

    A. Walras
    B. Pareto
    C. John R. Hicks
    D. Maynard Keynes and Keynesianism

V. Economics in America

    A. Emergence of the profession
    B. Capital Theory: The interesting cases of John Bates Clark and Irving Fisher
    C. Labor Economics: The normative economics of Commons and Douglas and the positive economics of the Chicago microeconomic traditions of Gregg Lewis and Becker
    D. Fisher's Monetarism and Business Cycles; Wesley Clair Mitchell and Arthur F. Burns
    E. The Several Facets of Simon Kuznets
    F. Microeconomics: Varieties of rationality
    G. Macroeconomics: Its empirical and theoretical foundations
    I. Statistics and Econometrics: The availability of data, of theory, and of processing equipment

VI. The rationales for studying the history of economics

The Lecture Program

1. 5 Jan. Introduction -- The Legacy

2. 8   von Thuenen and location and distribution theory
3. 10   Cournot price theory and modern formal technique
4. 12   Jevons. marginalism, and Wicksteed

5. 15   University Holiday, no classes
6. 17   Jevonian marginalism, continued
7. 19   Menger: Subjectivism, marginalism, and methodology

8. 22   The spectrum of von Boehm-Bawerk's capital and interest theories
9. 24   The two sides of von Wieser
10. 26   The Karl Menger seminar of the 1920s

11. 29   The von Mises influence
12. 31   Wicksell and natural growth
13. 2 Feb **First Examination**

14. 5   Marshall
15. 7   Marshall
16. 9   Pigou

17. 12   The nemesis of the "First Cambridge School"
18. 14   Microeconomics and imperfect competition
19. 16   No Class: Great Americans' Day

20. 19   The Socialist pricing controversy: Barone, Mises, Lange, Robbins & Hayek
21. 21   The "second Cambridge school": Keynes's writings until 1936
22. 23   The General Theory

23. 26   Keynesianism: World War II and after
24. 28   Uncertainty: von Thuenen, Knight, Keynes, and Shackle
25. 2 Mar Open

    5   Spring Recess
    7   Spring Recess
    9   Spring Recess

27. 12   Walras and general equilibrium analysis
28. 14   Pareto and the continuation of the Lausanne tradition
29. 16   The positive dominance of John R. Hicks' positivism

30. 19   **Second Examination**
31. 23   Academic normativism and academic positivism; two strands in the development of the economics profession in America.
32. 24   Capital Theory: The interesting cases of John Bates Clark, Irving Fisher. Frank Knight, and Robert Solow

33.	26 Mar	Topic continued
34.	28	Fisher's Monetarism and Business Cycles; Wesley Clair Mitchell and Arthur F. Burns
35.	30	Topic continued
36.	2 Apr	Labor Economics: The normative economics of Commons and Douglas and the positive economics of the Chicago microeconomic traditions of Gregg Lewis and Becker.
37.	4	Topic continued
38.	6	The several facets of Simon Kuznets (social accounting, and economic growth)
39.	9	The empirical and theoretical foundations of Macroeconomics: from Denison to Solow and Jorgenson, from Moore to Samuelson, and from Patinkin to Ackley and Musgrave
40.	11	The development of microeconomics: From Berle-Means and von Neumann-Morgenstern to Cyert-March and Arrow's and Buchanan's public choice.V
41.	13	Varieties of Rationality
42.	16	Statistics and Econometrics: The availability of data, of theory, and of processing equipment
43.	18	Topic continued
44.	20	The rationales for studying the history of economics

The Writing Program

> Economics 108 honors program students: three 2,500-word essays **due on 5 February, 12 March, and 16 April, respectively.**

> Economics 108 non-honors program students: one 5,000-word term paper **due on 16 April.**

> Economics 208 students: one 7500-word term paper **due on 16 April.**

Topics are assigned, but negotiations are not out of the question.

These papers are to be typed and I expect the traditional cultural amenities to be honored: Spelling conventions count; so do traditions pertaining to punctuation and grammar. Proof-reading, although admittedly a pain, remains, nonetheless, a requirement.

Assigned Papers

Essay assignments for the Honors Students

Topic for paper due on 5 February: The Methodology of formalism, subjectivism and empiricism in modern economics: the impact of the contributions of the likes of von Thuenen, Cournot Jevons, Carl Menger, von Boehm Bawerk, von Wieser as well as others.

4

Topic for paper due on 12 March: Marshall's rhetoric. Take care to note his views regarding mathematical formalism, historicism, the use of constructs, and the audience for whom he purported to write.

Topic for paper due on 16 April: Is there an economic science? If so, what is it, if not what is there?

The purpose of each paper is to lay out what you have gleaned from your reading and to discuss your reactions to the theme outlined in the topic. In sum, your responsibilities are two: Show adequately what you have read, and attempt to present your own reactions to the topic, as specified.

Term paper for all but the Honors Students

As noted earlier in this handout, all but the Honors Students are required to turn in a term paper to me before or on 16 April. The expected length for Economics 108 is 5000 words, for Economics 208, 7500 words. There are about 260 words to a double-spaced typewritten page, so the amount of paper can be calculated easily.

The idea is not only to present your ideas, but also to do so with a degree or persuasive charm and/or imagination. It is an effort to get over inarticulateness. The "great" length assures that you will have my full attention for sufficient time to make a point.

I suggest that you start by either asking a question and explaining why the question has some ultimate relevance to your own curiosity or making an evaluation, which you will then explain and/or defend. This part of the paper might well be sketched initially and then rewritten after you have done the rest of the paper. Thus, this first part is a frame into which you ultimately fit what you have "painted." This introductory section usually concludes with no more that a paragraph or two "outlining the order of the thinking or argument which you are offering in the remainder of the paper."

The second part of the paper presents the materials which you are subsequently going to analyze. It has the data; it offers references to your sources and what you think of them as sources; it may suggest, but does not evaluate contradictions which you can see in your source material. In this section, you are trying to demonstrate your knowledge of the material; you are not yet trying to be original, clever, persuasive, or even definitive.

The third part of the paper sets out your own views. It ties the question you asked in the first part with the data in the second. It may include a great deal of valuative material, criticisms taken from others (credit to be given, of course), and criticisms offered by you (care being taken to explain what "bothers" you or what you think others plainly misperceive). Here is where your chance for persuasion and/or charm comes in. You cannot write this section until you have mastered the previous section. But one way to handle this third part is to sketch out for your later amazement even before you have done any extensive reading what you thought you were going to find. The third section can then take the form of comparing what you had originally thought through a priori with what you later found empirically.

5

The final part of the paper is a sort of reprise. It focusses on your conclusions. Often it takes the form of saying, "the questions I asked were, and the answers I found were. Insofar as the questions frame the answers, I concluded thus and so, but insofar as the answer shows the inadequacy of the question, this is what I would now ask, were I to start the exercise over."

The paper should have either foot- or end-notes and a separate list of bibliographical references.

Possible topics*

1. Present and evaluate the views of Jevons and Marshall about the place of mathematics in economics, particularly seen in the light of current practice.

2. Sources and varieties of general equilibrium analysis; the period between Walras and Arrow.

3. Using Henry Phelps Brown's article, "Sir Roy Harrod: A Biographical Memoir," Econ. J., 30 [357] (March 1980), 1-33 as an "ideal prototype," write a comparable essay on any one of the following:

Benjamin Anderson	Frank H. Knight	Arthur C. Pigou
John Bates Clark	Simon Kuznets	Thorstein Veblen
Irving Fisher	Nicholas Kaldor	Alfred Marshall
Frank Fetter	Joan Robinson	Francis Edgeworth
Wesley Clair Mitchell	Paul A. Samuelson	Paul Douglas
John Maurice Clark	Abba Lerner	Nicholas Georgescu-Roegen

*This list is not meant to be conclusive. Any topic on the list is acceptable. Any other topic must be checked out with me.

The Reading Program

Undergraduates' reading assignments include all material preceded by an asterisk. Graduate students intending to present the history of thought as a Ph.D. field should read in addition to the undergraduate assignments the additional listed material and they should peruse carefully the original source material preceded by two asterisks. Graduate students taking the course for reason other than presentation as a Ph.D. field should look over all of the listed material even if they do not take notes on their reading.

The following are assigned as textbooks:

Henry William Spiegel. The Growth of Economic Thought. Durham, NC: Duke University Press, 1983. [This offers a good overview, with each discussion being pertinent and complete.]

Robert B. Ekelund and Robert F. Hebert. A History of Economic Theory and Method. New York: McGraw Hill, 1983, 2nd ed. [This book is far less complete, but offers some simple formal expositions.]

Schedule of Required Reading Assignments

1. **By 10 January 1988,** kindly have read the following material on "two who wrote before their time," von Thuenen and Cournot.

   *Henry William Spiegel. The Growth of Economic Thought. Durham, NC: Duke University Press. Chapter 22 (pp. 510-13).

   *Robert B. Ekelund & Robert F. Hebert. A History of Economic Theory and Method. New York: McGraw Hill, 1983, 2nd ed. Chapters 12 & 13 (pp 278-82)

   *Mark Blaug, "The Economics of Johann von Thuenen," in Warren Samuels [ed.]. Research in the History of Economic Thought and Methodology: A Research Annual. Vol. 3 (1985). Greenwich CT: JAI Press, 1985. Pp. 1-25.

   To be discussed 8 January

   *Arthur H. Leigh. "Thuenen, Johann Heinrich von," in the International Encyclopedia of the Social Sciences. (IESS) vol 16, pp. 17-19.

   Paul A. Samuelson. "Thuenen at Two Hundred," in Jour. Econ. Lit., XXI (Dec. 1983), 1468-87.

   To be discussed 10 January

   Note: take great care to master the Ekelund and Hebert diagram on Cournot's duopoly pricing and output model!

   *Henri Guitton. "Cournot Antoine Auguste," in IESS, vol 3, pp. 427-29.

   Robert B. Ekelund & Robert F. Hebert. "Dupuit and Marginal Utility: Context of a Discovery." Hist. Pol. Econ. 8 (1976), 266-73.

7

Robert B. Ekelund & Robert F. Hebert. "French Engineers, Welfare Economics, and Public Finance in the Nineteenth Century." Hist. Pol. Econ. 10 (1978), 636-68.

**Augustin Cournot. The Mathematical Principles of the Theory of Wealth. 1927 [Fisher] edition.

2. The next reading assignment to be completed by 17 January, involves the breakdown of the classical tradition and the emergence of the school of marginal analysis particularly starting with William Stanley Jevons. My lectures on the breakdown of the English classical tradition and the emergence of the marginalist school are based in good measure on two chapters (3 and 4) written by Terence W. Hutchison in On Revolutions and Progress in Economic Knowledge. Cambridge: Cambridge University Press, 1978. Those interested in filling out the Hutchison interpretation can find the book in my seminar room/library. My lectures on Jevons draw heavily on George Stigler's Production and Distribution Theories. New York: Agathon, 1968, [1941].

I am also distributing copies of a recent article of my own on Schumpeter as an historian of economic thought. It contains inter alia a summary of Schumpeter's estimates of the contributions and characteristics of the English classical school. These points supplement and perhaps even contrast with the four that he, incidentally, used later (in a book published posthumously in 1954) when he employed Nassau Senior's application of the principle of maximization to the problems of production, distribution, and consumption, (2) the original or early Malthusian theory of population pressure upon resources, (3) the application of the theory of diminishing returns upon agricultural output, and (4) the application of the theory of increasing returns in the area of manufacturing.

To be discussed 12 and 17 January

*Spiegel. op. cit., ch. 22 (pp. 513-25)

*Ekelund and Hebert. op. cit., ch. 14

*T. W. Hutchison. "Jevons, William Stanley." IESS, vol. 8, pp. 254-60.

John Maynard Keynes. "William Stanley Jevons," being in his 1936 centennial elocution essay. It can be found in any copy of Maynard Keynes's Essays [and Sketches] in Biography, but is volume 10 of the Royal Economic Society's great publication, The Collected Writings of JOHN MAYNARD KEYNES, pp. 109-60.

**William Stanley Jevons. The Theory of Political Economy. 1957 [1871], 5th ed.

**Philip H. Wicksteed. The Alphabet of Economic Science. New York: Augustus Kelley, [1888] 1955.

8

3. The third reading assignment concerning the various Austrian Schools, besides being very heavy, is to be completed by 30 January; as before, I rely heavily in my lectures on Stigler's Production and Distribution Theories, and, again, I urge all who can to read the relevant material from that book.

*Friedrich von Hayek. "The Austrian School" in IESS, vol. 4, pp. 458-60.

*Spiegel. op. cit., ch. 23.

*Ekelund & Hebert. op. cit., chs. 13 and 21.

*Terence W. Hutchison. The Politics and Philosophy of Economics. New York: New York University Press, 1984, chs. 6 and 7.

William Smart. An Introduction to the Theory of Value on the Lines of Menger, Wieser, and Boehm-Bawerk. Augustus Kelley: New York [1910], 1966, 2nd ed.

To be discussed 19 January

*George J. Stigler. "Carl Menger," being chapter 6 of Stigler's Production and Distribution Theories: The Formative Period.

Joseph Schumpeter. "Carl Menger," being chapter 3 of Schumpeter's Ten Great Economists from Marx to Keynes. New York: Oxford University Press. 1951.

To be discussed 22 and 24 January

Joseph Schumpeter. "Eugen von Boehm-Bawerk," being chapter 6 of Schumpeter, ibid.

**Eugen von Boehm-Bawerk. The Positive Theory of Capital, trans. by William A. Smart. London: Macmillan, 1891.

**Friedrich von Wieser. Natural Value, trans. by William A. Smart. London: Macmillan, 1893.

George Stigler. "Eugen von Boehm-Bawerk," being chapter 8 of Stigler, op. cit..

To be discussed 26 January

George Stigler. "Friedrich von Wieser," being chapter 7 of Stigler, op. cit..

**Carl Menger. Principles of Economics. trans. by James Dingwall and Bert F. Hoselitz. New York: New York University Press [1871], 1981.

Gerald P. O'Driscoll, Jr. "Money: Menger's Evolutionary Model." Hist. of Pol. Econ., 18 (1986), 601-616.

9

**Friedrich von Wieser. <u>Social Economics</u>. trans. by A. Ford Hinrichs. New York: Augustus M. Kelley, [1924] 1967.

To be discussed on 26 January

*E. Roy Weintraub. "On the Existence of a Competitive Equilibrium, 1930-1954." <u>Jour. Econ. Lit.</u>, XXI (March 1983), 1-39; also in E. Roy Weintraub, <u>General Equilibrium Analysis: Studies in Appraisal</u>. New York: Cambridge University Press, 1985. p. 59-107.

*Joseph W. Duncan and William C. Shelton. <u>Revolution in United States Government Statistics 1926-1976</u>. Washington: U.S. Department of Commerce, 1978. Chapter 2.

To be discussed on 29 January

*Murray Rothbard. "Rothbard on Mises," in Henry W. Spiegel and Warren J. Samuels. <u>Contemporary Economists in Perspective</u>. Greenwich, Conn.: JAI Press, 1984, vol. 1, pp. 285-296.

*Stephen B. Boehm. "The Private Seminar of Ludwig von Mises." Paper delivered at the 1984 meetings of the History of Economics Society: Mimeo., vol. 1.

*Earlene Craver. "The Emigration of the Austrian Economists." <u>Hist. Pol. Econ.</u> vol. XVIII, 1986 (Spring), pp. 1-32.

*Georg Winckler and Peter Rosner. "Aspects of Austrian Economics in the 1920s and 1930s." Paper delivered at the 1984 meeting of the History of Economics Society: Mimeo, vol. 1.

Fritz Machlup. "Hayek, Friedrich A. von." <u>IESS</u>, vol. 18, pp. 274-82.

*Fritz Machlup. "Machlup on Hayek," in Henry W. Spiegel and Warren J. Samuels [eds.], <u>Research in the History of Economic Thought and Methodology: A Research Annual</u>. Vol. 1 (1983). Greenwich, CT: JAI Press. Pp. 251-84.

*Warren J. Samuels. "Machlup on Knowledge: Science, Subjectivism, and the Social Nature of Knowledge," in Warren Samuels [ed.], <u>Research in the History Of Economic Thought and Methodology: A Research Annual</u>. Vol 3 (1985). Greenwich, CT: JAI Press, 1985. Pp. 243-55.

*Richard N. Langlois. "From the Knowledge of Economics to the Economics of of Knowledge: Fritz Machlup on Methodology and the 'Knowledge Society.'" <u>ibid.</u>, pp. 225-35. Read also Israel M. Kirzner's comment. ibid., pp. 237-41.

Paul A. Samuelson. "Schumpeter, an Economic Theorist," in Helmut Frisch [ed.], <u>Schumpeterian Economics</u>. New York: Praeger, 1981, pp. 1-27.

10

To be discussed 31 January

*Torsten Gaerdlund. "Knut Wicksell." IESS, vol. 16, pp. ~~474-85~~.
538-54V
Don Patinkin & Otto Steiger. :In Search of the 'Veil of Money' and the 'Neutrality of Money': A Note on the Origin of Terms." Scand Jour Econ 91 (1989), 131-46.

*Carl Uhr. "Wicksell and the Austrians." in Warren Samuels [ed.]. Research in the History of Economic Thought and Methodology: A Research Annual. Vol 3 (1985). Greenwich, CT: JAI Press, 1985. Pp. 199-224.

*Edwin Burmeister. "Synthesizing the Neo-Austrian and Alternative Approaches to Capital Theory: A Synthesis." Jour. Econ. Lit. 12 (1974), 413-56.

4. The fourth reading assignment to be completed by 28 February, is a very long one. It deals with the work established at the University of Cambridge under Alfred Marshall and continued there through much of the career of John Maynard Keynes, indeed his career until World War II. Marshall's approach focussed on partial equilibrium analysis and it is not until sometime after Maynard Keynes's death that Keynes's later contributions became established as a fusion of the Cambridge tradition and general equilibrium analysis into what is now called "macroeconomics," a term much newer than is often realized. Because Marshall's treatment of the topic continues to dominate the microanalytical approach to our subject, it is important to see Marshall's contribution not only for what it was but also for what it remains --- two quite different things. As noted, Marshall's treatment all but dominates our approach both positively and negatively. As a consequence, Marshall's synthesis is worth particular attention. It should be borne in mind that Marshall (even more that Menger), was for his time an accomplished mathematician, as was his student Maynard Keynes. Nonetheless, he consciously eschewed mathematics as a primary expository mode. The Mathematical Appendix to his Principles of Economics should be reexamined by anyone wishing to challenge my assessment of his skills.

*Spiegel. op. cit., chs. 25 and 26.

*Ekelund and Hebert. op. cit., chs. 15 and 18.

*Terence W. Hutchison. On Revolutions and Progress in Economic Knowledge. Ch. 3.

*Bernard Corry. "Marshall, Alfred," in IESS vol. 10, pp. 25-33.

The Marshallian Phase

To be discussed 5 and 7 February

John Cunningham Wood [ed.]. Alfred Marshall: Critical Assessments. Vol. 1, pp. xiv-xxxiii.

John Maynard Keynes. "Alfred Marshall, 1842-1924." ibid., (vol. 1) pp. 7-65; this essay is reprinted from John Maynard Keynes's Essays in Biography.

*Clifford Hildreth. "Edgeworth, Frances Ysidro." IESS, vol. 4, pp. 506-08.

**Alfred Marshall. Principles of Economics. 8th edition.

    Bk.1;
    Bk. III; chaps. 1, 2, 3, 4, 6;
    Bk. IV; chaps. 1, 2, 3, 13;
    Bk. V; chaps. 1, 2, 3, 4, 5, 6, 7, 8, 12, 13, 14.

The Post-Marshall/pre-General Theory Phase

*George L. S. Shackle. The Years of High Theory. Cambridge: Cambridge University Press, 1967, chs. 1, 2, 3, 4, 5, 6, 7, 8, 9, 10. [Obviously this book can only be scanned, but it gives one picture of the modern era in economics. I am, with reason, a Shackle enthusiast. Incidentally, this book was initially presented as lectures in the history of economic thought at Pitt in 1968.]

To be discussed on 9 February

*Austin Robinson. "Pigou, Arthur Cecil," in IESS, vol. 12, pp. 90-7.
**Arthur C. Pigou. The Theory of Unemployment. London: Macmillan, 1933.

**Arthur C. Pigou. The Economics of Welfare. London: Macmillan, 1920.

*S. R. Dennison. "Robertson, Dennis Holme," in IESS, vol. 13, pp. 529-33.

Thomas Wilson. "Robertson, Money, & Monetarism," in Jour. Econ. Lit., 18 (December 1980), 1522-38.

**Dennis H. Robertson. Lectures on Economic Principles. In three volumes. London: Staples, 1957.

To be discussed on 12 and 14 February

*Geoffrey C. Harcourt. "On the Influence of Piero Sraffa on the Contributions of Joan Robinson to Economic Theory." Econ. Jour. Supplement. vol. 96 (1986), 96-108.

*Maurice Dobb. "Dobb on Sraffa," in Henry W. Spiegel and Warren J. Samuels [eds.], op. cit., vol. 2, 623-37.

**Edward H. Chamberlin. The Theory of Monopolistic Competition. Cambridge: Harvard University Press, 1933.

**Joan Robinson. The Economics of Imperfect Competition. London: Macmillan, 1933.

12

*[Sir] John Hicks. "Hawtrey," in Economic Perspectives: Further Essays on Money and Growth. Oxford: Oxford University Press. Clarendon Press, 1977, pp 118-33.

A Digression into Socialism

To be discussed on 16 February

*Mark Perlman. Review of Don Lavoie's **Rivalry and Central Planning: The Socialist Calculation Debate Reconsidered.** Market Process, 4 (Spring 1986), 4-6.

The Second Cambridge School: The Keynesian Hegemony

For the lectures on 21 and 23 February

*G. Haberler. "The Place of the General Theory of Employment, Interest, and Money in the History of Economic Thought." REStat. 28 (Nov 46), 187-94.

*Harrod, R. F. "Keynes. John Maynard -- Contributions to Economics." IESS, vol 8, pp. 368-75. Actually, Harrod's adulatory biography is the better source: Roy F Harrod. The Life of John Maynard Keynes, (1951) -- although excellent, this is something like an "authorized biography," but it contains much indisputably trenchant information. Recently there has been a spate of books highly critical of Keynes's personal character and/or way of life as well as the impact he and his views have had on post World War II British economic policy. The former deal with the homosexuality within the "Bloomsbury set" as well as at the University of Cambridge; the latter with the promises implicitly existent in Keynes's General Theory anent the eating of one's cake and having it, too.

Axel Leijonhufvud. On Keynesian Economics and the Economics of Keynes: A Study in Monetary Theory. New York: Oxford University Press. 1968. (The great virtue of this study is that it initiated a sharp distinction between what Keynes actually wrote [ambiguities and all] and the uses others have put to what they asserted, were "really" his ideas.

George L. S. Shackle. The Years of High Theory [loc. cit.], chapters 11, 12, 13, 14, 15 & 16.

*Terence W. Hutchison. On Revolutions and Progress in Economic Knowledge. Ch. 4.

*Alan Coddington. "Keynesian Economics: The Search for First Principles." Jour. Econ. Lit. 14 (December 1976), 1258-73.

Don Patinkin. Keynes's Monetary Thought: A Study of Its Development. Durham: Duke University Press, 1976.

Alan Meltzer., "Keynes's General Theory: A Different Perspective." Jour. Econ. Lit. 19 (March 1981), 34-64. (Patinkin and Meltzer have much different views and there ensued after the appearance of the Meltzer something of a brouhaha between them). Meltzer expanded this article into a book, Keynes's Monetary Thinking: A Different Interpretation (New York: Cambridge University Press, 1988), which is currently considered by many to be the clearest account of the nature of the dilemmas in Keynes's thinking.

*Roy Forbes Harrod. "An Essay in Dynamic theory," Econ. Jour., 49 (March 1939 with an erratum in June 1939) 14-33, 377.

*Evsey Domar. "The Problem of Capital Accumulation." Amer. Econ. Rev., 38 (Dec. 1948), 777-94.

**Abba Lerner. The Economics of Control. New York: Macmillan, 1946.

**John Maynard Keynes. The General Theory of Employment Interest and Money. London: Macmillan [1936], 1973.

*Alan Coddington. "Hicks's Contribution to Keynesian Economics." Jour. Econ. Lit., 17 (September 1979), 970-988.

*Henry Phelps-Brown. "Sir Roy Harrod: A Biographical Memoir." Econ. Jour. 90 (#357, March 1980), 1-33.

G. L. S. Shackle. "Shackle on Harrod," in Henry W. Spiegel & Warren J. Samuels [eds.], op. cit., vol. 1, pp. 85-92.

To be discussed on 28 February

*James M. Buchanan. "Frank H. Knight " in IESS, vol. 8, pp. 424-28.

*William S. Kern. "On the Market As a Game: Hayek vs. Knight," in Warren Samuels [ed.]. op. cit., vol. 3 (1985), pp. 51- 59.

*Mark Perlman. "Perlman on Shackle," in Henry W. Spiegel and Warren Samuels [eds.], op. cit., vol. 2, p. 579-94.

5. The material on the Lausanne School and certain of its lineal descendants is to be completed by 14 March. It comes in non-chronological sequence, but is paced here to smooth the flow of the earlier materials and their ties to the later tradition. As I have already indicated, there were three marginal utility wellsprings: Jevons the Austrians and Walras. Their successors followed parallel, but somewhat competitive, courses.

*Spiegel. op. cit., ch. 24.

*Ekelund and Hebert. op. cit., ch. 16.

*Kenneth J. Arrow. "Economic Equilibrium," in <u>IESS</u>, vol. 4, pp. 376-89.

To be discussed on 12 March

*William Jaffe. "Walras, Leon," in <u>IESS</u>, vol. 16, pp.447-53.

Don Patinkin. <u>Money, Interest and Prices</u>. "Note B: Walras' Theory of Tatonnement."

**Leon Walras. <u>Elements of Pure Economics or the Theory of Social Wealth</u>, trans William Jaffe.

To be discussed on 14 March

*Maurice Allais. "Pareto, Vilfredo," in <u>IESS</u>, vol. 11, pp. 399-411.

**Vilfredo Pareto. <u>Manual of Political Economy</u>, trans. by Ann S. Schwier.

To be discussed on 16 March

*William Baumol. "Baumol on Hicks," in Henry W. Spiegel and Warren J. Samuels [eds.], <u>op. cit.</u>, vol. 1, pp. 37-64.

Assar Lindbeck. "Lindbeck on Samuelson," in Henry W. Spiegel and Warren J. Samuels [eds.], <u>op. cit.</u>, vol. 1, pp. 5-18.

Carl Christian von Weiszaecker. "Weiszaecker on Arrow." <u>ibid.</u>, vol. 1, pp. 65-83.

6. This block of reading is <u>to be completed by 16 April</u>. It deals with some distinctively American contributions to our discipline, contributions which have in major measure come to dominate much of what is taught here and in most of the "Western" world. While there are many interpretive volumes discussing the evolution of the discipline in the United States, I believe that the "standard treatment" is:

Joseph Dorfman. <u>The Economic Mind in American Civilization.</u> Volumes 1 and 2 -- 1606-1865; volume 3 -- 1865-1918; volumes 4 and 5 -- 1918-1933.

I also recommend as really first-class discussions of the development of important aspects of modern empirical economics:

Joseph W. Duncan and Shelton, William C. <u>Revolution in United States Government Statistics. 1926-1976.</u> Published by the United States Department of Commerce in 1978.

Carl F. Christ. "Early Progress in Estimating Quantitative Economics Relationships in America. <u>Amer. Econ. Rev.</u>, 75, No. 6 (Dec. 1975), 39-52.

Stephen M. Stigler. The History of Statistics: The Measurement of Uncertainty Before 1900. Cambridge: Harvard University Press. 1986. [An example of skilled historical analysis.]

However, the assignments, as such, are:

*Spiegel. op. cit., chapter 27.

*Ekelund and Hebert. op. cit., chapter 17.

For the lectures on 23, 26, 28, and 30 March

The discussion of modern monetary economics (which serves as one origin of modern macroeconomics) is to be completed by 19 April. It draws on earlier reading assignments and serves as a link to one of the key institutionalist American schools. The background is not treated in this course, since one has to make choices. Moreover, it is all but impossible to identify where to begin. Many point to Hume; others to Henry Thornton. For our purposes, which must be rather general, I chose to start with Knut Wicksell, an erstwhile (rather eccentric) pupil of Boehm-Bawerk, and to Irving Fisher, who became, once he was dead and his eccentricities were not so obvious, something of the beau ideal of the American profession. For that reason I suggest that you include in your reading two short biographies presented in Dorfman's monumental work.

*Spiegel. op. cit., ch. 26.

*Ekelund and Hebert. op. cit., ch. 19.

*Joseph Dorfman. The Economic Mind in American Civilization, 1865-1918. Vol. 3, chapter 7 ("John Bates Clark: The Conflict of Logic and Sentiment"), pp. 188-205; the middle part of Chapter 16 ("Irving Fisher: Mathematical economist and monetary reformer"), pp. 365-375, and Chapter 20 ("Wesley Clair Mitchell: Scholar of the Business Cycle"), pp. 455-473.

*James Tobin. "Neoclassical Theory in America: J. B. Clark and Fisher." Amer. Econ. Rev., 75, no. 6 (Dec. 1985), 28-38.

For the lectures on 2 and 4 April

*Mark Perlman. Labor Union Theories in America. Scan the book.

*R.B. Freeman, "Labour Economics." The New Palgrave, vol. 3, pp. 73-76.

For the lecture on 6 April

*Mark Perlman. "Political Purpose and the National Accounts." William Alonso and Paul Starr. The Politics of Numbers. New York: Russell Sage, 1987, pp. 133-51.

*Erik Lundberg. "Lundberg on Kuznets," in Henry W. Spiegel and Warren Samuels [eds.], op. cit., 523-42.

*Richard A. Easterlin, "Simon Kuznets," The New Palgrave, vol. 3, pp. 69-71.

Joseph W. Duncan and William C. Shelton. Op cit. Chapter 3.

For the lecture on 9 April

*Peter Howitt. "Macroeconomics: Relations with microeconomics." The New Palgrave, vol. 3, pp. 273-76.

*Stanley Fischer. "New classical macroeconomics." Ibid. vol. 3, pp. 647-51.

For the lectures on 11 & 13 April.

*Hal R. Varian. "Microeconomics. The New Palgrave, vol. 3, pp.461-63.

For the lecture on 16 & 18 April

*Joseph W. Duncan and William C. Shelton. Op cit. Chapters 5 & 6.

*M. Hashem Pesaran, "Econometrics," The New Palgrave, vol. 2, pp. 8-19.

7. What remains is to be completed by the end of the trimester.

*Spiegel. op. cit., chapters 28 and 29.

*Ekelund and Hebert. op. cit., chapters 22 and 23.

Terence W. Hutchison. On Revolutions and Progress ..., ch. 9.

Claudio Napoleoni. Economic Thought in the Twentieth Century. New York: Martin Robertson, 1972.

Jack Hirshleifer. "The Expanding Domain of Economics." Amer. Econ. Rev. 75, no. 6 (Dec. 1985), 53-68.

For the lecture on 20 April

> Donald N. McCloskey. "The Rhetoric of Economics." <u>Jour. Econ. Lit.</u>, 21 (1983), 481-517.
>
> *Mark Perlman. "Perceptions of Our Discipline: Three Magisterial Treatments of the Evolution of Economic Thought." <u>Hist. of Econ. Soc."Bulletin,"</u> 7 (Winter 1986), 9-28.

* * * * * * *
OLD EXAMINATIONS
First Hour Examinations

10 February 1986

1. Describe in detail Cournot's duopoly pricing proof. What inferences about the nature of competitive pricing can be drawn? What significance do you draw from the specifications of his assumptions? Given the "force" of the proof, the importance of his inferences, and the significance of his specifications, what usefulness does his work now have to (a) professional economists and (b) to businessmen?

2. Sketch out as completely as you can the contributions of William Stanley Jevons to modern economics. Identify the Utilitarian elements in his approach by contrasting them with the comparable elements in Menger's contributions.

3. Describe the Austrian School of Economics from the time of the elder Menger to the time of Hayek. What are the underlying consistent themes? Are there areas where the School has changed its position? Identify some of the principle shifts.

****

11 February 1987

Students may choose to write either Examination A or Examination B, but there is no opportunity for switching once the choice is made.

Examination A (notes, but not texts, may be used)

Answer both questions:

1. Identify five contributions associated with von Thuenen's <u>The Isolated State</u>. Explain the significance of each.

2. Explain thoroughly and carefully Jevons' and Wicksteed's perceptions of the economic science, taking care to show the likely sources of their views. How did their view differ from that of Menger/von Boehm-Bawerk/von Wieser?

Examination B (closed book)

Answer two questions: one from each part

Part I

1. What was Cournot's theory of monopoly and oligopoly price? Where desireable, use a geometric diagram.

2. What was the basic contribution of von Thuenen to the theory of regional economics?

Part II

3. How did Jevons introduce the concept of marginalism in his work? Explain fully.

4. What was the logic of Boehm-Bawerk's theory of interest how did it lead to his theory of the roundaboutness of production, and how was the "degree" of roundaboutness explained? Describe fully.

*****

5 February 1988

Answer three questions one from each part.

Part I

1. Central to von Thuenen's work was a theory of rent (location), how did it differ from Ricardo's?

2. Cournot's theories of (1) monopoly, (2) duopoly, and (3) of demand [D = f (p)] combine both logical and empirical elements. Summarize these theories and identify briefly what you think are the key logical and the critical empirical elements of each.

Part II

3. What did Jevons mean when using the phrase, "final degree of utility?" What beside diminishing "final degrees of utility" affect the amount of work that a laborer will offer to his employer? What would an increase in the price per hour do to affect a worker's willingness to work extra hours per day (or per week)? What would an increase in yearly pay do to a woman worker's willingness to give up a job and raise an (n + 1th) child?

4. Wicksteed asserted that he was Jevons's disciple. In what senses did the disciple "reinterpret" (go beyond in a different way) the master?

Part III

5. What were Carl Menger's perceptions of **subjectivity, imputed values of**

higher order goods, value as distinct from **utility** or even **price**, and how did his system differ from Jevons'? Discuss.

6. In what sense was Boehm Bawerk's perception of time and agio different from what Wicksell offered in the way of a theory of interest and the role that it plays in the production process?

*****

3 February 1989

Answer **two** of the following questions briefly and to the point:

1. Both von Thuenen and Cournot used a moderate level of abstraction to lay out their ideas. One example from each might include von Thuenen's analytical method to explain how an agricultural "estate" ought to be perceived as an economic entity, and the other might be Cournot's model to show not only how a duopolist could set prices, but also quantities -- both without reference to the other producer.

>First, identify each example in detail, and

>second, show their methodological similarities.

>Finally, why are they cited as the forerunners of modern economic science analysis?

2. >What were Jevons's ideas about science, and how was his judgement of the Coal Question and/or labor unions an example of his perception of the scientific process.

>Rene Descartes thought that mathematics was the link between all the sciences -- in what sense do you think that Jevons's and Wicksteed's uses of the calculus were a scientific advance, and were there any senses in which the uses of the calculus impeded scientific understanding? Discuss.

3. >Discuss the differences between Jevonian utilitarianism and Carl Mengerian subjectivism and explain how they approached the concept of marginal value differently.

>Indicate where Boehm Bawerk's contributions attach to Carl Mengerian subjectivism, and how did von Mises's praxeology fit into the Carl Menger subjectivist tradition?

>Wicksteed said he was the sole disciple of Jevons (surely a strange claim); but was he only a disciple -- or, did he go beyond Jevons in some senses and not in others -- Discuss.

****

20

Second Hour Examinations

8 March 1987

<u>Answer either three or four questions. Your grade will reflect an allowance for breadth as well as depth.</u>

1. Write a brief essay on the concept of equilibrium and how it got into the mainstream of economic analysis after the "marginal revolution." What relationship do you see it having to the central roles of value and price in the post-classical treatment of the topic --- what had classical economics emphasized? How does the concept of the role of equilibrium sharpen the differences among the contributions of Menger and Jevons? Discuss.

2. Discuss Marshall's "objectives" for the teaching of economics as put forth in his <u>Principle of Economics</u> taking care to stress what he wanted to synthesize in terms of the classical and various marginal contributions, what he wanted to stress in terms of the role of time in the production process, and what he thought of the relative importance of empiricism and deduction.

Identify at least four of his more-or-less original contributions such as (1) two ways to perceive elasticity of demand, (2) consumer and/or producer surplus. (3) the short and long runs, (4) joint, complementary and substitute products, (5) the bit-at-a-time method, (6) quasi-rents, and (7) prime <u>vs</u>. supplementary costs.

3. Describe Pigou's Welfare Economics, taking care to show its relationship to the system which Marshall had sought to install at Cambridge. Discuss it fully.

4. What was the implication of the imperfect competition and/or monopolistic competition attack on the traditional Marshallian synthesis? How does the concept of marginal revenue change the mechanics of microeconomics?

> Writers at the time thought that his assertion of the overwhelming "truth" of increasing costs "had finished" Marshall: others have argued that it was his assumption of perfect knowledge. What do you think made Marshall passe?

5. How did Keynes seek to revolutionize the Cambridge perception of economic analysis? What did his <u>Treatise on Money</u> offer, and what did his <u>General Theory</u> offer that was new and what was new only to Cambridge? How did Keynes's 1937 QJE article differ from the 1936 book (or did it?)? Discuss.

****

4 March 1988

1. Write an essay on the neo-classical contributions of Alfred Marshall to economics. Cover briefly.

    a. How his perceptions of what economics is about differed from Menger's and Jevons' perceptions, and how this difference affected the rigor of his presentation.

    b. His technical assumptions.

    c. His contributions regarding consumer surplus, elasticity, and time.

2. Write an essay on the dissatisfactions with Marshallian competitive partial equilibrium analysis and what emerged.

March 1989

Answer both questions:

1. The University of Cambridge came to dominate the teaching of Anglo-American economics from about 1890 until the end of World War II. Trace the development and identify the contributions of "Cambridge-on-the-Cam" economics from the time of Marshall's appointment until John Maynard Keynes's death. Specifically, what were the various systems-of-thought and the specific "discoveries" associated with the place.

2. Much of what has happened to American economic thinking after World War II can be identified with the interests and work at the University of Lausanne of Leon Walras and Vilfredo Pareto. Identify the contributions of each. Why does their economics have so much appeal?

*****

25 March 1987 (special exam)

Instructions: Answer each question:

This is an open-book examination: You have one week to turn in your answers. They should be in polished essay form.

1. What were Wicksell's contributions? Identify and discuss.

2. Discuss the differences between the positions taken by Maynard Keynes in his Treatise on Money and in his later General Theory. . . ..
What was the "contradiction" between Keynes' views in compensatory governmental investment programs and his views on uncertainty? Discuss.

3. What is the rationale for Marshallian partial equilibrium analysis and the one for general equilibrium analysis?

22

Final Examination

22 April 1986

Answer four questions at least one from each part.

Part I

1. Write an essay on the role of mathematics in the evolution of modern economics, taking care to identify the arguments, pro and con, for its use as an expository and/or an analytical instrument(s).

2. Write a brief essay on the purposes of studying the history of economic thought. First, what is the delineation of economics? Second, where and why, in your view, has "Professionalism" (define the term) occurred? Third, discuss the variety of sources of ideas which have been incorporated into the "core area" of economics (delineate that area) and explain why some contributions have been more and some less "acceptable."

3. Write a brief essay on the development of macroeconomics in the development of the discipline.

Part II

4. What were the schema introduced into economics by any _four_ of these "groups":

   a. William Stanley Jevons and Philip Wicksteed
   b. John Bates Clark
   c. Alfred Marshall
   d. Leon Walras and Vilfredo Pareto
   e. John Maynard Keynes and/or the "Keynesians"
   f. Wesley Clair Mitchell
   g. Roy F. Harrod and Evsey Domar
   h. John von Neumann and Oskar Morgenstern
   i. Paul H. Douglas and Charles E. Cobb
   j. Knut Wicksell, Gunnar Myrdal and the Swedish group
   k. Karl Popper or some other [economic] methodologist

5. Using as exemplar material from three of the following:

   1. The Austrians
   2. The "neoclassical economists"
   3. The Lausanne general equilibrium writers
   4. The American Institutionalists
   5. The English "neo-Ricardians"

   Identify what constitutes a school of economic thought -- does it include a reaction to a change in socio-economic problems, a change in assumptions and/or method, an advance in analytical process, or something else?

6. Write a brief essay on the evolution and ultimate disappearance of interest in (a) the "residual," (b) the wages-fund, _or_ (c) "the greatest good for the greatest number."

Part III

7. Discuss the "rise" and "fall" of "Pigovian welfare economics" or imperfect competition.

8. How did modern national income accounting come to be established? What are the issues which separated one of its principal architects, Simon Kuznets, from the work done by his successors in the Department of Commerce? What was the contribution of Richard Stone, and what part did John D. Hicks's The Social Framework play?

*****

26 April 1988

Answer each question:

1. Schumpeter mentions that von Thuenen and Cournot "wrote before their time." Indicate **fully and in detail** what was so prescient about their work.

2. How do you explain the rise and fall of Marshallian neo-classical economics. **Discuss fully**.

3. Discuss the impact of John Bates Clark and Irving Fisher on the development of American economic thought.

4. What is there to the American Institutional Economics of Thorstein Veblen, Wesley Clair Mitchell? **Discuss**.

5. Trace the development of macroeconomics from the time of Walras through the institutionalization of modern national income analysis.

26 April 1988

Answer each question:

1. Schumpeter mentions that von Thuenen and Cournot "wrote before their time." Indicate **fully and in detail** what was so prescient about their work.

2. How do you explain the rise and fall of Marshallian neo-classical economics. **Discuss fully**.

3. Discuss the impact of John Bates Clark and Irving Fisher on the development of American economic thought.

4. What is there to the American Institutional Economics of Thorstein Veblen, Wesley Clair Mitchell? **Discuss**.

5. Trace the development of macroeconomics from the time of Walras through the institutionalization of modern national income analysis.

Master's Degree Comprehensive Examination

1. Using as exemplar material from three of the following:

    1. The English Mercantilists
    2. The Physiocrats
    3. The English "Classicals"
    4. The Austrians
    5. The American Institutionalists

   Identify what constitutes a school of economic thought --- does it include a reaction to a change in socio-economic problems, a change in assumptions and/or method, an advance in analytical process, or something else?

2. Write a brief essay on the evolution and ultimate disappearance of interest in (a) the "residual" (b) the wages-fund, or (c) "the greatest good for the greatest number."

***

Answer one question

1. Schumpeter identifies Adam Smith as the last of the philosophers. Mitchell sees Smith as the beginning of modern economics. Given this dichotomy, how do you see the Smith of the Theory of Moral Sentiments and the Smith of the Wealth of Nations? Explain.

2. Identify fully the principal contribution to static microanalytic analysis of:

    1. Johann Heinrich von Thuenen
    2. Antoine Augustin Cournot
    3. Alfred Marshall
    4. Joan Robinson

***

Answer three questions, one from Part One and two from Part Two:

Part One

1. One of the questions intriguing the classical economists was who "pocketed" the residual? Some said the landlord, others said the owners of capital. Another view was that it depended upon the kind of monopoly power inherent in the particular market situation. And then there was the opinion that it depended upon the social bargaining power of each of the groups involved in the production and/or distribution process.

    Write a brief essay first identifying what was meant by the residual, then place the comments of each of the following into the appropriate group with a precis of what the opinion was, and finally offer your own assessment of who (if any) was "right:" Ricardo, Malthus, Senior, John Stuart Mill, and Marx.

25

2. Explain what is meant by the Marshallian "neo-classical synthesis." taking care to identify your thinking by reference to questions of factors shaping demand and supply, objectivity and subjectivity, <u>a priori</u> theory and empiricism, and the determinants of interest rates.

3. What were Cournot's contributions to modern economic theory and theorizing? Compare and contrast them with the contributions to modern economic theory made by Carl Menger.

Part Two

4. Discuss thoroughly the contributions of Johann von Thuenen.

5. Who developed national income analysis? Discuss thoroughly.

6. What was the Keynesian analysis? Identify the IS-LM interpretations offered by John Hicks and explain its rise and fall.

7. What is game theory? Identify the original work by von Neumann and Morganstern, the work on the core, and the more recent work coming under the social choice rubric.

COMPREHENSIVE EXAMINATION FOR THE Ph.D. IN ECONOMICS

February 1985

Instructions: Answer five questions. one from each part.

Part I

1. Aristotle argued that property ownership was essential to all types of people, not so his teacher, Plato. Why did they differ on this topic? On what other "economic" matters did they also differ? Did either have much of a concept of price as an incentive or as an equilibrating mechanism? What economic ideas did either Xenophon or Hesiod have?

2. What was the medieval perception of The Just Price? What did Thomas Aquinas consider usury to be? Include in your discussion explanations of the doctrines of dammum emergens and lucrum cessans. poena conventionalis and periculum sortis.

Part II

3. Identify the basic economic ideas of Thomas Mun, Dudley North, Nicholas Barber, Edward Misselden, and Gerard Malynes. Date their contributions. Can you explain the "sophistication" of their views by any reference to chronological development? If not how do you explain the variation of "competence?"

4. What was the "school" of Political Arithmeticians? What was novel about their contributions, and how do you explain their sudden emergence and similarly sudden disappearance? Identify the scope of Petty's economic interests, the economic efforts of Gregory King, and the general interest that virtually all members of this "school" had in the demographic aspects of economics. What was Edmund Halley's contribution to demographic analysis?

5. Compare and contrast the original perceptions and organization of the body of economic thought as developed by Richard Cantillon, Sir James Steuart, Francois Quesnay, and Adam Smith.

Part III

6. What were the contributions to economic analysis offered by Adam Smith?

7. Compare and contrast the contributions to modern or semi-modern economics made by David Ricardo and Thomas Robert Malthus.

8. Benthamite utilitarianism was probably at the heart of English classical economics. What was it, and how was it modified by John Stuart Mill? What, by way of comparison, was at the heart of the work done by Walras and Pareto? If they did not draw on the tradition of Bentham, what was the source of the "inspiration" in their economic writings? Discuss.

Part IV

9. Identify the similarities and differences in the contributions to marginal economic analysis of William Stanley Jevons, Karl Menger, and John Bates Clark. Terence Hutchison thinks that there was a "marginalist" revolution; what do you think is a "revolution," and, accordingly what tests does the marginalist revolution have to pass? Did it do so? Discuss.

10. What is "neo-classical economics?" How can it be distinguished from Jevonian or Mengerian "marginalism?" How do each of the following persons "fit" under the neo-classical <u>aegis:</u> Wicksell, Wicksteed, Frank Knight, Edward Chamberlin, John Neville Keynes, John Maynard Keynes, and Milton Friedman.

11. What were Piero Sraffa's contributions to economic theory? In what traditions did he write?

Part V

12. It is said the Johann von Thuenen and Auguste Cournot "wrote before their time." Just what were their contributions, and in what sense were they more "before their time" than "any" other economic writers?

13. Trace the development of the quantity theory of money starting with John Locke, Henry Thornton, and Irving Fisher. What did Wesley Clair Mitchell conclude as to its universal validity? What did Mitchell offer as an alternative explanation for price changes?

14. How did modern national income accounting come to be established? What are the issues which separated one of its principal architects, Simon Kuznets, from the work done by his successors in the Department of Commerce? What was the contribution of Richard Stone, and what part did John D. Hicks's <u>The Social Framework</u> play?

Brown University

Louis Putterman
Department of Economics

Economics 128
University Course 128

The History and Philosophical Context of Economic Thought

Office: 206 Robinson Hall
Phone: 863-3837
Office Hours: T and Th 1:00-1:50, and by appointment

Fall, 1988

Requirements: You may choose one of the following options. (a) A paper of 8 to 10 double-spaced pages on an assigned theme or themes after each three units of the course, totalling four papers, each worth 20% of term grade; (b) a midterm exam worth 30% and a final exam worth 50% of term grade; (c) a paper on a topic approved by the instructor, worth 20% of term grade, plus midterm and final exams, worth 20% and 40%, respectively. Under (c), your paper is due at the final exam, and will be 10-15 pages in length. Under each option, the remaining 20% of the term grade will be determined by class participation.

1. Classical Economics: Smith, Malthus, and Ricardo.

    Readings:

    1. Adam Smith, The Wealth of Nations [1776], Book I, Ch. 1, 2, 3, 7, and 10 (Part I); Book II, Ch. 2 (pp. 420-423).
    2. Thomas Malthus, Essay on Profits [1798], Chapters 2 and 5.
    3. David Ricardo, Essay on Profits [1815], pp. 10-31.
    4. William Barber, History of Economic Thought (1967), chapters on Smith, Malthus, and Ricardo (pp. 23-93).
    5. (Optional) Encyclopedia of Social Sciences: (a) "Economic Thought": subsections on Ancient and Medieval Thought, Mercantilist Thought, and Physiocratic Thought; (b) "Adam Smith"; "Thomas Malthus"; "David Ricardo". NOR.

2. Marx's Economics

    Readings:

    1. Karl Marx, Capital, Volume I: [1867], Ch. I, Sec. 1 (pp. 35-41); Chs. IV, V, VI, and VII (pp. 146-198) but especially pp. 146-7, 167-73, 175-6, and 190-5; Ch. XIV, Sec. 4, 5 (pp. 350-363); Ch. XXXII (pp. 761-764). Volume III: [1894], Ch. X (pp. 173-199) but especially pp. 188-191; Chs. XXI-XXIV (pp. 338-399), skim except for pp. 338-9, 391-3.

2. Maurice Dobb, *Theories of Value and Distribution Since Adam Smith*, (1973) Ch. 6: "Karl Marx."
3. Robert Hielbroner, *Marxism for and Against*, (1980) Ch.- "The Socioanalysis of Capitalism."
4. (Optional) Frederick Engels, Prefaces to Volumes II and III of *Capital* (pp. 5-19 and 8-21, only), and Appendix to Vol. III, "Law of Value and Rate of Profit" (891-907).
5. (Optional) Mark Blaug, *Economic Theory in Retrospect*, (1968) Chapter 7, "Marxian Economics."
6. (Optional) Paul Sweezy, *The Theory of Capitalist Development*, especially first chapters.
7. (Optional) Joseph Schumpter, *Ten Great Economists*, Chapter 1, "Karl Marx."

3. The Marginalists

Readings:

1. Alfred Marshall, *Principles of Economics* [1890], Preface to 1st Edition (pp. v-xi); Book I, Chapter I, Section 4 (pp. 5-10); Book III, Chapters 3, 4, and 6 (pp. 92-116, 124-137); Book V, Chapters 2 and 3 (pp. 331-350); Book VI, Chapter 13, Sections 11-15 (pp. 712-722); (Optional: Appendix B. The Growth of Economic Science. pp. 754-769).
2. Barber, Chapter 6, "Alfred Marshall and the Framework of Neo-Classical Economics."
3. William Jaffe, "Menger, Jevons and Walras Dehomogenized", *Economic Inquiry*, 1976.
4. Mark Blaug, "Was There a Marginal Revolution?" and G.L.S. Shackle, "Marginalism: The Harvest", in Black, Coats, and Goodwin, eds., *The Marginal Revolution in Economics* (1973).
5. (Optional) Emil Kauder, *A History of Marginal Utility Theory* (1965).
6. (Optional) *Encyclopedia of the Social Sciences*, "Economic Thought": subsections on the Historical School, The Austrian School, and the Institutional School. NOR.

4. Political-Economy versus Economics

Readings:

1. Phyllis Deane, *The Evolution of Economic Ideas* (1978), Chapters 6, 7, and 9 ("Scope and methodology of

classical political economy," "The marginal revolution and the neo-classical triumph," and "The Marxian Alternative").
2. Philip Mirowski, "Physics and the Marginalist Revolution."
3. Dobb, Ch. 7, "The Jevonian Revolution," Section I (pp.166-183), in <u>Theories of Value</u>...
4. Paul Sweezy, "Editor's Introduction", <u>Karl Marx and the Close of his System</u> (1949).
5. Rudolf Hilferding, [1904] "Bohm-Bawerk's Criticism of Marx," in Sweezy, ed., <u>ibid</u>: pp. 130-134, 137-140, and 184-189.
6. Assar Lindbeck, <u>The Political Economy of the New Left: An Outsider's View</u>, (1977) Part One, and "Comment" by Stephen Hymer and Frank Roosevelt.
7. (Optional) Frank Hahn, "General Equilibrium Theory," pp. 123-138 in Daniel Bell and Irving Kristol, eds., <u>The Crisis in Economic Theory</u>, 1981.
8. Ronald Meek, "Marginalism and Marxism," in <u>The Marginal Revolution in Economics</u> (cited above).
9. (Optional) Thorstein Veblen, "Professor Clark's Economics," <u>Quarterly Journal of Economics</u>, 1908 (reprinted in <u>The Place of Science in Modern Civilization</u>).

5. General Equilibrium Theory

Readings:

1. F.M. Scherer, "General Equilibrium and Economic Efficiency," <u>The American Economist</u>, 1966.
2. F.M. Bator, "The Simple Analytics of Welfare Maximization," originally in <u>American Economic Review</u>, March 1957.

6. The Shift to Ordinal Utility

Readings:

1. Vincent Tarascio, "Paretian Welfare Theory: Some Neglected Aspects," <u>Journal of Political Economy</u>, 1969.
2. Robert Cooter and Peter Rappaport, "Were the Ordinalists Wrong About Welfare Economics?" <u>Journal of Economic Literature</u>, 1984.
3. Amartya Sen, "Personal Utilities and Public Judgments: or What's Wrong with Welfare Economics?" <u>Economic Journal</u>, 1979.

7. Background on Method and Epistemology

   Readings:

   1. Blaug, The Methodology of Economics. Part I: "What you always wanted to know about the philosophy of science but were afraid to ask," and Part II: "The history of economic methodology," except Chapter 5 (all listed as "From Received View to View of Popper").
   2. (Optional) Karl Popper, "Three Views Concerning Human Knowledge," pp. 97-119 in Conjectures and Refutations, 1963.

8. Contending Views on Methodology; The Making of an Economist

   Readings:

   1. John Neville Keynes, The Scope and Method of Political Economy, (1890) pp. 9-30.
   2. Ludwig von Mises, "Epistemological Problems of Economics" pp. 17-22, and "The Scope and Meaning of the System of a Priori Theorems," pp. 23-30, in Epistemological Problems of Economics [1933].
   3. Milton Friedman, "Methodology of Positive Economics," pp. 3-43 in Essays in Positive Economics, 1953.
   4. Amartya Sen, "Description as Choice," Oxford Economic Papers, 1980.
   5. Axel Leijonhufvud, "Life Among the Econ," Western Economic Journal, 1973.
   6. Benjamin Ward, "Economics as a Science," in What's Wrong with Economics?" (1972), pp. 5-13.
   7. David Colander and Arjo Klamer, "The Making of an Economist," Economic Perspectives, 1987.

   Some additional, strictly optional, material of interest for this topic and topic 10 is:

   E.K. Hunt and Howard J. Sherman, excerpts from Economics: An Introduction to Traditional and Radical Views, 1972.
   Oscar Lange, "The Scope and Method of Economics," 1945.
   Karl Polanyi, "The Economy as Instituted Process," (ca.) 1957.
   Alfred Marshall, "The Scope and Method of Economics," 1890.
   Ronald Meek, "Economics and Ideology."

Lionel Robbins, "The Subject Matter of Economics," in *The Nature and Significance of Economic Science*, 1932.
Hugh Stretton, "Paul Streeten: An Appreciation," in *Theory and Reality in Development*, 1986, especially pp. 4-13 and 26-27.

9. Political Philosophy and Economics

   Readings:

   1. John Locke, *Treatise of Civil Government*, [1688], Chapter V, "Of Property."
   2. Selections from Thomas Hobbes, *Leviathan* [1651], Chapters 13 and 17.
   3. S.H. Peterson, ed., *Readings in the History of Economic Thought*: Bernard de Mandeville, "Fable of the Bees," [1714], pp. 2-18; Jeremy Bentham, "An Introduction to the Principles of Morals and Legislation," [1789], pp. 178-182; John Stuart Mill, "On Liberty" [1859] and "Utilitarianism," [1863], pp. 270-290 (all listed under Mandeville).
   4. Gunnar Myrdal, *The Political Element in the Development of Economic Thought*, 1953 [1929] Chapters 1, 2, 3, and 4 (further reading guidelines to be announced).

10. Economics and Values

    Readings:

    1. Frank Knight, "The Ethics of Competition", (1935).
    2. Herbert Gintis, "A Radical Analysis of Welfare Economics and Individual Development," *Quarterly Journal of Economics*, 1978.
    3. Dan Usher, "The Value of Life for Decision Making in the Public Sector," in E.F. Paul *et al*., eds., *Ethics and Economics*, 1985.
    4. Richard Thaler and Sherwin Rosen, "The Value of Saving a Life: Evidence from the Labor Market," in Terleckyj, Ed., *Household Production and Consumption*. National Bureau of Economic Research, 1976 (read for general idea).
    5. (Optional) J.A. Mirrlees, "The Economic Uses of Utilitarianism," and Frank Hahn, "On Some Difficulties of the Utilitarian Economist," in Amartya Sen and Bernard Williams, eds. *Utilitarianism and Beyond* (1982).

11. Utilitarianism and Other Views of Justics

    Readings:

    1. R.M. Hare, "Ethical Theory and Utilitarianism," and John C. Harsanyi, "Morality and the Theory of Rational Behavior," in Sen and Williams, Utilitarianism and Beyond.
    2. John Rawls, "Justice as Fairness" [1958] in Laslett and Runciman, Philosophy, Politics and Society.
    3. John Roemer, "An Historical Materialist Alternative to Welfarism," 1981 reprinted with revisions in Jon Elster, ed., Foundations of Social Choice Theory).
    4. James Buchanan, "A Hobbesian Interpretation of the Rawlsian Difference Principle," (1979) in Karl Brunner, ed., Economics and Social Institutions.

12. The Best of All Possible Worlds

    Readings:

    1. Murray Rothbard, "Property and Exchange," from For a New Liberty (1973).
    2. Shlomo Avineri, "The Stages of Socialism," from The Social and Political Thought of Karl Marx (1968).

Jane Rossetti
Williams College
Fall, 1989

Economics 235:   Economics as Literature

The idea of reading and analyzing economic texts as literary texts is rather new to economists. Since the late nineteenth century, economics has by and large been regarded as a social science where "science" outweighs most "social" factors. Mainstream economists have claimed to follow the 'scientific method' of research, making hypotheses, modelling them, testing them against available data. This approach has not so lately been questioned, both on its own grounds, and in economists' application. If economists aren't engaged in 'science', just what is it we are engaged in? Are we trying to persuade other economists to see the world as we do? Are we presenting our interpretations of some economy actually out there? Are we constructing our idea of the economy, and then deciding how to go about analyzing it? These approachs are variously rhetorical, hermeneutical, and post-structuralist, applying literary theory and criticism to economists' work. In this course we will examine briefly the fall of 'science', and the rise of interpretative theories, and then try to apply this new way of thinking about economics to particular examples of economic writings or aspects of the economy. Since the field, in economics, is relatively new, this will require a certain amount of creativity and resourcefulness by the participants in this course.

The course requirements include active participation in class, two short papers and their presentation to the class, and a (take home) final exam. At least one of the papers must be a literary analysis of an economic text.

The syllabus attached should be viewed as a guide to the most basic readings, but not as an exhaustive listing of the literature. You are encouraged to read beyond the assigned chapters or portions of the books identified, and into other topics which are not covered well in the course. Please do the basic reading before class meetings!

The text for the class is The Rhetoric of Economics, by D. McCloskey. Other major references are listed below, and are all on overnight reserve. Readings marked "xerox" are at the reserve desk in the Economics 235 Readings Notebook.

Blaug, Mark.   The Methodology of Economics.

Booth, Wayne.   The Rhetoric of Fiction.

Klamer, Arjo.   Conversations with Economists.

Klamer, Arjo, D. McCloskey, R. Solow, eds.   The Consequences of Economic Rhetoric.

Kuhn, Thomas.   The Structure of Scientific Revolutions.

Lakatos, I. and A. Musgrave, eds.   Criticism and the Growth of Knowledge.

Latsis, S.   Method and Appraisal in Economics.

Nelson, Megill and McCloskey, eds.   The Rhetoric of the Human Sciences.

Rorty, Richard.   The Consequences of Pragmatism.

I. Economics as Science

A. Falsificationism and its Failings

    McCloskey, ch. 1.
    Lakatos, I. "Falsification and the Methodology of the Scientific Research Programme" sections 1-2b; in Lakatos and Musgrave, pp. 91-132.
    Blaug, ch. 1.
    Maxwell, Nicholas, "A Critique of Popper's View" Philosophy of Science, June, 1972.

B. Kuhn and Scientific Revolutions

    Kuhn, T. chs. 3, 9, 10.

C. Lakatos and Scientific Research Programs

    Lakatos "Falsification and the Methodology of the SRP" op cit, pages 132-177.
    Hutchinson, T. in Latsis.
    A. Rosenberg, "Lakatosian Consolation for Economists" in Economics and Philosophy, April 1986.

II. Science as ?

Richard Rorty, "Science as Solidarity" in Nelson, et al.
----- Consequences of Pragmatism p. xxxvii-xliv.
McCloskey, ch. 2, 3.
----- exchanges with Hollis, Economics and Philosophy, vol. 1, 1985.
Stanley Fish, Is There a Text in this Class?, ch. 15, 16.

FIRST PAPER DUE

III. Economics as Literature

A. Persuasion and Conversation

    1. Levels of Discourse

        Klamer, A. Conversations with Economists, ch. 13
        ----- "Levels of Discourse..." History of Political Economy, Summer, 1984.

    2. Metaphors

        McCloskey, ch. 4, 5.
        Mirowski, Phil. "Shall I Compare Thee..." in Consequences of Economic Rhetoric. OR
        ----- "Physics and the 'marginalist revolution'" Cambridge Journal of Economics, 1984, 8, 361-379.
        Klamer, A. "As If Economists and Their Subjects were Rational" in

The Rhetoric of the Human Sciences.
  Bicchieri, C. "Should an Economist Abstain from Metaphor?" in
      Consequences of Economic Rhetoric.

   3. Rhetoric

      McCloskey, "The Rhetoric of Economics" Journal of Economic
          Literature, 1983, pps. 491-499, 507-515.
      McCloskey, ch. 6, OR 9
      Booth, The Rhetoric of Fiction, ch. 1, and one of chapters 2, 3, 4
          or 5, OR Modern Dogma and the Rhetoric of Assent, ch. 1-3.
      Craufurd Goodwin, "The Heterogeneity of the Economists' Discourse"
          in Consequences of Economic Rhetoric.
      Davis and Hersh, "Rhetoric and Mathematics" OR
      Campbell, "Charles Darwin, Rhetorician of Science" both in
          Rhetoric of the Human Sciences.

-----
      see also
      Symposium reports in Economics and Philosophy, April 1988.

B. Interpretation and Construction: the importance of context

   1. Foucault

      The Order of Things, Foreword to the English edition, Preface, ch
          6, plus section on Ricardo.
      Jack Amariglio, HOPE 20:4 "The body, discourse, and power..."
      Arjo Klamer, "The Rise of Modernism", mimeo.

      S. Todd Lowry, The Archaeology of Economic Ideas, Duke Univ.
          Press, 1987
      Pamela Major-Poetzl, Michel Foucault's Archaeology of Western
          Culture, UNC press, 1983

   2. Hermeneutics

      Eagleton, ch. 2.
      "Austrian Economics" in the Palgrave's Encyclopedia.
      Ebeling, R. M. "Toward a Hermeneutical Economics" in Kirzner,
          Subjectivism, Intelligibility and Economic Understanding.
      Lavoie, D. "Accounting of Interpretations..." or "Hermeneutics,
          Subjectivity..." (xeroxs)

   3. Deconstruction

      Eagleton, T. ch. 4. "Post-Structuralism"
      Derrida, J. "Differance" and translator's introduction (xerox)
      Rossetti, "Menger", xerox
      Elshtain, J.B. "Feminists Political Rhetoric" in Rhetoric of the
          Human Sciences, optional.
      Folbre and Hartmann "The Rhetoric of Self-Interest" in
          Consequences of Economic Rhetoric.

4. Changing meanings

>   Weintraub, E. Roy. "On the Brittleness of the Orange Equilibrium" in *Consequences of Economic Rhetoric*.
>   Fritz and Haulman, "The Marginal Revolution and Change in the Linguistic Structure of Economics" (xerox)
>   Bausor, Randy. "Conceptual Evolution in Economics: The Case of Rational Expectations." (xerox)

IV. Implications

>   Stanley Fish, "Comments from Outside Economics"
>   Arjo Klamer, "Negotiating a New Conversation..."
>   Donald McCloskey, "The Consequences of Rhetoric" all in Klamer, et al.

SECOND PAPER DUE - Class presentations.

FINAL EXAM

Michigan State University

Economics 421
History of Economic Thought

Warren J. Samuels
Course Outline and
Reading List

Texts: Henry W. Spiegel, THE GROWTH OF ECONOMIC THOUGHT, Revised and expanded edition, 1983

E. K. Hunt, HISTORY OF ECONOMIC THOUGHT: A CRITICAL PERSPECTIVE, 1979

PART ONE: INTRODUCTION

PART TWO: ECONOMIC THOUGHT PRIOR TO ADAM SMITH

    A. Pre-Scholastic

        1. Spiegel, chs. 1-2

    B. Scholastic

        1. Spiegel, chs. 3-4

    C. Mercantilism

        1. Spiegel, chs. 5-7

        2. Hunt, chs. 1-2

    D. Physiocracy

        1. Spiegel, ch. 8

        2. Hunt, ch. 2

    E. Other Precursors of Adam Smith

        1. Spiegel, chs. 6, 7, 9, 10

        2. Hunt, ch. 2

PART THREE: ADAM SMITH AND CLASSICAL POLITICAL ECONOMY

    A. Adam Smith

        1. Spiegel, chs. 10-11

        2. Hunt, ch. 3

    B. English Classical Political Economy

        1. Spiegel, chs. 12-16

        2. Hunt, chs. 4-8

Economics 422 Warren J. Samuels
History of Economic Thought Syllabus

Texts: Henry W. Spiegel, THE GROWTH OF ECONOMIC THOUGHT, revised edition, 1983

E. Ray Canterbery, THE MAKING OF ECONOMICS, 3rd ed., 1987

PART ONE: THE CLASSICAL HERITAGE

Skim Spiegel, chs. 10-16, and Canterbery, chs. 1-5, reading carefully to become familiar with the ideas of Smith, Malthus, Ricardo, Bentham and J. S. Mill.

PART TWO: ANARCHISM, SOCIALISM, MARXISM

1. Spiegel, chs. 17-21
2. Canterbery, ch. 10
3. Marx and Engels, "Communist Manifesto," any edition

PART THREE: MARGINAL UTILITY (AUSTRIAN) ECONOMICS

1. Spiegel, chs. 22-24
2. Canterbery, ch. 5, 14 (to page 259)

PART FOUR: HISTORICAL ECONOMICS

1. Spiegel, chs. 17-18

PART FIVE: NEOCLASSICAL ECONOMICS: THE DEVELOPMENT OF MICROECONOMICS

1. Spiegel, chs. 25, 27, 28
2. Canterbery, ch. 6

PART SIX: INSTITUTIONAL ECONOMICS

1. Spiegel, ch. 27
2. Canterbery, ch. 11

PART SEVEN: KEYNES AND THE DEVELOPMENT OF MACROECONOMICS

1. Spiegel, ch. 26
2. Canterbery, chs 7, 15, 16, 17, 18

PART EIGHT: FURTHER DEVELOPMENTS

1. Spiegel, ch. 29
2. Canterbery, chs. 8, 9, 12, 13, 14, 18

Economics 841A
History of Economic Thought

Warren J. Samuels
Syllabus

Texts: Mark Blaug, ECONOMIC THEORY IN RETROSPECT, 4th ed., 1985
S. Todd Lowry, ed., PRE-CLASSICAL ECONOMIC THOUGHT, 1987
Adam Smith, WEALTH OF NATIONS, Modern Library ed.

PART ONE: INTRODUCTION

1. Blaug, Introduction; chapter 17

2. E. Whittaker, A HISTORY OF ECONOMIC IDEAS, chs. 3, 9, 16

3. G. L. S. Shackle, THE NATURE OF ECONOMIC THOUGHT, ch. 1

4. W. J. Samuels, THE CLASSICAL THEORY OF ECONOMIC POLICY, appendix

5. W. J. Samuels, "The History of Economic Thought as Intellectual History," HISTORY OF POLITICAL ECONOMY, vol. 6 (Fall 1974), pp. 305-323

6. W. J. Samuels, "Ideology in Economics," in Sidney Weintraub, ed., MODERN ECONOMIC THOUGHT, 1977, pp. 467-484

7. W. J. Samuels, "The Scope of Economics Historically Considered," LAND ECONOMICS, vol. 48 (August 1972), pp. 248-268

8. W. J. Samuels, "The State, Law, and Economic Organization," RESEARCH IN LAW AND SOCIOLOGY, vol. 2 (1979), pp. 65-99

PART TWO: ECONOMIC THOUGHT PRIOR TO ADAM SMITH

1. Blaug, ch. 1

2. Henry Spiegel, THE GROWTH OF ECONOMIC THOUGHT, Revised and expanded edition, 1983, chs. 1-8

3. Lowry, chs. 1-8

PART THREE: ADAM SMITH AND ENGLISH CLASSICAL POLITICAL
              ECONOMY

1. Blaug, chs. 2-6

2. Adam Smith, WEALTH OF NATIONS

3. W. C. Mitchell, TYPES OF ECONOMIC THEORY, 1967, vol. 1, chs. 2-8

4. P. Sraffa, ed., THE WORKS AND CORRESPONDENCE OF DAVID RICARDO, vol. 1, pp. xxx-xlix

5. David Ricardo, ON THE PRINCIPLES OF POLITICAL ECONOMY AND TAXATION, 3rd ed., chs. 1-7, 20, 30, 31

6. W. J. Samuels, "Adam Smith and the Economy as a System of Power," INDIAN ECONOMIC JOURNAL, vol. 20 (January-March 1973), pp. 363-381

7. W. J. Samuels, "The Political Economy of Adam Smith," ETHICS, vol. 87 (April 1977), pp. 189-207

Economics 841C

HISTORY OF ECONOMIC THOUGHT

Warren J. Samuels

Texts: G.L.S. Shackle, THE YEARS OF HIGH THEORY, 1967

Phyllis Deane, THE EVOLUTION OF ECONOMIC IDEAS, 1978

John Maloney, MARSHALL, ORTHODOXY AND THE PROFESSIONALISATION OF ECONOMICS, 1985

Klaus Hennings and Warren J. Samuels, eds., NEO-CLASSICAL ECONOMICS, 1990

Note: Starred [*] items are optional in the sense that a selection but not all need be read in any section.

PART ONE: A HERITAGE OF DISSONANCE

1. Shackle, chs. 1-2
2. Mark Blaug, ECONOMIC THEORY IN RETROSPECT, 3rd ed., Introduction and ch. 8; or same in 4th ed.
3. Deane, chs. 6-7, 9
4. A. W. Coats, "Sociological Aspects of British Economic Thought," JOURNAL OF POLITICAL ECONOMY, vol. 75 (1967), pp. 706-729
5. A. W. Coats, "The Historicist Reaction in English Political Economy, 1870-1890," ECONOMICA, vol. 21 (1954), pp. 143-53

PART TWO: NEOCLASSICAL ECONOMICS: THE DEVELOPMENT OF MICROECONOMICS

A. Marshallian Economics

1. Blaug, chs. 9-10, either edition
2. Deane, chs. 7-8
3. Alfred Marshall, PRINCIPLES OF ECONOMICS, 8th ed.: Prefaces of 1st and 8th eds; Book 1, chs. 1-4; Book 3, chs. 1-6; Book 4, chs. 1, 9, 11-13; Book 5, chs. 1-15; Book 6, chs. 1, 2, 6-8, 11; Appendices B, C, D, J
*4. Joseph A. Schumpeter, HISTORY OF ECONOMIC ANALYSIS, Part 4, chs. 5, 6, 7 (including appendix)
*5. T. W. Hutchison, A REVIEW OF ECONOMIC DOCTRINES, ch. 4
*6. G. J. Stigler, PRODUCTION AND DISTRIBUTION THEORIES, ch. 4
*7. William Breit and Roger L. Ransom, THE ACADEMIC SCRIBBLERS, chs. 2, 3
*8. Leo Rogin, THE MEANING AND VALIDITY OF ECONOMIC THEORY, ch. 14
9. Maloney, chs. 1-11

239

B. Further Development of Neoclassical Economics

 1. Shackle, chs. 3-8, 17
 2. Deane, chs. 10, 11
 3. H. W. Spiegel, THE GROWTH OF ECONOMIC THOUGHT (1971), ch. 25
 4. Blaug, chs. 11, 13, either edition
*5. Ben B. Seligman, MAIN CURRENTS IN MODERN ECONOMICS, chs. 4 (v, vi, vii); 5 (iii, iv, v); 6 (iii, vi, vii), 8 (i-v, vii, viii); 9 (i, ii, iii, vi)
*6. Wesley C. Mitchell, TYPES OF ECONOMIC THEORY, vol. 2, chs. 11, 12, 13, 16, 17, 18
*7. Breit and Ransom, chs. 5, 6, 7, 9, 12, 13, 14
*8. O. H. Taylor, A HISTORY OF ECONOMIC THOUGHT, ch. 16
 9. Hennings and Samuels, entire book

PART THREE: KEYNES AND THE DEVELOPMENT OF MACROECONOMICS

 1. Blaug, 3rd ed., chs. 14, 15; 4th ed., chs. 15, 16
 2. Deane, chs. 12, 13
*3. Seligman, chs. 6 (iv); 7 (i, ii); 8 (iv, vii); 9 (v)
 4. Shackle, chs. 9-16
 5. Warren J. Samuels, "What Aspects of Keynes's Economic Theories Merit Continued or Renewed Interest? One Interpretation," JOURNAL OF POST KEYNESIAN ECONOMICS, vol. 9 (Fall 1986), pp. 3-16

PART FOUR: FACTORS AND FORCES IN THE DEVELOPMENT OF ECONOMIC THOUGHT

 1. Shackle, ch. 18
 2. Deane, Introduction and ch. 14
*3. Joan Robinson, ECONOMIC PHILOSOPHY
*4. Benjamin Ward, WHAT'S WRONG WITH ECONOMICS?
 5. Blaug, Introduction and ch. 16 (3rd ed.) or 17 (4th ed.)
 6. Warren J. Samuels, "The History of Economic Thought as Intellectual History," HISTORY OF POLITICAL ECONOMY, vol. 6 (Fall 1974), pp. 305-323
 7. Warren J. Samuels, "Determinate Solutions and Valuational Processes: Overcoming the Foreclosure of Process," JOURNAL OF POST KEYNESIAN ECONOMICS, vol. 11 (Summer 1989), pp. 531-546.
 8. Warren J. Samuels, "An Essay on the Nature and Significance of the Normative Nature of Economics," JOURNAL OF POST KEYNESIAN ECONOMICS, vol. 10 (Spring 1988), pp. 347-354.

Indiana University-Purdue University at Indianapolis   U
Department of Economics
E 420
History of Economic Thought

B 001, 3 credits　　　　　　　　　　Assoc. Prof. Martin C. Spechler
TR 11:30-12:45　　　　　　　　　　　　　　　Office: Cavanaugh 519
Prerequisite: E201-202　　　　Office hours: Tuesdays, 2:00-4:00 or
Fall Semester, 1990　　　　　　　　after class or by appointment
BS 3012　　　　　　　　　　　　　　　　　　　Telephone: 274-7379

　　This course is intended to convince students that great economists of the past are still important for our thinking. Not only did they develop the ideas of modern economics; they also provided alternative ways of thinking about the economy and its social context which go beyond modern models of analysis. Instead of dealing with many economists, this course concentrates on six major schools of economics which continue to this day. You will read substantial parts of text, often condensed and translated, and see how these ideas have been applied to today's problems. You will also identify the philosophical bases for present day liberal, conservative, radical, and libertarian economics. You will also review and criticize what you have learned in your previous courses in mainstream economics.
　　The course will be conducted as a lecture and discussion, with student participation and exercises based on common reading. Attendance and active participation in written work and oral discussion will count 40% of the grade; the hour exam in the seventh week will count 20%; and a take-home examination (40%) to integrate all material of the course will be due Tuesday, December 13, at 1p.m. It is expected that about half of all students completing all requirements will receive A's or B's.

　　Required Texts: All will be placed in the IUPUI library under the instructor's name. Please do not hold readings when not using them; you may make copies.
　　Jacob Oser and Stanley L. Brue, The Evolution of Economic Thought, Fourth Edition (Harcourt Brace Jovanovich, 1988), referred to below as "O & B."
　　All readings are contained in:
　　Martin C. Spechler, Perspectives in Economic Thought (McGraw-Hill paperback, 1990). [denoted R below]
DETAILED PLAN OF STUDIES

WEEK STARTING
TUESDAY　　　　　TOPIC　　　　　　　　　READINGS
1. Aug.23　　　Introduction　　　O&B, chapter 1 (pp. 1-10) and 2
　　　　　　　　　　　　　　　　　　(pp. 15-29)

　　　　　　　　Mercantilism　　　T. Mun, "England's Treasure by
　　　　　　　　　　　　　　　　　　Foreign Trade," [R]

2. Aug.30		Neo-mercantilism and trade policy	H.O. Schmitt, "Mercantilism: a Modern Argument," *Manchester School*, June, 1979, pp. 93-111. [R]
3. Sept.6		Classical School: Smith's System of Natural Liberty	O&B, ch. 4 (pp. 45-58) and ch. 5 (pp. 61-82); Adam Smith, *Wealth of Nations*, Book I, chs. I-VII, [R]
4. Sept.13		Film on *Wealth of Nations* Smith's Economics	Smith, *Wealth of Nations*, Book I, chs. VIII-X (pt.1); Book III, ch. 1; Book IV, chs. I, VIII, and IX, all in [R]
5. Sept.20		Malthus and the population bomb	O&B, ch. 6 (pp. 85-96); Thomas Malthus, *Essays on the Principle of Population*, Books I and II, in [R] Dennis Meadows and others, "The Limits to Growth," (1972) in [R] and Robert M. Solow, "Is the End of the World at Hand?" *Challenge* (1972), reprinted in Edwin Mansfield, *Principles of Macroeconomics: Readings Issues and Cases*, 4th ed., pp. 172-83.
6. Sept.27		Ricardo	O&B, ch. 7 (pp. 99-118) plus pp. 265-67; David Ricardo, *Principles of Political Economy and Taxation* chs. I, III-IV, XXI, in [R]
		Ricardo's American follower, Henry George	*Progress and Poverty*, Part III, in [R]
7. Oct.4		**HOUR EXAM**	TUESDAY IN CLASS
	Thursday	Marxism: Socialist Antecedents	O&B, chs. 9 & 10 (pp. 149-67, 171-76)
8. Oct. 11		Marx's Economics	O&B, ch. 10 (176-189); Karl Marx, *Capital*, vol. I, selected in [R]

242

9. Oct. 18	Marx's Economics Applied to History	Karl Marx, *Capital*, [R]	
10. Oct. 25	Marxian Economics Applied to the USA	O&B, pp. 467-69. Paul Baran and Paul Sweezy, *Monopoly Capital* (1966), chs. 2-4, 7 in [R]	
11. Nov. 1	<u>Austrian Neo-Classical Economics:</u> Capitalist Dynamics	O&B, ch. 12 (pp. 211-16), ch. 13 (pp. 229-49), plus pp. 463-67; Joseph A. Schumpeter, *Theory of Economic Development*, ch. II, pp. 57-94 [R], and *Capitalism Socialism and Democracy*, chs. VII-VIII, pp. 82-106. [R] Friedrich A. Hayek, *Individualism and Economic Order* (1948), ch. IV [R]	
12. Nov. 8	Neo-Classical Monetary Theory	O&B, pp. 127-30 (on Say's Law), ch. 16 (pp. 295-309).	
	<u>Keynesianism:</u> Departures from Classical School	John Maynard Keynes, *The General Theory of Employment, Interest and Money* (1936), selections in [R].	
13. Nov. 15	Keynes' Theory of Instability	J.M. Keynes, "Economic Possibilities for Our Grandchildren," (1930) in *Essays in Persuasion* [R]. J.M. Keynes, *General Theory*, chs. 11-12, 18, 22 [R] James Tobin, "Inflation and Unemployment," *American Economic Review*, 1972, no. 1, pp. 1-18. [R] Franco Modigliani, "The Monetarist Controversy, or Should We Forsake Stabilization Policies?" *American Econ.* [R]	
Nov. 21-26	THANKSGIVING VACATION	NO CLASSES	
14. Nov. 29	<u>Institutionalism:</u> Veblen and Other Critics of Capitalism	O&B, ch. 19 (pp. 361-84); Thorstein Veblen, *The Theory of the Leisure Class*, excerpted in [R]	
15. Dec. 6	Galbraith and the Attack on Big Business	John Kenneth Galbraith, *Economics and the Public Purpose*, chs. I, II, IX-XIX. [R]	
16. Dec. 13	**FINAL EXAM DUE**	TUESDAY, DEC. 13, AT 1:00 p.m.	

243

U&G

University of Chicago

(1) Required
(2) Recommended

Economics 325
George J. Stigler
Spring 1989

READING LIST

History of Economic Thought Before 1870

BEFORE 1776 (to be passed over silently)

    (2) J. Schumpeter, History of Economic Analysis
    (2) David Hume, Writings on Economics (Rotwein edition)
    (2) Cantillon, Essai sur la nature du commerce
    (2) Jacob Viner, Studies in the Theory of International Trade, Chapters 1 and 2
    (2) E. Heckscher, Mercantilism, Vols. 1 and 2
    (2) R. Meek, The Economics of Physiocracy
    (2) T. Hutchison, Before Adam Smith

THE CLASSICAL ECONOMICS

1. General

    (2) E. Cannan, Production and Distribution Theories
    (2) E. Halevy, Growth of Philosophical Radicalism
    (2) M. Bowley, Nassau Senior
    (2) L. Stephens, The English Utilitarians
    (2) L. Robbins, Robert Torrens and the Classical Economics
    (2) M. Blaug, Ricardian Economics
    (2) Occasional Papers of T. R. Malthus, ed. by B. Semmel
    (2) D. P. O'Brien, J. R. McCulloch
    (2) S. Hollander, The Economics of Adam Smith
    (2) D. O'Brien, The Classical Economists

2. Adam Smith

    (1) Adam Smith, The Wealth of Nations (Liberty Fund Reprint): Bk. I; Bk. II; Bk. IV, Chs. 1, 2, 7, 8, 9; Bk. V, Ch. 1
    (2) A. Skinner and T. Wilson, Essays on Adam Smith (Clarendon, 1975)

3. Population

    (1) T. R Malthus, First Essay on Population (Everyman's ed., Dutton)
    (2) F. Place, Principles of Population
    (2) Patricia James, Population Malthus

4. Rent

    (1) E. West, Application of Capital to Land (Johns Hopkins U. reprint)
    (1) T. R. Malthus, Nature and Progress of Rent (Johns Hopkins U.); or The Works of Thomas Robert Malthus, Vol. 7.
    (1) David Ricardo, Principles of Political Economy and Taxation, Ch. 2

5. The Ricardian System

    (1) David Ricardo, Principles, Chs. 1, 4, 5, 6, 21, 31
    (1) DeQuincy, "Dialogue of the Knight Templars," in Works
    (2) F. H. Knight, "Ricardian Theory of Production and Distribution," reprinted in History and Method of Economics
    (1) G. Stigler, "Ricardo and the 93% Labor Theory of Value," American Economic Review, 1958; reprinted in Essays in the History of Economics
    (2) S. Hollander, The Economics of David Ricardo

6. Say's Law

    (1) J. B. Say, Political Economy, Bk. 1, Ch. 15
    (2) J. B. Say, Letters to Malthus
    (1) T. R. Malthus, Principles of Political Economy, Bk. II, Ch. 1
    (1) J. S. Mill, "Consumption," in Essays on Unsettled Questions (Volume IV of Collected Works

7. John Stuart Mill

    (1) Mill, "The Quarterly Review on Political Economy," Collected Works of John Stuart Mill, Vol. IV
    (2) N. de Marchi, "The Success of Mill's Principles," HOPE, Summer 1974
    (1) Mill, Principles of Political Economy (Ashley or Toronto edition)
        Bk. I, Chs. 4, 5, 10, 11, 12
        Bk. II, Chs. 1, 2, 4, 11, 14, 15, 16
        Bk. III, Chs. 1, 2, 3, 4, 6, 14, 15
        Bk. IV, Chs. 4, 5, 7
        Bk. V, Chs. 1 10, 11
    (1) Mill, "Thornton on Labour and Its Claim," in Essays on Economics and Society (Collected Works, Vol. V)
    (2) Mill, "Essays on Unsettled Questions in Political Economy," in Essays on Economics and Society (Collected Works, Vol. IV)
    (2) Letters of J. S. Mill and Harriet Taylor, ed. by Hayek.
    (2) G. Stigler, "The Nature and Role of Originality," in Essays in the History of Economics

8. Von Thünen

    (1) Von Thünen's Isolated State, ed. by Peter Hall, Part I, Chs. 1-5
    (1) B. W. Dempsey, The Frontier Wage contains a transation of Part II of Der Isolierte Staat, pp. 193-214, 281-330

9. Cournot

    (1) Cournot, Researches into the Mathematical Principles of the Theory of Wealth, Chs. 1, 4, 5, 7, 8

10. Economists and Public Policy

    (1) G. Stigler, "Do Economists Matter?", reprinted in The Economist as Preacher
    (2) F.W. Fetter, The Economist in Parliament, 1780-1868, Chs. 1-13, 15
    (2) J. Viner, "The Tariff Question and the Economist," reprinted in International Economics
    (1) J. Viner, "The Short View and the Long in Economic Policy," reprinted in The Long View and the Short

11. The Beginnings of the Modern Period

    (2) The Marginal Revolution in Economics, History of Political Economy, Fall 1982. Especially essays by Blaug, Coats, de Marchi, Hutchison, and Stigler.

Economics 325
History of Economic Thought to 1870

George J. Stigler
Spring 1989

SUGGESTED TERM PAPERS

1. Appraise the contribution (to general theory, or monetary or international trade theory, or wage theory, for example) of one of the minor economists of the period, e.g.

Lauderdale	Longfield	West
Ellet (American)	Torrens	Say
Whewell	Wakefield	Rae
Jones		

2. Analyze the main criticisms raised against a theory in the first few years after its appearance. (Examples: comparative costs, Ricardo's theory of value, Malthus' overproduction theory, measures of value, Mill's last proposition on capital.) Examine *precisely* how each criticism is handled by the theorist or his disciples.

3. Analyze the policy proposals of a classical economist or, alternatively, the proposals on a given policy by various such economists. In the former case, to what extent are the policies compatible with the man's general theoretical system? (Why were there any incompatibilities?) In the latter case, why do men of similar general theoretical position differ on a specific policy? Pinpoint the explanations, or at least the questions.

4. Examine the role of economic theory in the deliberations of Parliament and its committees on some important legislation (export of machinery, combination acts, 10-hour day, poor laws, slavery, etc.). Look not only for explicit references to economists but also at the implicit theorizing by political leaders and its relationship to the currently ruling theory.

5. Analyze the economic theory implicit in the writings of a major political figure (Pitt, Gladstone, Palmerston, Peel, Disraeli -- or even an American), and determine the extent to which it reflects (1) current or earlier economists' writings, (2) ordinary layman's prejudices, (3) the rationalization of political expediency, and (4) other types of sources.

6. Examine the structure of use of empirical evidence in the writings of some classical economist. Limit your analysis to a compact topic (wages, foreign trade, etc.). When are "facts" resorted to, when not, and why? Do not limit empirical evidence to statistical data. Do not treat assertions of fact ("wages tend to subsistence") as fact. When are facts illustrative and when are they presented as evidence? Are hostile facts recognized? As a special instance, did the Navigation Acts deserve the flattery of Smith's sustained criticism?

7. Why did the mathematical method not receive much use or approval before 1890? Alternatively, why were available statistical methods (least squares, for example) not used in economics by Jevons or Edgeworth, etc.?

U&G

University of Chicago

Economics 326
History of Economic Thought after 1870

Spring Quarter 1990
George J. Stigler

READING LIST

*Required reading

GENERAL SURVEYS

    T.W. Hutchison, A Review of Economic Doctrines

    G.J. Stigler, Production and Distribution Theories

    R.S. Howey, The Rise of the Marginal Utility School, 1870-1889

    W. Jaffe, ed., Correspondence of Leon Walras and Related Papers, 3 volumes

    Papers on the Marginal Revolution in Economics, Special issue of History of Political Economy (Fall, 1971)

    A. Kadish, The Oxford Economists of the Late Nineteenth Century

    D.P. O'Brien & J.R. Presley, eds., Pioneers of Modern Economics in Britain

    J. Maloney, Marshall, Orthodoxy, and the Professionalization of Economics

    Essays in The New Palgrave Dictionary (1987), 4 volumes

1. THE HISTORICAL SCHOOL

    T.E.C. Leslie, Essays in Political Economy, Ch. 15

    C. Menger, Problems of Economics and Sociology, esp. Book IV

    J.K. Ingram, History of Political Economy, Ch. 6

    G.M. Koot, English Historical Economics, 1870-1926

    *W. Bagehot, "The Postulates of Political Economy," in Economic Studies

2. THE MARGINAL UTILITY THEORY

    F. Jenkin, Graphic Representation...and Essays on Political Economy

    *W.S. Jevons, Theory of Political Economy, Preface, Chs. 1-4

    *C. Menger, Principles of Economics, Ch. 3

    *L. Walras, Elements of Pure Economics, Lessons 8-10, 12

*F.Y. Edgeworth, Mathematical Psychics, pp. 1-56

*V. Pareto, Manual of Political Economy, Ch. 4

G.J. Stigler, "The Development of Utility Theory," in Essays in the History of Economics

3. JEVONS AND EMPIRICAL ECONOMICS

W.S. Jevons, Papers and Correspondence (7 volumes)

*W.S. Jevons, The Coal Question

*W.S. Jevons, "A Serious Fall in the Value of Gold Ascertained," in Investigations in Currency and Finance

4. THE MARGINAL PRODUCTIVITY THEORY

*P.H. Wicksteed, Coordination of the Laws of Distribution

L. Walras, Elements, Appendix III

5. GENERAL EQUILIBRIUM THEORY

L. Walras, Elements, Part IV

V. Pareto, Manual, Ch. 6

6. AUSTRIAN CAPITAL THEORY

*E. Böhm-Bawerk, Positive Theory of Capital, Books V, VI, VII -- or Capital and Interest, Vol. II, Book IV

K. Wicksell, Lectures on Political Economy, Vol. I

*I. Fisher, The Rate of Interest, Ch. 4

R. Kuenne, Eugen v. Böhm-Bawerk

7. MARSHALL

*A. Marshall, The Early Economic Writings of Alfred Marshall (John K. Whitaker, ed.; 2 vols.), esp. Introductory Essay

* A. Marshall, Principles of Economics

A.C. Pigou, ed., Memorials of Alfred Marshall

H. George, "Mr. Henry George at Oxford: Disorderly Meeting," Jackson's Oxford Journal, 1884; reprinted in J. Law & Economics, April 1969 (after "Marshall's Lectures")

8. **FISHER**

   *I. Fisher, The Theory of Interest

   *F.H. Knight, "Professor Fisher's Interest Theory," Journal of Political Economy, 1931

9. **FRANK H. KNIGHT**

   F.H. Knight, The Ethics of Competition, Chs. 2, 8.

   F.H. Knight, Risk, Uncertainty, and Profit, Parts I and II.

REFERENCES ON THE SOCIOLOGY OF SCIENCE

   *R. Merton, The Sociology of Science (University of Chicago Press), esp. Parts III and IV

   *T.S. Kuhn, The Structure of Scientific Revolutions (2nd ed.; University of Chicago Press, paperback)

   G. Stigler, "The Literature of Economics: The Case of the Kinked Oligopoly Demand Curve," reprinted in The Economist as Preacher

Economics 326
HISTORY OF ECONOMIC THOUGHT AFTER 1870

Spring Quarter 1990
George J. Stigler

Suggested Term Paper Topics

1. Appraise the contribution of a major economist (Jevons, Marshall, Edgeworth, Wicksell) to monetary or international trade theory.

2. Study the evolution of the measurement of: (a) price levels; (b) national income; (c) consumption function.

3. Did the appearance and development of prices indexes have an appreciable influence upon the development of monetary theory? Did national income accounting influence economic analysis before Keynes?

4. Examine the process and rate of adoption of a new scientific advance by the profession at large. What is the relationship between the accepted theory of leading theoretical innovators and that of the practitioners?

5. Examine the role of economic theory in the deliberations of Parliament or Congress for some important legislation (land tenure reform, trade union legislation, etc., in Britain; regulation of railroads, laws on silver purchase, etc., in America). Look for implicit theorizing as well as explicit references to economists' writings.

6. Apply Kuhn's theory of scientific revolutions to a major development (e.g., marginal utility theory; imperfect competition in the 1930s; Keynes' General Theory). Does it fit?

7. Examine the influence of the shift of economics to the universities on the nature of economic analysis and writings.

8. Examine the barriers encountered in the introduction of mathematical methods or statistical methods in economics. Where did mathematization come first, and last?

9. Analyze the economic theory implicit in the writings of a major political figure (Gladstone, Disraeli—here the novels are interesting, an American president). Does a politician's theory reflect (a) current or earlier economists' writings, (b) ordinary laymen's views, (c) rationalizations of political expediency, or (d) other types of influences?

10. Trace the theory of price indexes to 1940.

11. Examine the influence of self-interest on the choice of work or viewpoint of economists.

12. Analyze the policy proposals of an economist such as Marshall, Walras, or Pigou. To what extent were they consistent with the economist's general theoretical system? If there were inconsistencies, why did they arise? Pay special attention to taxation.

13. Study the impact of game theory on economics since the appearance of the von Neumann-Morganstern book.

14. Write a suitable obituary essay on Chamberlin's monopolistic competition.

UNIVERSITY OF CHICAGO

History of Economic Thought Prelim

Summer 1989

Answer Question 1 or Question 2, not both:

1. Sam Hollander argues that David Ricardo's *Principles* is really a neoclassical analysis (such as Marshall's), although written in a different style and laying different amounts of emphasis upon various parts of the theory (for example, more emphasis on cost, less on demand).

    (a) If this is true of Ricardo, why not also of Adam Smith? How do these two differ?

    (b) What is neoclassical (Marshallian) or not neoclassical about Ricardo's treatment of wages on average, or of wages in individual occupations?

2. In his recent review of Samuel Hollander's study of J.S. Mill, Pedro Schwartz argued that Hollander failed to see that J.S. Mill had a very different view of the scope of economics than Smith or Ricardo. Mill "treated [economics] as a limited science whose rationale is irreconcilable to the guiding principles of ethics and politics."

    From your knowledge of Mill's *Principles*, defend Schwartz or Hollander.

Answer <u>all</u> of the remaining questions:

3. Do people know what is good for them? Show how Smith and J.S. Mill draw their conclusions on this question.

4. Arguments have often persisted for long periods over what an economist really meant. Ricardo is a favorite example, but there is hardly an economist of note who has escaped this sort of dispute. Compare the roles of

    (a) a careful analysis of what the economist meant (relying on his writings, letters, etc.)

    (b) a careful analysis of what his contemporaries and immediate successors thought he meant

    in resolving such disputes. Which is the more important basis of judgment, and why? Apply both techniques to Malthus' use of the arithmetic and geometric ratios.

5. Every individual is continually exerting himself to find out the most advantageous employment for whatever capital he can command...the study of his own advantage naturally, or rather necessarily leads him to prefer that employment which is most advantageous to the society.

    First, every individual endeavors to employ his capital as near home as he can, and consequently as much as he can in the support of domestic industry. ...

Thus, upon equal or nearly equal profits, every
wholesale merchant naturally prefers the home trade to the
foreign trade. ...In the home trade his capital is never
so long out of his sight as it frequently is in the
foreign trade...yet for the sake of having some part of
his capital always under his own view and command, he
willingly submits to this extraordinary charge (double
charge of loading and unloading as well as to the payment
of some duties and customs).

In this passage, famous for arguing free trade, Smith seems to make a
case (a) for preferring domestic industry to foreign trade, and (b) to
define the advantage of "society" as that of one's own nation. Is Smith
not an advocate of free trade?

6. Read all the way through this question before beginning your answers.

 (a) In explaining the advance of knowledge in a science, one must choose
 between:

 (1) The Kuhnsian view of revolutions, which says that wholly new
 paradigms (incommensurable with earlier paradigms) work major
 revolutions such as that of Marginal Utility, and

 (2) All science is basically cumulative (which Kuhn believes is true
 only of "normal" science within a paradigm).

 Appraise these alternatives.

(b) Again, in explaining progress in a science one must choose between:

   (1) A "great man" theory, in which a genius (he's one by definition) makes a fundamental contribution and lesser scholars fill in the details, and

   (2) The science has a main direction that is the product of the whole community of scholars. If a theory needs to be invented or discovered, one or more scholars will do so (Robert Merton).

   Again, appraise these alternatives.

(c) In both parts above, try to illustrate your argument by an episode in economics -- preferably from this century. Thus, the theory of the firm, statistical study of economic functions, oligopoly theory, Keynes' General Theory, monetarism, etc., are examples.

UNIVERSITY OF CHICAGO

Preliminary Examination　　　　　　　　　　　　　　　　　Summer 1987

HISTORY OF ECONOMIC THOUGHT

1. Appraise Mill's proposition that the laws of production are beyond social control but the laws of distribution are not. Why do you think that he emphasized this distinction?

2. What would you name as Ricardo's most important contribution to economics:

    a. From the viewpoint of his contemporaries?

    b. From our viewpoint today?

3. William Grampp has recently challenged the view that Adam Smith favored "laissez faire" citing not only his many instances of favoring some sort of intervention, but his advocacy of tariffs to offset foreign excise taxes and tariffs to retaliate for foreign protection, and the arguments he brings to the critique of state policy on religion and university education. How do Smith's arguments about tariffs and state intervention in religion and education relate to his seeming support of "laissez faire"?

4. There was considerable mutual ill-will between members of the Marshallian school and those of the Walrasian school, especially over the comparative merits of the theories of partial vs. general equilibrium.

    a. How "general" was Walras' theory?

    b. Did Marshall have also a general equilibrium theory?

    c. How differently would the two schools handle a problem such as analyzing output under monopoly vs. competition?

5. When Ricardo considered how the use of machinery would affect the wages of labor, did he misapply his own theory or did he find an area where his theory didn't work?

6. Answer <u>one</u> of the following:

    a. Smith made the cost of training one factor in the determination of wage rates in specific occupations. Should we credit him with having the central element of modern human capital theory? Why didn't he introduce the concept of human capital?

    b. In a course in the history of economic thought, one necessarily concentrates on the leading economists of each period. There were some non-leading economists in early times, and innumerable competent non-leaders today. What is their role in the economic profession and in the advancement of economic science?

UNIVERSITY OF CHICAGO June 26, 1986

PRELIMINARY EXAMINATION

HISTORY OF ECONOMIC THOUGHT

1. Compare the statements of the marginal utility theory by two of the discoverers of the theory in the 1870s (Jevons, Menger, Walras). Which formulation was most influential at the time?

2. The classical economists explained the structure of wages across occupations by cost factors. The marginal productivity theory explained the demand for labor (and other productive services). (Thus the situation is symmetrical with the classical and marginal utility theories of value.) What elements of observable wage behavior, if any, were there that the classical theory could not explain but the marginal productivity theory (as used, say, by Marshall) could explain?

3. "The classical economists made policy choices on the basis of efficiency and ignored equity." Consider the validity of this statement with respect to Adam Smith, D. Ricardo, and J.S. Mill. (Omit the national defense case.)

4. It is common nowadays for economists to distinguish positive and normative economic analysis. What do you understand by the distinction, and do you think the distinction is important? Is there evidence of the recognition of such a distinction in the writings of Ricardo, Mill, and Marshall?

5. "Perhaps the most important, and...most heretical, remark to be made about [the Wage-Fund theory] was that it was correct...it yielded correct predictions of the effects of changes in wage rates, capital, and population" (G. Stigler). -- Would this assessment also apply to the Ricardian theory of value and distribution?

6. How do you explain the fact that economists did not begin to use statistical analysis until nearly the end of the nineteenth century and did not attempt to estimate economic functions empirically until the beginning of the twentieth century?

UNIVERSITY OF CHICAGO

HISTORY OF ECONOMIC THOUGHT

PRELIMINARY EXAMINATION

Answer any <u>five</u> of the following six questions:

1. Ricardo argued that the primary determinant of the rate of profits was the cost of growing corn.

    a. How did he fashion this theory?

    b. Why did it fail to explain the rate of profits throughout the 19th century?

2. How well can the criteria of public good, transactions cost and allocative efficiency be applied to the agenda J.S. Mill set out for government intervention and laissez faire?

3. What were the major theories of monopoly and oligopoly that emerged in the 19th century? Identify their authors.

4. Ricardian economics was tested in its practical application to social questions of the mid-19th century in the Ten Hours Bill and in the "Machinery Question" -- both of them affecting the welfare of laborers. How did economists apply their theories to analyze the effects of these two questions?

5. Comment on the following elements of Mill's work:

    a. His distinction between the laws of production and the laws of distribution.

    b. His recantation of the wages-fund doctrine.

    c. His fundamental propositions on capital.

6. How did economists demonstrate the correctness of their theories before 1900? What use was made of empirical evidence? Illustrate your answer with the methods of an early economist (before 1825) and a later economist (after 1870).

THE UNIVERSITY OF MICHIGAN
Department of Economics

History of Economic Thought   Winter 1987
Preliminary Examination, Part I

This examination comprises ten study questions. Four will be selected by the
examination committee for the actual examination, of which the student will be
expected to write on two.

Part II of the examination is a take-home examination and is to be written
separately.

1. Compare and contrast the value theory of Classical economies with the price theory of neo-Classical economics.

2. Monetary theory was not central to the analytic models of either Classical or neo-Classical economics, yet it played a significant role in both systems. Explain.

3. Discuss the role played by the heterodox ideas of Marx and Veblen in the historical development of "mainstream" or orthodox economic thought.

4. Compare the theories of distribution of income and wealth of the chief Classical economists (Smith, Ricardo, Malthus, J.S. Mill) with those of the neo-Classical school (Clark, Marshall).

5. In what sense did Keynes' General Theory constitute a "revolution" in economic thought?

6. Discuss: "Both Classical and neo-Classical economics were conservative political theories masquerading as scientific economic analysis."

7. Compare the method of economic analysis used by Marx with the method used by the neo-classical economists.

8. What insights into contemporary economic thought are derived from study of the history of economics? Explain.

9. How does contemporary mainstream economics deal with the problems of uncertainty raised by Knight and Keynes?

10. Any system of economic thought (i.e., classical, neoclassical, Keynesian) embodies a unified combination of world view, theory, method and policy. Explain and illustrate with a specific example.

In this part of the examination the student is to prepare the outline of a one-semester upper-level undergraduate course in History of Economic Thought for a liberal arts college. The semester is 15 weeks long. Assume a class size of about 25 students.

1. Prepare a statement of the objectives of the course, that is, the things the students are expected to learn or be able to do at the end of the course. The objectives should include

   a. General education objectives.

   b. Objectives for students majoring in economics.

   c. Objectives specific to the subject matter of this particular course.

2. Select a textbook and/or other readings for the course, explaining the specific reasons for each selection and how each contributes to the achievement of the goals of the course.

3. Prepare a detailed outline of the course, allocating each hour (3 hours per week, 15 weeks per semester) to a topic or activity. The outline should allow time for an introduction, examinations, review, and should include an hour-by-hour outline of subjects or topics to be covered. The outline should include a statement explaining why you decided to allocate the available time in the fashion chosen and how your allocation contributes to achievement of the course objectives.

4. Add any further comments you feel are appropriate to a full explanation of your goals for the course and how they are to be achieved.

Part II of the examination is to be turned in no later than one week after the written examination.

THE UNIVERSITY OF MICHIGAN
Department of Economics

History of Economic Thought
Preliminary Examination

January 7, 1987

Answer any two of the following four questions

1. Discuss the role played by the heterodox ideas of Marx and Veblen in the historical development of "mainstream" or orthodox economic thought.

2. Compare the theories of distribution of income and wealth of the chief Classical economists (Smith, Ricardo, Malthus, J.S. Mill) with those of the neo-Classical school (Clark, Marshall).

3. What insights into contemporary economic thought are derived from study of the history of economics? Explain.

4. Any system of economic thought (i.e., classical, neoclassical, Keynesian) embodies a unified combination of world view, theory, method and policy. Explain and illustrate with a specific example.

THE UNIVERSITY OF MICHIGAN
Department of Economics

History of Economic Thought
Preliminary Examination

September 4, 1986

INSTRUCTIONS: Answer two of the following four questions.

1. Compare and contrast the value theory of Classical economics with the price theory of neo-Classical economics.

2. Compare the theories of distribution of income and wealth of the chief Classical economists (Smith, Ricardo, Malthus, J.S. Mill) with those of the neo-Classical school (Clark, Marshall).

3. Discuss: "Both Classical and neo-Classical economics were conservative political theories masquerading as scientific economic analysis."

4. What insights into contemporary economic thought are derived from study of the history of economics? Explain.

THE UNIVERSITY OF MICHIGAN
Department of Economics

History of Economic Thought
Prelim Examination, Part I

Fall 1986

This examination comprises eight study questions. Four will be selected by the examination committee for the actual examination, of which the student will be expected to write on two.

Part II of the examination is a take-home examination and is to be written separately.

1. Compare and contrast the value theory of Classical economics with the price theory of neo-Classical economics.

2. Monetary theory was not central to the analytic models of either Classical or neo-Classical economics, yet it played a significant role in both systems. Explain.

3. Discuss the role played by the heterodox ideas of Marx and Veblen in the historical development of "mainstream" or orthodox economic thought.

4. Compare the theories of distribution of income and wealth of the chief Classical economists (Smith, Ricardo, Malthus, J.S. Mill) with those of the neo-Classical school (Clark, Marshall).

5. In what sense did Keynes' General Theory constitute a "revolution" in economic thought?

6. Discuss: "Both Classical and neo-Classical economics were conservative political theories masquerading as scientific economic analysis."

7. Compare the method of economic analysis used by Marx with the method used by the neo-Classical economists.

8. What insights into contemporary economic thought are derived from study of the history of economics? Explain.

History of Economic Thought
Prelim Examination, Part II   Fall 1986

In this part of the examination the student is to prepare the outline of a one-semester upper level undergraduate course in History of Economic Thought for a liberal arts college. The semester is 15 weeks long. Assume a class size of about 25 students.

1. Prepare a statement of the objectives of the course, that is, the things the students are expected to learn or be able to do at the end of the course. The objectives should include
   a. General education objectives.
   b. Objectives for students majoring in economics.
   c. Objective specific to the subject matter of this particular course.

2. Select a textbook and/or other readings for the course, explaining the specific reasons for each selection and how each contributes to the achievement of the goals of the course.

3. Prepare a detailed outline of the course, allocating each hour (3 hours per week, 15 weeks per semester) to a topic or activity. The outline should allow time for an introduction, examinations, review, and should include an hour-by-hour outline of subjects or topics to be covered. The outline should include a statement explaining why you decided to allocate the available time in the fashion chosen and how your allocation contributes to achievement of the course objectives.

4. Add any further comments you feel are appropriate to a full explanation of your goals for the course and how they are to be achieved.

Part II of the examination is to be turned in no later than one week after the written examination.

PRINCETON UNIVERSITY
Department of Economics

General Examination for the Degree of Doctor of Philosophy

History of Economic Thought

Time: 3 hours   January 1987
----

1. Distinguish the roles of the labor command and the labor content discussions of value in Adam Smith. What was Smith's general model of the determination of long run exchange value under competition?

2. In terms of the formal Ricardian model, explain the consequences of elimination of a tariff on grain (corn) (a) in the short run; (b) in the long run.

3. (a) Explain why, in Marx's view, profits under capitalism can be expected to decline with the passage of time. (b) Why did he reject Ricardo's model leading to the same conclusion? (c) On what grounds has Marx's model of the declining profit rate been criticized?

4. In one sentence each, characterize some of the main work of the following:

    a. Jeremy Bentham
    b. Frederick Bastiat
    c. J. B. Clark
    d. J. R. McCulloch
    e. Enrico Barone

5. (for Arthur Moretti) Describe the logic of the Hayek business cycle model. What role is played by technological elements? by monetary elements? What is the pertinence of the "Ricardo effect?"

6. (for Kin Yip Louie) Explain the source of Marshall's error in using consumers' surplus to argue that increasing returns industries should be subsidized. Would the Hicksian analysis of the four consumers' surpluses have helped to avoid the error? Why or why not?

7. (for Susan Skeath) Explain the role played by utility in J. S. Mill's value theory. Does his utility concept lead him to particular policy conclusions? How do Mill's views on the appropriate role of government differ from those of his classical predecessors?

8. (for Teow-Hock Koh) To what extent does Malthus' analysis (in contradistinction to his conclusions) anticipate the structure of the Keynesian model? In answering this, provide a summary of the workings of the pertinent parts of the Keynesian analysis. What features of Marxian Theory overlap with the Keynesian model?

9. (for Vicente Morales) a) Describe any of the mathematical solutions to the transformation problem showing how prices and the rate of profit are related to values and the rate of surplus value. b) Explain Samuelson's criticism of the entire analysis and Morishima's reply.

PRINCETON UNIVERSITY
Department of Economics

General Examination for the Degree of Doctor of Philosophy

History of Economic Thought

Time: 3 hours   January 1986

1. (for Peter Rathjens) Earlier writings on rent focussed on rent payments as a reward to units of superior quality that was attributable to the heterogeniety of the resource. Thus, land was alone among inputs in the focus upon its heterogeneity. Discuss the role of this issue in later writings and the degree to which they did or did not treat land as essentially different from all other inputs. Which of them, if any, concluded that there is such a thing as an "absolute" rent (in contradistinction to differential rent)?

2. (for Jai-June Kim) Validity of the infant industry argument for tariffs as a benefit to the general public required that when the industry grows up it not merely yield net benefits, but that they be more than sufficient to offset the welfare lost during the period of protection. Was this point recognized by those who wrote on the subject? If so, by whom? Discuss what other qualifications some of the writers raised in relation to the argument and how they treated the way in which the issue had been analyzed by others.

3. Discuss the role of alienation in Marx. In which of his writings was it discussed? Does the term always refer to the same phenomenon? How might it relate to accumulation and, consequently, to the "laws of motion of capitalism?"

4. Ricardo's test of the labor theory of value was whether a rise in wages will change the relative prices of commodities. Explain the logic of this test. What does Ricardo conclude from the test about the validity of the labor theory in reality? Why was this way of looking at the matter of importance to Ricardo?

5. Describe the tasks that Adam Smith considers to constitute the proper roles of government. Was he an extreme or a moderate advocate of laissez-faire? What is the logic of his arguments for governmental economic activity? How do they compare with modern analysis of the subject?

6. In one sentence each characterize some of the work of the following:

    1) Cantillon
    2) Quesnay
    3) Menger
    4) Wesley Mitchell
    5) Kondratieff

7. (Jeehwan Rhee) Summarize some of Malthus' arguments on the issue of general overproduction. To what extent do they constitute a logically unified position? Indicate (giving specific examples) to what extent Malthus' arguments anticipate those of Keynes.

PRINCETON UNIVERSITY
Department of Economics

General Examination for the Degree of Doctor of Philosophy

History of Economic Thought

Time: 3 hours   January 1985

---

1. Have you completed the course readings for Economics 506?   Yes _____   No _____

2. In the Wealth of Nations what is the invisible hand said to achieve? How do the achievements differ from those that modern welfare theory attribute to perfect competition?

3. Chapter 1 in Ricardo's Principles is framed in terms of the effect of a change in wages on the relative values of commodities.

    a) How does this orientation affect Ricardo's conclusions relating to a labor theory of value?

    b) What fundamental role does this view of the matter play in Ricardo's Theory of Distribution?

4. a) What is the transformation problem?

    b) What was its significance to Marx?

    c) What is your view of its significance?

5a. (for Paul Brewer) Give three examples of non-cooperative equilibrium concepts which have counterparts in 19th century literature. Discuss in detail the relation between the earlier and the later work.

5b. (for Dahai Yu) Discuss two of the following: Mill's views on the Wages Fund; Mill on Say's Law; Mill on the role of government; Mill on utilitarianism.

    Contrast Mill's views on these subjects with some of his predecessors.

5c. (for Daniel Vincent) Does the development of the utilitarian concept over the course of the nineteenth century constitute a process of increasing approximation to the foundations of either modern welfare economics or modern theories of fairness? Illustrate your discussion with descriptions of the pertinent views of the nineteenth century writers.

6. In one sentence each suggest one of the main contributions to economics of each of the following:

    a) David Hume   d) M. Tugan Baranovsky

    b) J. H. von Thunen   e) Wesley C. Mitchell

    c) Auguste Walras

ECONOMICS READING LISTS, COURSE OUTLINES, EXAMS, PUZZLES & PROBLEMS

Compiled by Edward Tower, Duke University, August 1990

Volume 1	Microeconomics Reading Lists, 227pp.
Volume 2	Microeconomics Exams, Puzzles & Problems, 283pp.
Volume 3	Macro, Monetary & Financial Economics Reading Lists, 259pp.
Volume 4	Macroeconomics, Exams, Puzzles & Problems, 264pp.
Volume 5	Development Economics Reading Lists, 238pp.
Volume 6	Development Economics Exams, Puzzles & Problems with additional reading lists, 193pp.
Volume 7	Industrial Organization & Regulation Reading Lists, 297pp.
Volume 8	Industrial Organization & Regulation Exams, Puzzles & Problems, 253pp.
Volume 9	International Economics Reading Lists, 292pp.
Volume 10	International Economics Exams, Puzzles & Problems with additional reading lists, 283pp.
Volume 11	Public Finance Reading Lists, 280pp.
Volume 12	Public Finance Exams, Puzzles & Problems, 258pp.
Volume 13	Econometrics Reading Lists, 222pp.
Volume 14	Econometrics Exams, Puzzles & Problems, 298pp.
Volume 15	Labor Economics Reading Lists, 208pp.
Volume 16	Labor Economics Exams, Puzzles & Problems with additional reading lists, 204 pp.
Volume 17	Comparative Systems & Planning, 244pp.
Volume 18	Monetary & Financial Economics Exams, Puzzles & Problems, 264pp.
Volume 19	Mathematical Economics & Applied General Equilibrium Modelling, 242pp.
Volume 20	Public Choice, Political Economy, Law & War, 266pp.
Volume 21	Environmental & Natural Resource Economics, 253pp.
Volume 22	Agricultural Economics & Agriculture in Economic Development, 200pp.
Volume 23	Economic History, 240pp.
Volume 24	History of Economic Thought, 269pp.
Volume 25	Urban, Regional, Health, Education & Transport Economics, 222pp.

The price of each volume is $20. The discount price for the complete set of 25 Economics volumes is $350. For individuals buying economics volumes, buy 2 volumes at the regular price, and get additional volumes for a special price of $15 each when ordering directly from Eno River Press. These prices include postage and handling for domestic orders only. Other postage charges are: foreign surface @ $1 per volume; Canada air @ $3 per volume; Europe & Latin America air @ $4 per volume; and Asia, Africa & Pacific air @ $10 per volume. U.S. funds only please.

Eno River Press
Box 4900, Duke Station
Durham, N.C. 27706-4900
U.S.A.

BUSINESS ADMINISTRATION READING LISTS AND COURSE OUTLINES
1990

Compiled by Richard Schwindt, *Simon Fraser University*

Volume 1	ACCOUNTING, 229 pages
Volume 2	MARKETING, 315 pages
Volume 3	CORPORATE FINANCE AND INVESTMENTS, 206 pages
Volume 4	FINANCIAL THEORY, INSTITUTIONS AND MONEY MARKETS, 202 pages
Volume 5	INTERNATIONAL BUSINESS, 268 pages
Volume 6	INTERNATIONAL BANKING AND FINANCE, 153 pages
Volume 7	ORGANIZATIONAL BEHAVIOR, 265 pages
Volume 8	INDUSTRIAL RELATIONS AND HUMAN RESOURCES MANAGEMENT, 266 pages
Volume 9	QUANTITATIVE METHODS, RESEARCH DESIGN AND COMPUTER APPLICATIONS IN BUSINESS, 286 pages
Volume 10	BUSINESS, GOVERNMENT AND SOCIETY, 252 pages
Volume 11	BUSINESS POLICY AND STRATEGY, 242 pages
Volume 12	RISK, DECISION MAKING AND BARGAINING, 271 pages
Volume 13	ENTREPRENEURSHIP, SMALL BUSINESS AND VENTURE CAPITAL, 221 pages
Volume 14	MANAGEMENT COMMUNICATION, 125 pages

All volumes are priced at $20 each. The complete set is $225. These prices include postage, handling and taxes for DOMESTIC ORDERS. Other postage and handling charges are: foreign surface @ $1/volume; Canada air @ $3/volume; Europe & Latin America air @ $4/volume; Africa, Asia & Pacific air @ $10/volume. Payment accepted in U.S. funds only.

Eno River Press
Box 4900 Duke Station
Durham, N.C. 27706-4900
U.S.A.

POLITICAL SCIENCE READING LISTS AND ES
including course exams and comprehensive exams   I.D.
from leading professors and Universities

Compiled by Allan Kornberg, Duke University, August 1989

Volume 1	Political Philosophy, 221pp.
Volume 2	Methodology in Political Science, 189 pp.
Volume 3	American Politics I: The American Political System, 183pp.
Volume 4	American Politics II: Congress, The Presidency, Political Parties, 172 pp.
Volume 5	American Politics III: Law, State & Local Politics, Voting Behavior, 215 pp.
Volume 6	International Relations I: Theories of International Politics, 239 pp.
Volume 7	International Relations II: US Foreign Policy, National & International Security, War & Technology, 231 pp.
Volume 8	Comparative Politics I: Europe, Canada, Soviet Union, Latin America, 279 pp.
Volume 9	Comparative Politics II: Asia, Africa, Middle East, 211 pp.
Volume 10	Comparative Politics III: Development, Political Participation, Ethnicity, 291 pp.
Volume 11	Comparative Politics IV: Theories of Comparative Politics, 236pp.
Volume 12	Political Economy & International Political Economy, 236 pp.
Volume 13	Public Policy, 182 pp.

The price of each volume is $14.95. The discount price for the entire set is $149.00. These prices include postage and handling for domestic orders only. Other postage charges are: foreign surface @ $1 per volume; Canada air @ $3 per volume; Europe & Latin America air @ $4 per volume; and Asia, Africa & Pacific air @ $10 per volume. U.S. funds only please.

Eno River Press
Box 4900, Duke Station
Durham, N.C. 27706-4900
U.S.A.